SOCIAL WORK MACRO PRACTICE

SOCIAL WORK MACRO PRACTICE

F. Ellen Netting
Peter M. Kettner
Steven L. McMurtry

Arizona State University

Longman

Longman, 10 Bank Street, White Plains, N.Y. 10606

Associated companies:
Longman Group Ltd., London
Longman Cheshire Pty., Melbourne
Longman Paul Pty., Auckland
Copp Clark Pitman, Toronto

Sponsoring editor: David Estrin
Development editor: Virginia L. Blanford
Production editors: Professional Book Center, Linda W. Witzling
Cover design: Joseph DePinho
Production supervisor: Anne Armeny

Library of Congress Cataloging-in-Publication Data

Netting, F. Ellen.
    Social work macro practice / F. Ellen Netting, Peter M. Kettner,
Steven L. McMurtry.
        p.   cm.
    Includes bibliographical references and index.
    ISBN 0-8013-0464-4
    1. Social service. 2. Social service—United States.
3. Macrosociology. I. Kettner, Peter M., 1936– . II. McMurtry,
Steven Lloyd. III. Title.
HV41.N348 1992
361.3'2—dc20   92-18943
                                                CIP

8 9 10–CRW–96

To my father, Millege H. Daniel, who taught me
to value the printed word
F. E. N.

To G–Y and Caitlin
S. L. M.

Contents

CHAPTER 9 **DEVELOPING AN INTERVENTION
STRATEGY   222**

CHAPTER 10   SELECTING APPROPRIATE TACTICS   248

Preface

Tracing the history of social work practice requires constant attention toward shifts in the dominant focus of the profession from intervention with individuals to intervention with and within larger systems. This distinction between "micro" and "macro" levels of intervention continues, and some current literature on social work practice suggests a trend toward perceiving two clearly separate domains of practice engaged in by distinct sets of practitioners. A major goal of this book is to attempt to recapture broader definitions of social work practice that recognize the need for workers to be able to bridge these distinctions if they are to provide effective services.

Too often, social work practice with macro systems has been considered solely the realm of administrators, community organizers, program planners, and others. Though these are important roles, they are not the only ones that require social workers to interact with macro systems. In fact, all social workers must to some degree involve themselves in macro practice. This is not exactly new. Social workers have always worked with and within communities and organizations, and arenas of practice such as administration and community organizing date back to the earliest days of social work. However, we believe that the importance of macro systems to the everyday experiences of social workers is growing. So, too, is their reliance on these systems in order to do their jobs effectively. Even social workers whose roles place them almost exclusively in activities such as intensive one-on-one counseling must work within formal organizations and interact with other organizations that in turn comprise complex community service systems.

Our intent is to provide students a basic grounding in social work macro practice—students who plan to specialize in macro practice and those who specialize in direct practice. In particular, we will attempt to operationalize macro practice in a way that makes it accessible and meaningful for all social workers. We strongly believe that if change is to take place in organizations, communities, or other macro systems, practitioners directly involved must participate in and often initiate the change effort. Because many practitioners work directly with individuals, families, and groups, it is necessary to bring their knowledge of client needs to the attention of critical actors in their communities and organizations. It is equally important to include client perspectives in every part of the change process.

We have attempted to develop our approach to macro practice in several ways. First, we have compiled a brief history of social work as a profession throughout which we highlight components of macro practice. We did this to point out the rich traditions of macro-level change all social workers inherit when they enter the profession. We also emphasize ethical dilemmas that arise on a daily basis. Every choice that a practitioner makes (whether to act or not to act) carries implications that are steeped in ethical decision making.

Second, we have attempted to conceptualize—in separate sections—macro practice in both communities and organizations. For each section, we have provided an overview of the theoretical and conceptual literature, and a model for analysis of each of these arenas. We believe it is important to include in the analysis a thorough understanding of informal vehicles of service provision (the household unit, the neighborhood, voluntary associations) as well as the more visible providers (formal organizations, both private and public).

Finally, we have designed a practice model for planned intervention that we believe is applicable to both communities and organizations, and that we sincerely hope addresses the realities of practice. When a caseworker or administrator recognizes the need for change, casework or administrative responsibilities do not stop. By sharing organizing responsibilities with others and by clearly identifying, analyzing, and planning, we believe that the busy practitioner can bring about organizational and community changes necessary to improve the quality of life for those being served. We view this model as a guideline to be used by creative practitioners. As with any model, we encourage practitioners to be critical of the approach we have taken and to keep us informed of how the model should evolve.

We believe that the knowledge and skills promoted in this book are becoming increasingly important for social workers. In the conservative, at times even punitive, political environment in which we have found ourselves since the early 1980s, it is vital that social workers be able to function as watchdogs over their own services and service systems. It is our responsibility to the oppressed and disenfranchised clients we serve to critically examine decisions, decision-making processes, appropriations, organizational mission statements, strategic plans, and other indicators of community and organizational commitments. When the need for change is recognized, someone must act. In many cases, the first to recognize the need for change or action will be the social worker closest to the problem.

Also, we believe that language is critical in setting the stage to study the way differences are viewed and the actions that emanate from those views. Throughout this text, we will be referring to many different groups within American society who, over the years, have been referred to as minorities, oppressed persons, or special populations. We will also address distinctions that identify them, including such factors as race, ethnicity, gender, sexual orientation, age, and physical abilities. As we refer to various population groups, it is our intention to do so in a way that is sensitive to the power of descriptive terms. In reviewing the history of macro practice with these groups, in Part I of the book, we will address in greater detail the importance of such terms.

We gratefully acknowledge the help of a number of people who strengthened this book. To our reviewers, we express our gratitude for their careful and thoughtful assessment of the strengths and weaknesses of our earlier drafts:

Allen Rubin, University of Texas, Austin

Claudia Ellano, California State University, Long Beach

Nancy Johnston, University of Minnesota

To our editor, David Estrin, we express our great appreciation for his patience, his humor, and his forgiveness for belated drafts. We are also grateful to his colleagues at Longman, including Virginia Blanford, Owen Lancer, Linda Witzling, and others, for their helpfulness. We only hope that what our efforts lacked in timeliness, they made up for in quality.

Most of all we thank those students and practitioners who, often in the face of seemingly insurmountable barriers, continue to practice social work the way it was intended. They intervene at whatever level is needed. They persist with what may appear to be intractable problems and intervene with clients who have lost hope until hope can be rediscovered and pursued. Their spirit and dedication continually inspire us in our efforts to provide an increasingly clear sense of direction for macro practice.

SOCIAL WORK MACRO PRACTICE

PART I

Values and Historical Perspectives

The first part of this book is intended to provide the definitions, background information, and contextual bases on which the subsequent parts are built. Chapter 1 offers a definition of macro practice, presents case vignettes to illustrate its relevance to social work practice as a whole, and explains the rationale for preparing all social workers to undertake macro-practice activities. Chapter 2 traces the historical development of traditional macro-practice roles, and identifies ways in which contemporary trends have affected these roles. Chapter 3 provides introductory information on the two major macro systems that we will address—communities and organizations—and discusses the value base of practice in these systems.

CHAPTER 1

An Introduction to Macro Practice in Social Work

WHAT IS MACRO PRACTICE?

Macro practice is professionally directed intervention designed to bring about planned change in organizations and communities. Macro practice, as all social work practice, is built on theoretical foundations, proceeds within the framework of a practice model, and operates within the boundaries of professional values and ethics. Macro-level activities engage the practitioner in organizational, community, and policy arenas.

These activities go beyond individual and group interventions but are often based on needs, problems, issues, and concerns identified in microactivities. Organizational activities include, but are not limited to, supervision of professional and paraprofessional staff, working with committees, participating in budgeting, writing proposals, and developing programs. Community activities engage the practitioner in negotiating and bargaining with diverse groups, encouraging consumer participation in decision making, establishing and carrying out interagency agreements, conducting needs assessments, and advocating for client needs in a variety of community systems. Policy-related activities include coalition building, lobbying, testifying, tracking legislative developments that directly affect clients, and carrying out other efforts designed to affect legal or regulatory frameworks.

Typically, macro social workers occupy positions in social agencies and are involved in the agency's functioning. The agency may be a funding source, a planning organization, or a direct service provider, or it may perform multiple functions. The unifying concern of macro workers is how the agency relates to its environment and the forces that shape that environment. These forces include changing needs, shifting demographics, interest group politics, legislative influences, funding patterns, and a host of other factors. The macro worker, therefore, must understand the community within which an organization operates and the policies that affect the service delivery system within that community (Meenaghan 1987).

Although most practitioners will work within organizations and have some understanding of communities, it is clear that not all committee and task force work is macro practice, and not all people who serve on committees and task forces are doing macro social work practice. Macro practice is carried out by people operating in a sanctioned professional capacity, following a soundly based set of procedures, and focusing on planned change.

Social work practice is broadly defined and allows for intervention at the micro (individual, group, or family) level, and at the macro (organization and community) level. Given this division of labor, some professional roles require that the social worker be involved full-time in macro practice. These professional roles are often referred to by such titles as *planner, community organizer, manager,* or *administrator.* The direct service worker or clinical social worker, however, also bears responsibility for initiating change in organizations and communities. The direct service worker is often the first to recognize patterns indicating the need for change. If one or two clients present a particular problem, the logical response is to deal with them as individuals. However, as more persons present the same situation, it quickly becomes evident that something is awry within the systems in which these clients are interacting. It then becomes incumbent upon the social worker to help identify the system(s) in need of change and the type of change needed. The nature of the system(s) in need of change may lead to communitywide intervention or intervention in a single organization.

Given these statements, practitioners may begin to feel overwhelmed. Is it not enough to do good clinical work? Is it not enough to listen to a client and offer options? Professional practice focusing only on an individual's intrapsychic concerns does not fit the definition of social work. Being a social worker requires seeing the client as part of multiple, overlapping systems that comprise the person's social and physical environment. If the social worker is not willing to engage in some macro-practice types of activities relating to these environments, then he or she is not practicing social work.

Similarly, social workers who concentrate in macro practice must understand micro practice, which may be defined as intervention directed primarily at the individual or group level. Without this understanding, macro practice may be carried out in the absence of an adequate grounding in the nature of client needs. MBA and MSW administrators would act similarly in all situations, and cost alone—rather than an understanding of client need balanced with cost—would drive community planning. The interconnectedness of micro and macro roles are the heart of social work practice. In short, it is as important for social workers in macro-practice roles to understand the importance of individual and group interventions as it is for social workers in micro practice roles to understand the importance of organizational, community, and policy change.

Because we believe that all social workers are professional change agents, we use the terms *social worker, professional,* and *change agent* interchangeably throughout this text. Social workers are always change agents because they are constantly identifying changes that need to occur in order to make systems more responsive or sensitive to target population needs. Change is so much a part of social work practice that one cannot separate the two. Professional is a term that implies identification with a set of values and the judgment and skill to act on those values. In Chapter 3, we discuss the meaning of professional values that unite social workers across roles, arenas, and emphases.

MACRO PRACTICE IN CONTEXT

This book is intended for all social workers, regardless of whether they specialize in micro or macro tracks within schools of social work. It is designed to be an introduction to the macro-practice roles social workers play. Although some practitioners will concentrate their efforts primarily in one arena rather than another, in some situations all social workers will engage in macro-level interventions as the appropriate response to a need or a problem.

This book is not designed to educate full-time agency administrators, program planners, community organizers, or policy analysts. Those social workers who assume full-time macro roles will need a more advanced understanding than what this text will provide. This is not a book on specialization. The roles discussed in this and the following chapters are those that competent social work practitioners will play during their professional careers.

In preparation for writing this text, we talked with a number of our former students who are now practicing social workers, some of whom work directly with clients and some of whom are planners, managers, or administrators. We asked them what they would say to current students about the differences between their expectations of social work practice when they were students and their actual experiences over the past few years. One student responded: "As a student, I have this very vivid memory of being idealistic. I liked social work's emphasis on serving clients as the primary focus of attention, and I thought that would carry over to my professional practice. Instead, I find that my professional life is dominated by two things: fellow employees and money. In making decisions, we find that we have to deal much more with staff egos than with client needs. And the 'bottom line' mentality that pushes budget issues into every discussion and decision has been a real disappointment."

A second student said: "What makes this profession worthwhile for me is that there is a core of very committed people who really live up to the ideals of the profession. They're very talented people who could make a lot more money elsewhere, but they believe in what they're doing, and it is always a pleasure to work with them. Our biggest frustration has been that there are so many people (like state legislators, for example) who wield so much power over this profession, but who have no understanding of what social problems and human needs are all about. Even though professionals may have spent the better part of their careers trying to understand how to deal with people in need, their opinions and perspectives are often not accepted or respected."

A social worker recently employed by a community-based agency on an Indian reservation shared his experience: "Culture is so important to the work we do. I constantly have to ask indigenous people for advice so that I do not make assumptions about the people with whom I work. The concept of community and what it means to this tribe, even the value of the land as a part of their tradition, is so crucial. It is much more complex than I had assumed when I was in school."

Another former student reinforced the importance of community: "I guess I never realized how porous agency boundaries are. We have board members coming in and out and we see clients. But the thing that has surprised me is how much I need to know about the community—people's values, where funding comes from, how to assess community needs. Even though I do direct practice, I am constantly pulled onto task forces and committees that have to deal with the broader community issues."

Concerns about limited public resources combined with overwork were expressed by a program specialist in foster care: "A big problem is the workload— the sheer size of people's job responsibilities. The state can't or won't provide the money to keep workloads at reasonable levels. It never occurred to me the frustration there would be in working with policies you can't change because you don't have any input at those levels. Our organization has two separate parts—volunteers and professional staff—and there's often no clear definition of who does what. It's very difficult to know which issues should be brought to the board and which ones should be settled by staff." Despite these problems, though, this same person quickly added, "A real positive is the feeling you are having a role in helping people. Seeing progress on the part of individual clients is one of the main things that keeps you going. It's also very reinforcing to have the opportunity to be an advocate for kids."

Another former student was disappointed about the impact of limited resources on practice and employee morale: "It really wears you down after awhile when everything is decided in terms of money. Furniture in our waiting room is falling apart, the place needs to be painted, there are so many things we should do to improve our efficiency and effectiveness, but we can't because we can't afford them. Just once I'd like to have the resources to really do things right, the way they can in big corporations."

However, lest we begin to believe that the commercial sector does not have its own limitations, the clinical director of a private for-profit adoption agency had this to say: "Unlike a lot of social workers, I work in a for-profit agency, and business considerations always have to be factored into our decisions. We have a fairly small operation, and I think the agency director is responsive to my concerns about how clients are treated, but I've still had to get used to the tension that can arise between making a profit and serving clients. Our agency works primarily with adoptions, and I've been very surprised by the ignorance and prejudice that exist about adoption even among other social workers. A lot of these people are constantly imposing their values on women about how they should always keep their child, and they usually do this without knowing anything about the case."

A child protective services worker said: "It's really hard to describe. Within a few days last year in my caseload there was a death of a child, another of my kids was abandoned in our waiting room, and there were threats of violence against our staff from people who think we just indiscriminately take children away from their parents. I often think of going into other lines of work, but there are lots of intangible rewards in social work, and other professions have their headaches, too."

The director of a social services unit in a hospital talked about another client group, the elderly: "I have been here long enough to see the advent of diagnostic-related categories. This is the Medicare system's way of making sure older patients are discharged efficiently, and if they are not, the hospital has to pick up the tab. Social workers graduate from MSW programs ready to counsel patients in the hospital and they are sorely disappointed. What we have to do is work fast; counseling is done 'on the run,' and we are pushed and prodded by everyone from admissions to discharge planning to move these folks along. Many of these older persons don't have people who can help them when they are discharged and they are really vulnerable to being placed in a nursing home. It is as if policies and procedures make our decisions—where is the patient involved?"

On a final note, a direct practice student who recently graduated made this statement: "This may sound negative, but it is not meant to be. My education in social work taught me how little I know. I feel as if I have just scratched the surface. Learning is a long ongoing process. I work in a head injury center and what I learned from having had exposure to macro-practice roles is that you have to know the organization in which you work, particularly the philosophy behind what happens there. This is more important than I ever imagined."

These quotations tell their own stories. Many of the issues facing social workers in their daily practice are not only client problems but problems in agencies or communities that affect the worker's ability to serve their clients. We thank our former students for helping us raise these issues.

THREE CASE EXAMPLES

Other aspects of social work macro practice that need to be understood by the student and the beginning practitioner can best be illustrated by case examples. We selected the following because they contain similar themes but focus on different target population groups: children, the aged, and women.

CASE EXAMPLE 1: CHILD PROTECTIVE SERVICES

Child protective services (CPS) workers have responsibility for dealing with the abuse and neglect of children. When reports of alleged abuse or neglect come to the unit, the CPS worker has the responsibility for investigating the report and making decisions about the disposition of the case. It is a very demanding and emotionally draining area of specialization within the field of social work. Several years ago, one CPS worker took the time to record the details of a particular case, and also shared with us a list of dilemmas and contradictions he had recorded over the years, in the interest of helping prepare new workers for what they will face as they enter practice.

Friday, 10:40 a.m. Supervisor called to inform me about a report of neglect. She felt it should be checked out today because it sounded too serious to be left over the weekend. According to the neighbor's report, parents have deserted and abandoned three minor children.

11:10 a.m. Got in my car and headed for the address on the intake form. I know the neighborhood well. It is the poorest in the city and not a safe neighborhood at night. A high percentage of families receive some kind of assistance. Homes are run-down, streets are littered, any sense of pride has long been abandoned.

11:40 a.m. The house at the address given is among the most run-down in a seriously deteriorating neighborhood. The house had no front steps, just a cinder block placed in front of the door. Window casings were rotting out for lack of paint. There was no doorbell. I knocked. There was rustling inside, but no answer. I waited and knocked again. I walked around and peered through a window and saw a small child, about three years old I guessed, curled up in a chair. An older girl, about age eight or nine, peeked out from behind a doorway.

I remembered that the oldest child was named Cindy, so I called out to her. After a bit of conversation, I persuaded her to let me in. I quickly recognized that this would not be an ordinary case. A foul smell hit me so hard it made my eyes water. I used my handkerchief to filter the air. The worst odors were coming from the bathroom and kitchen. The water had evidently been shut off—toilets were not working and garbage was piled up. The kitchen was littered with fast-food containers, possibly retrieved from the dumpsters of nearby fast-food outlets.

There were three very frightened children: Cindy, age nine; Scott, age six; and Melissa, age three. None would talk.

12:35 p.m. I made arrangements to transport them to the shelter and went back to the office to do the paperwork.

2:15 p.m. A previous neglect report revealed the following:

Father: Stan, age 27, unemployed, in and out of jail for petty theft, public intoxication, and several other minor offenses. Frequently slept in public parks or homeless shelters. Rarely showed up at home any more. Several police reports of violence against wife and children. Admits paternity for only the oldest child.

Mother: Sarah, age 25. AFDC recipient, high-school dropout, never employed. Tests performed in connection with one attempt at job training revealed borderline retardation. While child care skills have always been minimal, there is no previous history of abandonment of children. Whereabouts at this time are unknown.

3:35 p.m. Filed the appropriate forms with agency and the police. Dictated case for the record. Children placed at Vista Shelter until a more permanent placement can be arranged.

Over the years as this CPS worker had dealt with similar cases, he had kept a running list of the kinds of dilemmas, frustrations, and contradictions he and his colleagues regularly faced. These are excerpts from his list:

1. A high percentage of lower socioeconomic status teens get pregnant and drop out of high school, go on welfare, parent poorly, and recycle many of their problems to the next generation. How can we interrupt this pattern? Current programs seem to focus primarily on survival in terms of shelter, food, clothing, and medical care, but do not change the behavior patterns.

2. Chronically unemployed people need something different from what they have received in terms of preparation for self-sufficiency. There is an enormous gulf between government employment training program expectations and the abilities of many of our clients to become trained and employable. Major flaws include assumptions about ability to learn and perform in a competitive environment and about the work ethic. The workplace is not able to deal with people who have not absorbed work ethic values. Could there be some middle position between the "all or nothing" extremes of most employers?

3. I have discovered from working in a bureaucracy that the more competent a person is on the job, and the more work a person is capable of doing, the more work he or she is assigned. Conversely, the less competent person is assigned less work. There is little correlation between work performed and salary. If I were a supervisor, what would I do to reward hard work and high levels of performance?

4. Abused and neglected children are the saddest victims of all. They brought nothing on themselves, yet their chances of success are extremely limited. Success, to a large extent, correlates with children's ability to perform in school. Their performance will be hindered by moving from shelter to foster home to home, changing schools, missing many days, lacking consistent parental support and help, having poor clothing, diet, and self-esteem, and other barriers. We can predict failure, but we can't do anything to change it.

5. Lots of people in this wealthy country are worse off than lots of animals in this country. There ought to be minimum standards for food, clothing, housing, and medical care below which no one should be allowed to fall. Governments at all levels claim lack of resources, when it is clearly a matter of priorities.

6. Bureaucracy has a tendency to become an end in itself. Its manuals become a way of life for many of its employees. People in severe emotional pain bring their needs to our agency and we look up an answer in the manual and quote it to them. Sometimes all they want is to make contact with a human being, and they are unable to do so in our agency. What would it take to humanize a large bureaucratic organization like ours?

7. The corporate sector has reaped enormous benefits from our economic system. Gross national product continues to grow and many corporations are moving from a national to an international market. As a sort of a "return" or "payback" for their success, the corporate sector donates a few dollars to charitable organizations. Rarely do they get involved directly in the habilitation or rehabilitation of human beings, even though they control the means to self-sufficiency and success. If all employable people were somehow tied to a job with benefits, the need for income assistance and human services would be greatly reduced.

CASE EXAMPLE 2: FRAIL ELDERLY CASE MANAGEMENT

Case managers work in a variety of both public and private settings. They are responsible for screening potential clients, assessing client needs, developing care plans, mobilizing the resources to meet identified needs, and monitoring and evaluating the services provided. The case manager in this example works for a nonprofit senior citizens' center that is primarily funded by state and federal funds. She is assigned to the long-term care unit, and carries a caseload of approximately 100 clients. As part of the program evaluation, she was asked to keep a diary of what happened during a typical day. The following are excerpts from her diary:

Wednesday, 7:30 a.m. Arrived early to catch up on previous day's paperwork. Organized documents from eight cases from past two days, including two new care plans and five medical reports.

8:00–8:10 a.m. Mrs. Garcia, a seventy-nine-year-old woman, called. She was distraught over a letter received from the Social Security office, thinking it meant her benefits would be cut off. Explained that it was a form letter, indicating a routine change, not affecting the amount of her check. Knowing that she is often forgetful and has a hearing problem, made a note to make home visit tomorrow to be certain she understands what was said.

8:10–8:30 a.m. Met with Jim from In-Home Support Services. Mr. Thomas, a ninety-three-year-old man, had fallen last night and was in Mercy Hospital. Homemaker had found him when she arrived at 7:00 this morning. He is not expected to live. Homemaker is very upset. Called his daughter and will plan to meet her at hospital later this morning.

8:30–9:30 a.m. Staff meeting regarding ten clients discharged from City Hospital with inadequate discharge plans. Discussed how to work better with discharge planners from hospital since this situation continues to be a problem. As I left meeting, another case manager told me that my client, Mrs. Hannibal, had refused to let the home health nurse into her apartment.

9:30–9:45 a.m. Called Mrs. Hannibal, but no one answered the phone. Called the emergency assistance program to meet me at her apartment.

9:45–10:00 a.m. Drove to Mrs. Hannibal's apartment. No one answered, so got manager to let me in. Mrs. Hannibal was very paranoid, had been drinking, threw bottle at me and screamed that "no one is going to get me out of here. I'll never go to a home. I'll die first." Worked with emergency assistance staff to get Mrs. Hannibal calmed down. She is a sixty-seven-year-old widow. She goes in and out of the hospital every two months. Has a severe drinking problem.

10:00–11:00 a.m. Arrived at Mercy Hospital. Met Mr. Thomas's daughter. She was in tears, saying it was all her fault, that if he had been living with her this would have never happened. Talked with her regarding fact that her father had wanted to live alone, that this had been his choice. Contacted hospital social worker to work with daughter.

11:15–12:00 a.m. Back to office. Wrote up visits to Mrs. Hannibal and Mr. Thomas. Called two new referrals and set up appointments to do assessments tomorrow. Received call from Mrs. Roman, age eighty-three. She is very lonely and wondered when I would be seeing her. Her husband died last week and she is crying. Has no family. Assured her I would be by to see her on Friday.

12:00–12:30 p.m. Ate lunch with adult protective services (APS) worker. Discussed Mr. and Mrs. Tan's abusive relationship. They are in their sixties and live in public housing. Agreed to work closely with APS regarding this situation.

12:45–2:00 p.m. Conducted in-home assessment for new client, Ms. Johnson. Ms. Johnson was just released from the hospital yesterday and is receiving home-delivered meals and in-home nursing. She needs chore and housekeeping services. Her small home is a total mess and roaches are everywhere. Because there is a waiting list for chore services, I called and pleaded with volunteers at the center to assist her temporarily. Client was too weak to continue with full assessment, so will come back tomorrow.

2:30–3:30 p.m. Attended public hearing in preparation for area agency on aging planning process. Presented written and verbal documentation of problems identified in working with my caseload.

3:45–4:15 p.m. Stopped by Sunnyside Nursing Home to see Mrs. Martinez. Has been my client for five years and has just been admitted to Sunnyside. She does not know me and seems very confused. Checked with facility social worker regarding what medications she is on and agreed to call physician regarding potential drug interactions.

4:45–5:15 p.m. Returned to office to find that Mr. Thomas had died. Called his daughter. Called physician regarding Mrs. Martinez's medications. He is angry and tells me it is none of my business. As I hang up, receive call from home health aide referring client to us. Had to tell her that client did not qualify for our services, but referred her to for-profit agency in town.

5:00–5:30 p.m. Tried to clean up desk. Decided to stop by Mrs. Garcia's on way home to check on her before tomorrow.

Just as the CPS worker had kept a running list of the kinds of dilemmas he faced through the years, the case manager had kept a list of her dilemmas as well. In preparation for the area agency on aging public hearing, she had updated the list in hopes that something could be done to deal with her ongoing frustrations. Excerpts from her list follow:

1. So many of the older people I see have had problems all their lives. It is as if you can almost identify what is going to happen in their old age by what happens to them as they go through life. Certainly drug and alcohol problems seem to get worse, but if they had only had someone to intervene when they began having these problems. These behavior patterns are so set by the time I encounter them, that I really don't have a lot of hope. I know that people can change at any age, but I believe that it would have been easier to deal with these problems earlier.

2. Although we have some limited funds to serve any older person in need, regardless of income, the majority of our funding is tied to income eligibility. Our slots for those persons who are not destitute are quickly filled and there is a long waiting list. Therefore, clients above the income eligibility level are referred to for-profit agencies or to other nonprofits that have sliding fee scales. What is ironic is that it is those persons who have worked hard all their lives who get left out in the cold—persons with not enough to pay

the full cost but who fall just above our eligibility guidelines. This "notch group" includes persons who are not poor enough to qualify for help but who don't have enough to pay for other agencies' services. In our society I've concluded that if you aren't really poor or really rich, you had better hope your health holds out or you'll have nowhere to turn. How can we, as a nation, develop a system that respects the aged?

3. What I am finding out about case management is revealing. Case managers attempt to coordinate what is a nonsystem of services. If we had a "system," then we would not need to pay people like me and we could put those resources toward client services. Even our professional organizations have bought into it. The National Association of Social Workers and the National Council on Aging have developed guidelines and standards for case management. There is even a new journal on case management. We are investing a lot in institutionalizing case management when it covers up the real problem—that we don't have a service delivery system in place. What would a truly comprehensive, coordinated system of care look like?

4. How does one maintain a client-centered perspective in a cost-obsessive environment? Working closely with health care organizations, the term *managed care* comes up over and over again. It is really hard to explain that case management is more intensive and long term and that it requires balancing advocacy and gatekeeping roles. Managed care refers to a service delivery system in which treatment decisions are monitored in order to conserve clinical and fiscal resources. Is it possible for acute, long-term, and community-based care systems to balance client advocacy and fiscal constraint?

5. Old people are not a homogeneous group. There are really vulnerable subpopulations that get lost when one talks about "the aged." The clients in my caseload are primarily women who live alone and who are often members of minority groups. Because women and minorities have been oppressed all their lives, they are practically "invisible" now. This lifelong pattern of oppression will continue if we don't find ways to expose what is happening when people are younger. But my real fear is that if we do expose what is happening, no one in power will care.

CASE EXAMPLE 3: DISPLACED HOMEMAKER SERVICES

Many communities have designed programs and services to address the special needs of women. One such program targets displaced homemakers, persons who have experienced sudden and often traumatic change in their lives through separation, divorce, or widowhood. Having devoted their time to homemaking, they often encounter emotional and financial distress when their relationships alter.

A social worker was hired by a coalition of community groups interested in women's issues. Her task was to assess the status of displaced homemakers within the community and to make recommendations to the coalition. Excerpts from her field notes follow:

Tuesday, 9:00–10:00 a.m. Met with representatives from two state agencies to locate data on women in the workforce. Very productive meeting which resulted in identification of three studies on workforce characteristics. In addition, was referred to two groups that had conducted needs assessments on women's concerns in adjacent communities.

10:30–12:00 a.m. Drove to the community center to observe a support group for women experiencing divorce. Group was led by a member of the coalition. Twelve persons attended. Topics discussed were: no work experience outside the home and the accompanying economic fears, problems with taking care of children as single parents, emotional distress and grief over marital breakup, and lack of marketable skills and/or education needed to locate employment.

This meeting made me aware of how desperate these women feel. Several of the women had been married for over twenty years. Many emotions were expressed during the meeting. Some women said they were angry, others indicated they felt depressed.

12:30–2:00 p.m. Left support group to meet with five representatives from the AFDC program. We discussed the results of a recent survey of AFDC recipients. Although many of the women interviewed had been separated and divorced after only five years, 20 percent were teen mothers who had never married. We discussed the concept of displaced homemakers and whether the AFDC respondents could be described in this way. Certainly many of their needs for marketable skills, education, and money paralleled the needs of the morning's support group. However, the workers felt that they could not be described as displaced homemakers because they had seldom had the opportunity to be in a homemaking role for extended periods of time. This precipitated a long discussion regarding how we should define the target group.

2:30–4:00 p.m. Drove to the senior citizens' center to meet with the widows' support group. They had requested a speaker from the coalition. After my brief presentation, the group discussed their concerns. Five of the twenty persons present had worked outside the home all their lives and another eight had worked outside the home part time. The remaining seven described themselves as displaced homemakers who had been widowed in their fifties and had experienced severe financial problems when their spouses had died. They encouraged the coalition to focus on preparing women to understand finances and to obtain skills that would make them more marketable.

4:15–5:30 p.m. Tried to collect my thoughts. Returned several phone calls and began reading the state reports obtained this morning. The reports focused on the menial jobs women assumed, often without adequate benefits.

The dilemmas experienced by this social worker are somewhat different from those outlined in the previous two case examples. This professional was hired to assess a community situation described to her by members of a coalition. Her direct practice background gave her considerable insight in understanding women's issues, yet her first days on the job required a great deal of reflection. She outlined a number of questions and concerns.

1. Defining a target group sounds simple enough, but it isn't always clear. As I met with various community groups I realized that the concept of "displaced homemaker" cuts across population groups—young mothers, middle-aged widows, women of divorce at all ages, etc. The coalition needs to remain open to various groups and must recognize the implications of how this concept may shape the definition of the problem. How inclusive do we want

to be? Is this concept relevant to persons who have never had the option to remain at home? Should we begin without a concept in mind so that we don't script ourselves into fitting people into the mold of a "displaced homemaker"?

2. Not only is it difficult to define the problem, but there will be continued danger as we analyze it. Too often we view women's issues in a "we–they" context that would really alienate men and some women. How can we analyze the problem so that we don't impose dichotomous thinking on the process— as if women are one way and men are another way. There are many differences among women, too. Just because one woman feels a certain way does not mean that others feel similarly. I wonder if this may be why women of color are not well-represented in the coalition. The very way we define the problem may be insensitive to some women.

3. One thing I'm learning is that as the coalition designs its needs assessment, it will be necessary to use a multimethod approach. It is important to maintain a balance between the statistics about a target population and what is learned through face-to-face interaction. The latter is particularly time-consuming. What balance is appropriate and who should be involved in this process?

4. There are themes that seem to emerge across all the groups. Women keep talking about how devalued they feel and support groups focus on finding one's voice. Why does it take a crisis before we socialize women to find their voices and to value who they are? It seems we need to rethink the very messages that children are given in their early gender identity development and this means change that penetrates the very fibers of our society.

5. Coalition building is essential to community ownership of a problem. The coalition that wants to assess the status of women is composed of community-based women's groups. Where are the men? Many of the powerful leaders and groups in the community are not part of this coalition. What other groups should be involved? How can we build a base that assures broad support from the community?

6. In the women I've observed, I have seen tremendous strength. Yet, we always focus on the weaknesses of their economic and social dependency. Is it possible that helping professionals may see deficits before they see strengths? How can we develop the strengths of people in a society that may not always be open to hearing the female voice? How can we empower people regardless of gender?

7. There are real economic and policy issues here. The AFDC program is underfunded in this state and women have to make tremendous sacrifices. Without adequate child-care services, some mothers are reluctant to leave ·their children in order to find work. Even when women locate jobs, their options are limited. Several women explained that they worked for just above minimum wage but that the most frightening aspect of their employment was they still had no health benefits. Are these the issues that the coalition should be addressing? We can't do everything. How do we establish priorities?

SURVIVING THE DILEMMAS

We have presented these rather lengthy scenarios and the accompanying concerns expressed by social workers in an attempt to characterize the kinds of issues and problems social workers face almost every day. The nature of a capitalist economy is that some people are able to compete and to succeed; others are not. For the most part, social workers deal with those who are not able to care for at least a part of their own needs. Sometimes the stark contrast between their deprivation and the affluence we are all exposed to can be a source of frustration and confusion to a social worker who daily must live in both worlds. Faced with these contrasts, Sherman and Wenocur (1983) say that a practitioner has a number of choices:

1. *Capitulation.* The social worker can decide to deal with clients and ignore the larger issues. Capitulation means that the practitioner will accept organizational norms, do the best that can be done, but relinquish the advocacy role. This is a tempting option because taking on the larger issues can add many hours of work to an already busy week for what often seems like an impossible task.

2. *Noncapitulation.* The noncapitulator becomes an activist, joining as many organizations and efforts as time and energy will allow. Rejecting the norms of what is viewed as a flawed organization, the noncapitulator tries to effect systemic change through whatever means possible. Adopting an independent stance from the organization in which he or she works, the social worker quickly becomes a maverick or "house radical." Often these persons become labeled as uncooperative and immature, losing credibility as they fight for change.

3. *Niche Finding.* The niche finder sidesteps conflict by focusing on an area of expertise or assuming a set of responsibilities that establishes an independent base of power within the organization. Basically, these practitioners distance themselves from the political and economic issues that affect service delivery. They acknowledge the problems and concerns that arise, but typically stay out of the central life of the organization and community.

4. *Withdrawal.* Frustrated and burned-out practitioners may decide to leave the organization in which they work or to leave social work altogether. Unable or unwilling to continue to deal with the ambiguities inherent in their professional practice, withdrawal becomes their option of choice.

5. *Self-Victimization—Martyrdom.* Social workers can get caught in believing that they are working at impossible jobs. They stay in the system and feel powerless—accepting the role that they, too, are victims of the things they cannot control. Unlike noncapitulators who overidentify with clients, these workers become mired in their own martyrdom. The worker-martyr overworks, stays late, complains frequently, and perpetuates the cycle of powerlessness.

6. *Functional Noncapitulation.* Together with other concerned colleagues, practitioners can apply professional knowledge and skill toward an orderly, systematic change effort designed to resolve at least a part of a problem and, hopefully, work toward its reduction and eventual elimination. This is the approach taken by most committed social work professionals. Together with colleagues, workers form committees and task forces with the intent of changing organizational and community problems.

Much of the work done by functional noncapitulators is what we refer to as macro practice, and is carried out with widely varying degrees of skill. The purpose of this text is to present a theoretical base and a practice model designed to assist the professional social worker in bringing about change in organizations and communities. We encourage its readers to become functional noncapitulators within the organizations and communities in which they will work.

WHY MACRO PRACTICE?

The beginning student will find that most social work literature reinforces the importance of practitioners' macro-level responsibilities. Why is this such an important issue? The answer has a great deal to do with the mission and history of the profession, and the development of a value base which has become the cornerstone of professional social work practice.

Although Chapter 2 will focus on historical development, understanding the professional mission of social work is essential to recognizing why macro practice is important. In a provocative argument, Specht (1990) challenges social work's contemporary interest in the "popular psychotherapies."

> [They have] diverted social work from its original vision, a vision of the perfectibility of society, the building of the "city beautiful," the "new society," and the "new frontier." There is a yet unfulfilled mission for social work that might be resuscitated. It is a mission to deal with the enormous social problems under which our society staggers: the social isolation of our aged, the anomie experienced by our youths, the neglect and abuse of children, homelessness, drug addiction, and AIDS.
>
> Our mission must be to build a meaning, a purpose, and a sense of obligation for the community, not one by one. It is only by creating a community that we establish a basis for commitment, obligation, and social support. We must build communities that are excited about their child-care systems, that find it exhilarating to care for the mentally ill and the frail aged. (pp. 354–56)

Earlier in this chapter we presented three case examples of what included seemingly unresolvable dilemmas. Yet, the lists of questions and concerns expressed by the three social work practitioners reflect their attempts to hold on to the mission described by Specht. This mission is built on a set of values.

Barker (1987) defines values as "the customs, standards of contact and principles considered desirable by a culture, a group of people, or an individual" (p. 171). He goes on to explain that in 1982, social workers, as a professional group, stated some of the overriding values for their practice. These values were published in the *NASW Standards for the Classification of Social Work Practice*. They were:

> Commitment to the primary importance of the individual in society,
> Respect for the confidentiality of relationships with clients,
> Commitment to social change to meet socially recognized needs,

Willingness to keep personal feelings and needs separate from professional relationships,

Willingness to transmit knowledge and skills to others,

Respect and appreciation for individual and group differences,

Commitment to develop clients' ability to help themselves,

Willingness to persist in efforts on behalf of clients despite frustration,

Commitment to social justice and the economic, physical, and mental well-being of all in society, and

Commitment to a high standard of personal and professional conduct.
(Barker 1987, 171)

These values do not cover the entire NASW Code of Ethics, but they do provide a general orientation to the positions taken by the profession on the larger issues relating to responsible and conscientious professional behavior. In all social work practice, there is clearly an expectation that the social worker will, when the situation calls for it, become involved beyond the simple needs of a "case" or client and initiate change at the organizational or community level.

In many ways it is this commitment to the understanding and changing of larger systems that separates social work from other professional disciplines. Few other professions have adopted the same "systems perspective." Thus, while a committee or a task force might be made up of many disciplines, the professional social worker who is doing macro practice is operating from a knowledge and value base that includes a number of considerations:

Informed Approach. First, the macro practitioner approaches the need for change with an understanding and expectation that decisions will be based on as complete a set of data and information as time and resources allow. Informed decision making is pursued in a systematic and scholarly manner, utilizing the best available theoretical, research-based, and practice-based knowledge.

Consumer Input and Participation. Although it may be more time-consuming and take more energy to include clients in change processes, the social worker must always look for client input. Finding new and meaningful ways to facilitate citizen participation in organizational and community arenas is an ongoing challenge for the dedicated professional.

Fit of Problem to Solution, Based on a Thorough Analysis. Defining the problem to be changed requires integrating what clients have to say with scholarly research and practice results. This analytical process is dynamic and interactive, often causing the change agent to reframe the original problem statement. But once the problem statement is agreed upon, social workers must ascertain that their interventions make sense in relation to the problem at hand. Interventions often require a creative imagination that goes beyond traditional approaches.

Goal Directed. Goals are broadly defined aims toward which practitioners guide their efforts. They are usually long term and sometimes idealistic.

However, goals provide a vision shared by clients and colleagues—a hope of what can be—and they assist the practitioner in maintaining a focus.

Outcome Oriented. Outcomes are defined as quality of life changes in clients' lives, based on the interventions planned by social work practitioners. Outcomes can be determined by professionals, based on what they think clients would want, but the best test of an outcome is whether or not the clients themselves really see it as meaningful and valuable.

Social workers have the opportunity to facilitate change. Based on a set of values, macro social work practice progresses in an informed manner, incorporating clients into the dynamic process, designing interventions to meet well-analyzed problems. Broad goals and specific outcomes provide the focused direction.

SUMMARY

In this chapter we have tried to provide the basic foundations on which students can build an understanding of social work macro practice. We defined macro practice as professionally directed intervention designed to bring about planned change in organizations and communities, and we began a discussion of the circumstances leading to the need for planned change.

To do this, we used comments from former students who are now practicing social workers. These comments illustrate how the circumstances that are often most troubling to social workers are not only the concerns of their clients but also the management of their organization or the resources available within their community. These points were reinforced through three case vignettes showing how policies, program structures, resource deficits, and other macro-related criteria have much to do with social workers' abilities to be effective in their jobs.

One way that social workers sometimes respond to these realities is to give up fighting against them. This is done through capitulation, withdrawal, self-martyrdom, or other approaches, all of which reduce the worker's professional effectiveness. However, social workers who are skilled in macro practice have another option, that of *functional noncapitulation,* in which they use their understanding of macro systems to bring about needed changes in these systems. These skills are not, and should not be, limited to those who are working in traditional macro-practice roles such as administration or planning. Instead, they are critical for all social workers to know, including those engaged mostly in micro practice.

Parts II, III, and IV of this textbook will provide a macro-practice model to guide social workers in undertaking change processes. But first, Chapters 2 and 3 will provide more detailed historical and values perspectives for macro practice in social work.

REFERENCES

Barker, R. L. (1987) *The social work dictionary.* Silver Spring, MD: National Association of Social Workers.

Meenaghan, T. M. (1987) Macro practice: Current trends and issues. *Encyclopedia of social work* (18th ed., 2: 82–89). Silver Spring, MD: National Association of Social Workers.

Sherman, W. R., and S. Wenocur. (1983) Empowering public welfare workers through mutual support. *Social Work, 28*(5): 375–79.

Specht, H. (1990) Social work and popular psychotherapies. *Social Service Review, 64*(3): 345–57.

CHAPTER 2
The Historical Roots of Macro Practice

INTRODUCTION

In Chapter 1, we defined macro practice and illustrated how all social workers must understand and interact with macro systems in society, even if they are involved primarily in practice with individuals or small groups. Chapter 2 provides the background and context for macro practice, though it is not designed to provide an exhaustive historical perspective. It is assumed that social work students will have a working knowledge of how the profession developed overall and that other textbooks will be devoted to more extensive treatments of social welfare history. In this chapter we will briefly examine the trends and events that paved the way for the emergence and integration of macro roles within the profession.

Some activities of macro practitioners have been carried out on an informal basis since people first began forming communities and organizations. However, the history of professional macro practice, like the history of the social work profession, dates back little more than 100 years. This period spans an era of pervasive and sustained social change, and the development of modern social work practice models (both macro and micro) is in large part a response to this change. Thus, to understand the roots of macro practice, it is necessary to review certain historical developments that contributed to the evolution and differentiation of professional social work.

First, we will briefly examine the broad social trends that contributed to the growth of social welfare institutions and the appearance of social work roles. These trends began to be felt strongly in the late 1800s when urbanization, industrialization, and ideological shifts forced the development of more organized responses to human need.

Second, we will review the development of professional social work. The divergence of micro- and macro-level interventions began early in this development, with charity organization workers focusing on what would become known as the casework method while settlement house workers joined forces with newly arrived immigrants to push for change at the community level. Since then the emphasis on macro practice has undergone periods of ebb and flow within the field, and historical events connected with these trends will be reviewed. Among these are the rise of professionalism beginning early in this century, the psychoanalytical focus of direct practice in the 1930s and 1940s, and the expanding role of the federal government in providing social welfare services.

Third, we will examine the contemporary recognition of the need for integrating micro and macro practice, including a review of the forces that led to this recognition. Finally, the current environment of professional practice will be considered. A number of important forces for change exist within this environment, and both their present influence and their implications for future directions will be discussed.

Central to this historical review are two main points. First, the history of the social work profession in general and of macro practice in particular are both inseparably tied to the history of the larger society. Any understanding of the changes that have taken place in professional practice must, therefore, be based in an understanding of how these changes reflected new conditions arising in society as a whole. Second, both society and social work practice continue to change, and learning from the conflicts and uncertainties of the past will assist practitioners in planning for the future. In a very real sense, the social work heritage is a tradition of growth and change.

TRENDS UNDERLYING THE EMERGENCE
OF SOCIAL WORK ROLES

Preceding the birth of social work as a profession, a number of trends had developed that eventually brought about recognition of the need for macro-level responses to societal problems. Among these, Garvin and Cox (1987) call attention to: (1) broad social conditions, (2) ideological conflicts, and (3) oppressed populations. We will also use these divisions in our discussion.

Broad Social Conditions

The first U.S. census in 1790 revealed a national population of less than 4 million. By 1900 this number had grown to almost 92 million, and the census count in 1990 exceeded 250 million. The period of fastest growth was in the 1800s, when the nation's population increased by more than one-third every ten years throughout the first half of the century and, despite the death and destruction of the Civil War, continued to grow by more than 25 percent per decade during the century's second half. The rate of growth moderated after 1900, with increases diminishing to about 11 percent per decade since 1960. Still, in raw numbers, the nation continues to add roughly twenty-four million persons to its population every ten years.

Of particular importance to this population growth was the effect of *immigration*. The first massive wave of immigrants began in the 1840s. To the East Coast came Irish and German immigrants fleeing famine and political upheaval, respectively. To the West Coast came the Chinese to obtain labor during the California gold rush. Successive waves followed from Southern and Eastern Europe as well as Asia, reaching a peak during 1900–1910 when immigrants totaled over six million and accounted for almost 40 percent of the nation's population growth. Though arrivals slowed after 1920, the proportion of population growth accounted for by immigration rose to almost 20 percent in the 1980s, with most immigrants coming from Latin America and Asia (Bogue 1985).

Accompanying the country's population growth was a rapid shift toward *industrialization* of its economy. Axinn and Levin (1992) illustrate the effects of this shift by noting that production of cotton in the South was only 6,000 bales the year before the invention of the cotton gin in 1793, whereas output grew to 73,000 bales by 1800 and to almost four million bales near the start of the Civil War in 1860. This type of change also transformed working life throughout the country. In 1820, for example, nearly three of every four workers were employed in agriculture, a ratio that dropped to less than two in five by 1900 and to about one in thirty-five by 1985. Similarly, the contribution of the agricultural sector to overall national income fell from 20 percent in the 1880s to just 2.4 percent in 1985 (U.S. Bureau of the Census 1987). The economic opportunity generated by increasing industrialization in many ways made the nation's population growth possible.

The combination of population growth and industrialization brought about increased *urbanization*. As recently as 1910, over half the population still lived in rural areas; by 1980, almost three-fourths lived in urban areas. Warren (1978) notes that no U.S. city had a population of 50,000 as of the 1790 census, whereas almost 400 such cities existed by 1970. Initially, much of this growth occurred in the urban core of large industrial cities, compared to the more recent increases taking place in suburbs and medium-size cities. Still, no American city reached a population of one million until the 1880s. Today more than half of all U.S. residents live in the thirty-seven metropolitan areas having populations of a million or more (Bogue 1985).

Accompanying these trends were fundamental changes in the *institutional structure* of society, the system of organizations that meet people's needs. In the early 1800s, these organizations tended to be informal, few in number, and small in scope (e.g., families, churches, and schools). Engaged primarily in agriculture and living in rural areas, people were largely self-sufficient and depended on these organizations for a relatively narrow range of needs. With the advent of industrialization, however, new technologies were linked with advances in methods of organizing, and a new social structure began to emerge. The hallmark of this structure is a complex system of highly specialized organizations designed to meet very specific needs. These range from accounting firms to computer manufacturers to adoption agencies, and they exemplify the enormous diversity and complexity of modern society.

Changes in broad social conditions that contributed to the development of social work thus included population growth, industrialization, urbanization, and changes in the institutional structure of society. The institutional changes were particularly relevant to social work because they most directly influenced the development of organizations that deliver services to people in need.

Ideological Conflicts

Not surprisingly, changes in broad conditions coincided with considerable ideological change. Garvin and Cox (1987) identify several viewpoints that arose during the late 1800s in response to these conditions. These include Social Darwinism, radical ideology, and liberalism.

In the late 1800s, Herbert Spencer, an English writer, applied Charles Darwin's biological theories to society. *Social Darwinism* emphasized survival of the fittest, reasoning that persons with wealth and power in society achieved this status because they were more fit than those without such resources. It was also hypothesized that, though in the biological world genetic mutations could survive and overcome inferior traits, in societies some groups are inherently inferior. Not surprisingly, this philosophy was embraced by many of the wealthy. Social Darwinism was used to argue that little should be done for the poor and dispossessed on the grounds that such help would simply perpetuate social inferiority.

Social Darwinism also provided the ideological underpinning for the philosophy of *manifest destiny,* which helped to fuel westward expansion during the 1800s. Coined by a democratic politician in 1845, this term described the belief that God had willed the land to the Anglo-Saxon race to build a utopian world. Such a world would fuse capitalism, Protestantism, and democracy, and in it Anglo-Saxon peoples were not to dilute their superiority by marrying members of other races (Jansson 1988).

Partly as a reaction to the racism and classism inherent in these views, but also in response to the growing influence of Karl Marx and other socialist writers, a *radical ideology* developed. This view is closely associated with the rise of the labor movement, which drew its strength from the terrible conditions afflicting most industrial laborers at the time. One goal of the proponents of this view was the transfer of industrial control from capitalists to trade unions. However, the growing plight of the poor also led to community organizing efforts designed to mobilize and empower this population (Garvin & Cox 1987).

Liberalism arose partly as a secular expression of Judeo-Christian values of egalitarianism and social responsibility that were seen as a means of tempering the excesses of a laissez-faire economic system. In this view, human rights supersede property rights, and society is seen as having a responsibility for promoting the collective good. One of the expressions of liberalism was *scientific charity,* which advocated "a method of investigation and planned helping, case by case, that would build on and strengthen the informal or natural 'fountains of charity' and not displace or weaken them" (Leiby 1987, 764). This view was to contribute powerfully to the rise of the first private human service agencies— the Charity Organization Societies—in the late 1800s.

Oppressed Populations

New social conditions such as the changing face of the U.S. population and shifts in ideology intensified prejudicial attitudes and discriminatory behavior toward certain groups. As is often the case, these beliefs and actions were commonly directed toward groups already suffering the negative effects of rapid social change. The following review thus focuses on trends affecting populations whose members would later become particular sources of concern for professional social workers.

Among Native Americans in the 1800s and early 1900s oppression was literally governmental policy, enacted via war, forcible relocation, and confinement to reservations. The Removal Act of 1830 gave the federal government the right to relocate any native peoples living east of the Mississippi River. For many tribes this move meant virtual genocide. Relocation of the Cherokee nation in 1838, for example, produced massive losses from disease and exposure, becoming known as the Trail of Tears. Beginning in the 1890s, generations of Native American youth were forced into off-reservation boarding schools where they were forbidden the use of their own language and made to "think, act, look and be, in every way possible, like members of white society" (Beane 1989, 38). Though the goal of this policy was to speed assimilation into white culture, the main effect was to severely damage Native American family life.

More than 100,000 indigenous Spanish-speaking people in the Southwest became part of the United States following the Treaty of Guadalupe Hidalgo at the end of the Mexican-American War in 1848. Though the treaty included specific protections regarding property rights and civil liberties, many people were still forced from their lands. Language was an especially common tool of oppression, with Latinos being denied participation in voting and public education because they were not proficient in English. Following the Mexican Revolution in 1910, large waves of Mexican immigrants began to face similar barriers. During the Depression years of the 1930s, unemployment pressures led to huge deportations of supposedly illegal residents, as many as half of whom were in fact U.S. citizens (Gibson 1987).

African Americans were treated poorly despite their emancipation from slavery in the Civil War. In 1865, the final year of the war, the Ku Klux Klan was formed and began its reign of terror in the South, effectively denying many blacks the freedoms they had only recently gained. On a policy level, segregation began to achieve similar ends. In the landmark *Plessy v. Ferguson* decision of 1896, the U.S. Supreme Court upheld the segregationist doctrine of "separate but equal" facilities, in this case with regard to public transportation. Trattner (1989) notes that even in the Progressive Era and the New Deal years, social welfare gains had a much greater impact on poverty among whites than among blacks.

On the West Coast, Chinese immigrants had been exploited as cheap labor. When economic conditions changed, hostility resulted in violence. In 1882, Congress enacted the Chinese Exclusion Act, which became permanent in 1902 (Garvin & Cox 1987). This act outlawed all Chinese immigration until its repeal in 1943. Japanese immigration increased between 1890 and 1907, resulting in changes to California state laws that restricted the ability of the Japanese to own or even lease property. Later, in one of the most egregious examples of governmental discrimination by race, hundreds of thousands of Japanese were forcibly relocated to internment camps during the Second World War.

Though the roots of feminism emerged during the 1800s, most women remained relegated to traditional subordinate roles. Women's suffrage was identified as a central goal at an early national Women's Rights Convention in 1848, but this goal was not to be reached for another seventy-one years. Viewed as keepers of the hearth and nurturers of the family, women were placed on a pedestal of romantic idealization that also served as a prison to constrain their thoughts and actions (Jansson 1988).

Gays and lesbians, because of longstanding and widespread persecution, were traditionally the most hidden of oppressed groups. For many years, homosexuality was viewed primarily through the lens of religious taboos and was thus considered sinful behavior. However, English law, unlike that of many other European countries, made homosexuality a crime as well, and as recently as 1816, English sailors were executed for the crime of "buggery" (Marotta 1981). English legal codes on homosexuality were adopted in the United States, and, though not always enforced, they were often used selectively as a means of harassment. More recently, drawing in part on theories advanced by Sigmund Freud, gays and lesbians were considered mentally ill, and could be forcibly subjected to hospitalization or other measures designed to cure their "perversions" (Szasz 1965).

The oppression of ethnic minorities, women, and sexual minorities predated the development of the social work profession. The profession, thus, was born into an environment in which social change was needed.

THE DEVELOPMENT OF THE
SOCIAL WORK PROFESSION

The effects of oppression, ideological shifts, and broad social changes created social pressures that could not be indefinitely ignored. The first organized efforts to respond to these pressures also formed the basis for development of social work. Among these efforts were the Charity Organization Societies (COS) and the settlement house movement.

Local COS agencies, which began forming in the 1870s, were usually umbrella organizations that coordinated the activities of a wide variety of charities created to deal with the problems of immigrants and rural transplants who were flooding into industrialized northern cities in search of jobs. Social Darwinism provided the philosophical roots of the movement, thus the "scientific charity" provided by COS agencies tended to be moralistic in tone and oriented mostly toward persons deemed able to become members of the industrial workforce (Axinn & Levin 1992). Workers in the COS agencies were often volunteers, especially middle- and upper-class women, who served as "friendly visitors" to poor individuals and families. These volunteers commonly shared idealistic goals of providing the poor with an opportunity to better themselves, but they had a high stake in weeding fraudulent claimants from the ranks of those seen as both truly needy and open to reform (Chambers 1985).

While the COS movement represented one response to human need, settlement houses adopted a somewhat different approach. Conditions in the crowded slums and tenement houses of industrial cities in the late 1800s were as dire as any in the nation's history, and the goal of the settlement houses was to attack these problems on a systemic level. This meant an approach to practice that emphasized societal as well as individual and group reform. Many of the settlement houses served as religious missions and, like the COS members, did their share of proselytizing and moralizing. Nonetheless, they were also more willing to meet their mostly immigrant constituents on their own grounds and to believe that chasms of class, religion, nationality, and culture could be spanned. In addition, their societal vision tended to be pluralistic; whereas COS workers feared organized efforts such as the labor movement, settlement leaders tended to support these endeavors. In particular, settlement house workers played prominent roles in the birth of organizations including the National Association for the Advancement of Colored People, the Women's Trade Union League, and the American Civil Liberties Union (Chambers 1985).

Women played a major role in building the foundations of social work in both the COS and settlement house movements. Benevolent work was viewed as compatible with women's nurturing roles in society, and, ironically, even the social change roles played by women were justifiable as " 'civic housekeeping' [that] was but an extension of women's concern for family welfare into the public sphere" (Chambers 1986, 13).

Service responsibility gradually began to shift from volunteers to paid employees. COS workers emphasized the need for a systematic approach to the work. Settlement house workers demanded training on how to effect social change. Both traditions "developed and promoted neighborhood-based research" (Brieland 1990, 135). The need for education and training contributed to the organization of social work education. In 1903, the Chicago School of Civics and Philanthropy was established, followed in 1904 by the founding of the New York School of Philanthropy and the Boston School for Social Workers (Jansson 1988). Accompanying these efforts, a debate ensued over whether the fledgling profession should focus on macro or micro social work models. Macro models, concerned with fundamental social policy issues, demanded an academic curriculum based on social theory with an orientation toward analysis and reform. A parallel movement, represented by Jane Addams, emphasized training for political activism. It promoted not only economic reforms but also a pacifist agenda (e.g., advocating peace negotiations instead of military involvement in World War I). Finally, micro models focused on case-by-case assistance and required that caseworkers learn how to conduct field work.

An important turning point in this debate was the 1915 meeting of the National Conference of Charities and Corrections, described as the "most significant event in the development of the intellectual rationalization for social work as an organized profession" (Austin 1983, 359). Abraham Flexner, the most prominent national figure in medical education, was asked to address the issue of whether social work was truly a profession. He argued that social work still lacked certain characteristics of a profession and could more appropriately be called a semiprofession, a view that Austin (1983) says was typically applied to careers in which women predominated. Flexner's six characteristics of a true profession were: (1) professionals operate intellectually with large individual responsibility; (2) they derive their raw material from science and learning; (3) this material is applied practically; (4) an educationally communicable technique exists; (5) there is a tendency toward self-organization or association; and (6) professions become increasingly altruistic in motivation (Austin 1983).

In a more or less unquestioning response to Flexner's remarks, social workers hurried to adopt these characteristics. In 1917, Mary Richmond published *Social Diagnosis,* which brought one-on-one casework practice to the fore and cast it firmly in a traditional, professional mold. As Reisch and Wenocur (1986) argue, the book "redefined investigation as diagnosis and thereby linked social work to the occupational symbols of the medical and legal professions" (p. 77). The focus on diagnosis was further strengthened by the influence of Freudian psychotherapy, which became the dominant theoretical basis for casework practice throughout almost the next half-century.

COMMUNITY ORGANIZATION AND SOCIAL REFORM

Though inconspicuous and not specifically professionally focused, the development of macro-practice models continued. By 1920, the first social work textbook on community organization had appeared, and at least five more books on the subject were written within the next ten years. Prominent social work educators such as Mary Follett and Eduard Lindeman also continued to discuss the role of social workers in promoting community development (Garvin & Cox 1987).

In addition, a radical social work movement emerged in the mid-1920s that reached a peak in the New Deal Era and was embraced as a part of professional identity in the early 1940s. Unionization efforts in the late 1920s and early 1930s resulted in social workers such as Bertha Capen Reynolds collaborating with other professions to reduce management abuses and ameliorate the effects of workforce reductions and pay cuts. Social workers also marched side by side with residents of urban slums demanding improved housing conditions. These social workers were mostly young, held low-level positions such as case managers and community action organizers, and did not strongly identify with "professional" social workers (Wagner 1989).

The Great Depression was a watershed event in the history of macro practice. In the four-year period from 1929 to 1933, the gross national product of the United States fell by almost half, and unemployment reached 25 percent. The resulting impoverishment of vast segments of the population raised doubts about traditional notions that poor people were responsible for their own plight and could solve it through personal reform. As Axinn and Levin (1992) note:

> The depression brought forcibly to consciousness the point that one could be poor and unemployed as a result of the malfunctioning of society. The temporary relief programs developed to meet the exigencies of the depression acknowledged the existence of this kind of poverty and of a "new poor." The later permanent programs of the Social Security Act recognized the possibility of inherent societal malfunctioning. (p. 171)

This was the point that settlement leaders and social reformers had long argued, and this view was to play an influential role in the development of Franklin D. Roosevelt's New Deal programs. A number of social workers and agency administrators who had supported New Deal-like reforms during Roosevelt's term as governor of New York later assumed key positions in his presidential administration. Harry Hopkins, head of the Federal Emergency Relief Administration (FERA), and Frances Perkins, secretary of labor, were the most visible of this community (Jansson 1988).

In an atmosphere of sweeping change, radical social workers cooperated with mainstream social work leaders during the late 1930s. The radical journal, *Social Work Today,* began to pay attention to social work practice, muting somewhat its traditional view that casework constituted a "Band-Aid" approach to client problems. Radical elements within the profession remained identifiable as the left wing in social work, but they were less dramatically differentiated from the liberal social work professional leadership. These shifts were facilitated by the achievement of mutual goals such as the Social Security Act in 1935 and passage of the Wagner Act, which guaranteed labor's right to organize.

After the mid-1930s, large governmental agencies began to dominate the provision of human services, and the battle of social work roles shifted to this arena. Reisch and Wenocur (1986) note that advocates of the casework model were well-placed in many of these organizations and developed job specifications that largely excluded community organizers. However, members of the Rank and File Movement of radical social workers also became involved in the public services arena (Wagner 1989).

The 1930s and 1940s set the stage for the development of later social movements. Though the 1950s were not a time of great tumult, events occurred during the decade that opened the door for considerable social change in the 1960s. For example, the landmark 1954 Supreme Court decision overturning school segregation became the foundation of the Civil Rights Movement. Beginning with the Montgomery, Alabama, bus boycott the following year, Martin Luther King, Jr., and the Southern Christian Leadership Conference began a campaign of nonviolent resistance through sit-ins, freedom rides, and demonstrations. In response to the struggles of blacks in the South and elsewhere, other social change movements began, including organization of Chicano farm workers in the Southwest by Cesar Chavez and others, the American Indian Movement (AIM), Gay Liberation, the Women's Movement, the student counterculture movement, Vietnam War resistance, and others. Participation in these movements provided on-the-job training for many community practitioners.

In the 1960s, expanded governmental social programs, though sometimes ill-conceived, provided new opportunities for community-level interventions. One catalyst for these changes was renewed awareness of the plight of poor people, brought on in part by books such as Michael Harrington's *The Other America.* John Kennedy's election in 1960 on a platform of social activism also played a part, resulting in programs such as Mobilization for Youth, inner-city delinquency prevention efforts, and the Peace Corps. On an international basis, these efforts helped refine models of community development (Trattner 1989).

In 1964, Lyndon Johnson's call for a war on poverty led to the passage of a vast array of social welfare programs. These programs left a mixed legacy of results but provided an opportunity for testing macro-practice models. One of the most important examples was the Community Action Program (CAP), part of the Economic Opportunity Act of 1964 that was a keystone of antipoverty legislation. The goal of CAP programs was to achieve better coordination of services among community providers and to facilitate citizen participation in decision making through "maximum feasible participation of the residents of the areas and the members of the groups being served" (U.S. Congress 1964, 9). Accordingly, CAP agencies were created in neighborhoods and communities throughout the country, recruiting residents to serve as board members or as paid employees alongside professionally trained staff members.

In their evaluation and critique of CAP initiatives, Peterson and Greenstone (1977) argue that the design and implementation of the programs largely undermined the first objective of improving coordination of services. However, they also argue that CAP agencies achieved considerably more success in their second objective of facilitating citizen participation, particularly in African American communities. In their view, "the contribution of [CAP agencies] to the organizational resources of local black communities was substantial . . . CAP's distinctive mission began the formation of new political linkages between black

Americans and the political order" (pp. 272–74). Other programs were less successful and in some cases resulted in harsh criticisms of social workers and their efforts. Within the field itself, however, accomplishments such as those of the CAP agencies helped to reestablish the importance of macro-practice roles.

Reflecting this trend, the Council on Social Work Education (CSWE), in 1962, recognized community organization as a method of social work practice comparable to group work and case work. In 1963, the Office of Juvenile Delinquency and Youth Development of the U.S. Department of Health, Education, and Welfare funded CSWE to develop curriculum for training community organizers. Between 1965 and 1969, the number of schools of social work providing training in community organization rose by 37 percent, eventually including virtually every school in the country (Garvin & Cox 1987). Community organization thus emerged as a legitimate part of social work practice.

MACRO PRACTICE IN ORGANIZATIONS

Communities are macro systems in which all social workers interact and for which practice models have evolved. However, communities are comprised of networks of organizations, and it is these organizations that usually hold the direct responsibility for carrying out basic community functions. As such, organizations are a second type of macro system with which social workers must be familiar. With respect to human service organizations, one important consideration is historical patterns of shifting emphasis between centralization and decentralization of agencies and services.

England's Elizabethan Poor Law of 1601, the first written law establishing a governmental system of services for the poor, adopted a decentralized approach to providing services. Under this law, assistance to the poor was a local function (as was taxation to pay for the assistance), and responsibility for service provision rested with an individual "overseer of the poor." This model was retained more or less intact in the American colonies, and until the 1800s, relief efforts for the needy remained primarily local and small in scale.

The reformist movement of the early nineteenth century began a slow transition to larger-scale services in the form of state-run asylums for dependent children, the mentally ill, and others. Later, as population, urban concentration, and service needs increased, so did the diversity of both public and private programs. Eventually, it became apparent that some sort of coordinating mechanism was needed for these various efforts. As Trattner (1989) notes:

> The situation in Massachusetts was typical. In 1859, the commonwealth had three state mental institutions, a reform school for boys, an industrial school for girls, a hospital, and three almshouses for the state or nonresident poor. In addition, four private charitable institutions—schools for the blind, the deaf and dumb, the feeble-minded, and an eye and ear infirmary—received state aid. Each of these was managed by its own board of trustees. So uncoordinated a system not only increased the cost of operation, but it did not provide for a channel of

communication between institutions; a reform in one, then, might not be implemented in the others. The situation obviously called for some method of state supervision. (p. 81)

The result was the creation of what became known as the State Boards of Charities, first in Massachusetts in 1863, then in another fifteen states by the mid-1890s. These boards represented the first real involvement of state governments in centralized coordination of welfare services, and they helped to establish standards for the administration of human service organizations.

For roughly the next sixty-five years, much of the development of human service organizations took place in the private sector. The formation of the COS agencies and settlement houses was a partial recognition of the advantages of establishing standard service practices within the framework of a strong organizational base. Efforts toward developing more comprehensive public agency involvement in social welfare services occurred during the Progressive movement in the early 1900s. One example was the creation of the first state public welfare department in Illinois in 1917. Still, the focus remained very much on decentralized service provision. There was relatively little growth among human service organizations in the public sector.

It was not until the Great Depression that public organizations for the provision of human services were established on a large scale. The New Deal programs created an infrastructure of organizations at the federal level that became both the foundations of the welfare state and the first large, governmental human service bureaucracies. In addition, a key function of these agencies was to distribute relief funds to various states, and this in turn helped to spur the creation of state-level public welfare organizations. Some programs, such as the Federal Emergency Relief Administration (FERA) and the Work Projects Administration (WPA) were established to respond directly to Depression-era problems and thus were relatively short-lived. Others, such as the Social Security Administration, formed the institutional basis of ongoing federal social welfare programs, and they continue to play major roles. With the creation in 1956 of the Department of Health, Education, and Welfare (now the Department of Health and Human Services), most of these agencies were combined into a single, cabinet-level organization through which governmental social welfare programs were centralized.

Since its early development, professional social work practice has been conducted within some type of organizational base. However, these organizations varied over time, and the skills needed for effective practice within them also changed. For example, in the early years of social work education, attention toward models of practice in social work organizations focused primarily on preparing a limited number of macro practitioners to assume roles as administrators of small agencies, usually in the private sector. The goal was to provide skills such as fund raising, working with voluntary boards, and supervising direct-service workers.

With the growth of large public bureaucracies and nationwide networks of affiliated agencies in the private sector, the size and complexity of human service organizations changed. The role of macro practitioners within these organizations was also forced to change. For example, trends such as the increased size of human service organizations, their increased complexity and diversity of services, and changes in standard budgetary policies forced administrators to seek new skills. Lewis (1978) calls particular attention to the growth of concern for fiscal accountability that first became a dominant issue in the late 1960s. He argues that these concerns forced social work administrators to shift from being "problem solvers" to being "managers." Implicit in this shift was a change in administrative orientation, moving away from external considerations of how best to deal with specific social problems and toward internal considerations of budgetary compliance and operational efficiency. Considerable concern was expressed that if social work administrators did not acquire these skills, leadership of human service agencies would pass to persons from other disciplines who did possess such training.

Concern has also arisen that administrative decisions in human service agencies have become overwhelmed by managerial concerns and no longer reflect the consideration of client needs. In response, Patti (1987) and others have called for the development of an *effectiveness-driven* model of administrative practice in which the achievement of desirable outcomes for clients becomes the primary criterion for decision making. The intent of this model is to view administrative practice in social work as a unique blend of managerial skills combined with broader knowledge of social problems and the means of addressing these problems.

Finally, just as views of the role of human service administrators have changed, so too have notions about the organizations in which they work. Since most social workers now operate within the context of some type of organization, their understanding of that organization may have much to do with the ability to do their job well.

For example, in a classic work entitled "The Good Bureaucrat," Robert Pruger (1973) made the point that social workers have two major roles. The helper role defines their activities as a social worker who assists clients with various problems. The organizational role defines the responsibilities the worker has for completing forms, making reports, attending meetings, and other organizational tasks. These roles may compete, and the clash between them may lead to a worker's inability to meet either satisfactorily. For example, a worker may have so many forms to fill out that he or she has little time for listening to detailed client problems. Pruger argues that a third role, the bureaucratic role, is possible, in which the worker develops skills in mediating the conflicts between the other two roles, learning to meet organizational demands without sacrificing professional skill. This is what the functional noncapitulator, discussed in Chapter 1, has to do in order to survive in a demanding environment. In subsequent chapters, we will discuss how Pruger's model of the good bureaucrat fits well within the larger framework of the modern macro practitioner.

CONTEMPORARY TRENDS

At the beginning of this chapter, we discussed major historical trends affecting the development of the social work profession. These were: (1) broad social conditions, (2) ideological conflicts, and (3) oppressed populations. In this section, we examine these same trends in terms of their influence on contemporary developments in the field.

Broad Social Conditions

The combined effect of population growth, urbanization, industrialization, and changes in institutional structures have created communities that are very different today than during the early years of the profession. Though these changes have fostered improvements in areas such as health, income, transportation, and others, not all aspects of the transformation have been positive. Warren (1978) calls attention to these concerns, noting that "discerning Americans have come to the uneasy realization that all is not right with their community living, that undesirable situations appear with growing frequency or intensity and that these are not the adventitious difficulty of one community or another so much as the parts of a general pattern of community living" (p. 14). Warren calls this the *community problem,* and as an element of the contemporary society, it is an important concern for macro practitioners.

One aspect of this problem has to do with the consequences of *urbanization.* Though they offer many benefits, large, complex cities also breed large, complex problems, and the very size and complexity of a community can interfere with solving these problems. One casualty of metropolitan growth, for example, is a sense of solidarity within the community. Small-town shared views of the common good may, in large cities, devolve into narrow parochialism based on units such as a single apartment building, an area of gang turf, or family and ethnic group affiliations. The greater the number of these communities *within* communities, the more difficult it is to identify and serve the interests of the whole.

Closely tied to these consequences of urbanization is the *loss of geographic relevance* of many communities. In small-town America, communities were largely defined in terms of residents' physical proximity, as well as commonalities such as topography, soil conditions, water supply, and other circumstances of proximity. People lived in the same place they worked, frequently remained there throughout their lives, and shared with their neighbors both fortune and misfortune (droughts, floods, good and bad harvests, and so forth). In contrast, many cities are now so immense that residents in one area may share little with those in another in terms of their economic base, political environment, lifestyle, or even climate and terrain. Because geographic, legislative, and social boundaries often intermingle and evolve, it may be difficult even to define the boundaries of a given community.

As residents' identification with local connections has ebbed, the importance of *extracommunity affiliations* has greatly expanded. These affiliations define the relationships between community organizations and related organizations outside the community. For example, an auto plant may be essential to the economy of a particular community, but its most important ties may not be to the community but to the home office of its corporation in another city far away. A decision to close the plant might come entirely from the home office, yet it is the community that would bear the most severe consequences of this decision.

Loss of control over such decisions renders the community extremely vulnerable, yet an excessive concern for external affiliations may blind community members to critical local needs.

In addition to community issues, contemporary developments in the organizational structure of human services are also important to consider. One parallel between communities and organizations is that both have continued to grow and become more complex. In the organizational realm, this has given rise to the *bureaucratization* of service systems. The term *bureaucracy* has taken on a number of mostly negative connotations which, as we shall discuss in Chapter 6, may or may not always be accurate. Here we refer to bureaucratization as the growth in size and structural complexity of human service organizations. This has been especially true in public agencies, which have generally continued to expand since the New Deal.

Bureaucratic organization is a means of structuring tasks and relationships among organizational members in order to maximize operational efficiency. In many ways, this model has made possible the development of modern organizations, and its advent coincides with the vast increase in productive capacity associated with the Industrial Revolution. The problem with bureaucracies is that they often become as machinelike as the tools they employ, and the result can be a rigid and dehumanizing style of operation. This style usually grows more pronounced as the organization gets larger, and vast governmental human service agencies have become some of the most notorious examples of the negative aspects of bureaucratic structure.

Partly in response to this problem, *privatization* became a significant trend during the last two decades. Although the term can be used in many ways, we define privatization as "the deciding, financing, or providing of human services by the private sector to clients for whom the public sector is responsible" (Netting et al. 1990). The trend may be more accurately termed reprivatization because of its focus on returning to the private sector for responding to human need.

Beginning in the 1960s, recognition of the limitations of government bureaucracies prompted growth in *purchase of service contracting.* Public agencies paid for services but they were provided to their clients by private organizations. Between 1973 and 1984, for example, nonprofit purchase of service contracts grew from $262.9 million to $664.1 million (Kettner & Martin 1987). Decision-making and financing functions remained governmental responsibilities, whereas the function of providing services shifted to the private sector. This arrangement was probably well accepted in many communities, since going to a local nonprofit agency to receive services is often less stigmatizing for clients. However, other trends accompanying the move toward privatization complicated the community service delivery system.

During the early 1980s, conservative views toward human services, combined with an economic slowdown, led to decreased public funding and decentralization of decision making. This meant that many nonprofit agencies, which had previously grown larger on public dollars, were suddenly faced with stiff competition for very limited resources. For example, facing a shortage of patients, hospitals began diversifying into service areas other than primary health care (i.e., substance abuse centers, home health, etc.). For-profit organizations began moving into human service provision, seeking clients who could pay for their own services.

The effect of this trend on community human service systems has been most acute in the provision of services to low-income clients. Formerly, many of these clients were served by nonprofit agencies either through contracts with public agencies or through excess revenues from clients who were able to pay. Now, government funds are more scarce and paying clients are often siphoned off by hospitals and for-profit providers. Many nonprofit agencies no longer have resources to pay for services to poor clients and there is increasing competition between nonprofits for the funds that are available (McMurtry et al. 1991).

A final trend is the advent of *computerization.* Society is moving toward a model in which information and services rather than manufactured goods are the most important commodities. As this takes place, communities will change. Heavy industries will diminish in importance and even the traditional character of the workplace will be altered, such as by workers remaining home and carrying out their tasks on computers. Moreover, the ability to tie into national and international computer networks will further enhance the importance of extra-community ties.

Social workers' roles will inevitably be affected by these changes. For example, Ginsberg (1988) discusses how computer technology has facilitated storage of vast numbers of client records by large public and private human service organizations. He cites government researchers who challenge social workers to use computer technology, noting that "social workers

> write reports and progress notes
>
> pull and read numerous files
>
> take case histories and develop diagnoses
>
> tap into local area resource networks
>
> keep in touch with professional developments
>
> provide factors and figures to contribute to agency accountability process."
> (Parker et al. 1987, cited in Ginsberg 1988, 71)

Still, other writers argue that these changes pose grave dangers for the profession. For example, Fabricant (1985) asserts that the computer revolution is simply another manifestation of an ongoing process of "deskilling" social workers. One example he offers is the role of workers who determine eligibility for benefits such as AFDC and food stamps. These positions are often filled by poorly trained and poorly paid clerical employees who simply input data into computers, and these computers determine clients' eligibility. The point is that if social workers cannot learn to adapt to and control new technologies (as well as other social trends we have discussed) they risk being controlled by them.

Ideological Conflicts

As with the discussion of broad social conditions, Warren's (1978) notions of the community problem also provide a starting point for addressing contemporary ideological trends. One issue concerns community members' increasing difficulty in achieving a *sense of community,* the psychological feeling of belonging that is important to both the individual and the community. This feeling ideally arises from individuals' awareness of the roles they play as functioning contributors to the well-being of the community. In historic times, people's roles were easier to perceive, as when they were perhaps the only grocer, teacher, baker, blacksmith, or midwife in the community. In complex modern communities, however, few people have unique roles, or their activities may be so specialized that no apparent contribution to the community good can be recognized.

The loss of a sense of community may in turn induce feelings of *alienation* from both the community and the larger society. Alienation is often described as a sense of rootlessness, whereby individuals consider themselves isolated from the social groups with which they might naturally identify. Persons who are alienated feel estranged or set apart from social and cultural connections, and they tend to be both less productive and less able to cope with the strains of daily living. Indeed, a vicious cycle can occur in which the complexity and impersonality of community living breeds alienation, and sufferers, in turn, feel even less able to manage such complexity. Feelings of separation that are also part of the experience of alienation fall especially hard on traditionally disadvantaged populations who are already worse off than other community members. Not surprisingly, one consequence of alienation is a rise of self-serving and anti-social behaviors in which any concern for community good is subordinated to individual interests.

Current writers agonize over the mounting tension between individualism and the collective or common good. This basic philosophical dispute has gained momentum over the last thirty years and has greatly influenced the way the individual, the community, and societal responses to social welfare are perceived. Fundamental disagreements have arisen over whether there should be a return to basic community decision making in which local people decide what is best in their own communities and how to maintain and balance a societal commitment that glues the social fabric together.

Oppressed Populations

A valuable contemporary lesson that has emerged in dealing with oppressed populations is the importance of language. The words that social workers use in describing special population groups can actually reinforce stereotypes and further oppress the very persons being served.

Abramovitz (1991) provides a glossary of terms to increase awareness about "hidden messages conveyed in everyday speech" (p. 380). For example, she discusses the "feminization of poverty" as a phrase that called attention to the economic concerns of women but argues that it may imply poverty is a new issue for women. She suggests a more appropriate phrase might be "povertization of women," which encapsulates the long history of women's economic disadvantage. Similarly, the sociological term *underclass,* which has been suggested as a replacement for *multiproblem, disadvantaged,* and *hard to reach* poor people, may stigmatize the persons so described (pp. 380–81).

Since the 1960s, there have been movements toward more accurate and politically sensitive language when referring to special populations. Relative to ethnic and racial groups, blacks adopted the term *black* as the most preferred descriptor in the 1960s and 1970s, but many now argue in favor of the term *African American.* Similarly, *Native American* is often both preferred and considered more accurate than the term *Indian,* but many native people continue to refer to themselves as American Indians. The term *Hispanic* is used as a generic expression to represent persons of Latin ancestry, including Puerto Ricans, Cuban Americans, Mexican Americans (who also call themselves "Chicanos"), and others. However, *Latino* is gaining acceptance as the preferred general term. *White,* despite its common usage, is a poorly defined term, but it also remains more broadly applicable than *Anglo* or other terms.

Relative to issues of sexuality, *gay* and *lesbian,* have been preferred terms for at least the past two decades. However, these groups were previously distinguished by the term *sexual preference,* which was later changed to *sexual orientation* and more recently to *affectional preference.* Also, with respect to gender, some feminist writers have argued for use of the terms *womyn* or *wimin* on the basis that they are less derivative of "men," but these terms do not yet appear to have been adopted into wide usage.

We recognize the extreme importance of language, and it is our intent to reflect that importance in our use of terms. Given the changing times in which we live, when some terms seem to be nearing the end of their useful lives and others seem to be emerging, we use most of these terms interchangeably. In some instances, where the use of a more traditional term seems more appropriate, we use such terms as black, white, Hispanic, Indian, or sexual orientation. In other cases, especially where the newly emerging terms seem more appropriate, we will use African American, Native American, Latino, or affectional preference. Our intention is to be sensitive to the convictions and wishes of as many people within these population groups as possible, and to offend as few as possible. We hope the reader is not confused by this mixed use of terms, but instead recognizes it as evidence of the dynamic, changing nature of modern society.

Relative to earlier periods in our nation's history, the recent past has been marked by significant gains by ethnic minorities, women, and gays and lesbians in their struggle to achieve equal standing in society. However, though progress has undoubtedly been made, the struggle has by no means been won. For example, success in reducing societal acceptance of prejudicial attitudes and overt acts of discrimination is tempered by the fact that these attitudes and behaviors often became simply more covert and thus more difficult to confront. Also, hard-won political victories have not always been matched by comparable economic gains, and for some groups conditions have in fact grown much worse.

These contrasts are perhaps most obvious among blacks, for whom victories in the Civil Rights Movement of the 1950s and 1960s meant the rejection of segregationist policies that had continued since the Civil War. These gains helped spur electoral successes, particularly on the local level. For example, in 1991, four of the six largest cities in the nation—New York, Los Angeles, Philadelphia, and Detroit—were led by African American mayors. Some economic progress has also been made in areas such as the expansion of the African American middle class, which was fueled in part by growth in the numbers of African Americans working in professional and managerial jobs.

Unfortunately, from a social work perspective the more telling figures concern African Americans who did not share in these economic gains, especially the inner-city poor. Consider, for example, the following statistics published by the Children's Defense Fund (1990) concerning the plight of young African American children. Relative to white children, they are:

78 percent more likely to die at birth;

twice as likely to be a low-birthweight child;

three times more likely to be born into a poor family;

four times more likely to be born to an unmarried mother; and

four times more likely to experience nutritional deficiencies.

These disparities would be troubling enough if they applied to adults, but the fact that African American children are afflicted by such disadvantages presents an even graver picture relative to future progress in achieving equality.

Native Americans also benefitted from the social upheavals of the 1960s, with groups such as the American Indian Movement (AIM) helping to focus attention on the troubled relationship between tribal organizations and the federal government. As a result, tribal governments were able to diminish the paternalistic influence of agencies such as the Bureau of Indian Affairs and gain greater autonomy over their own operations. For example, the Indian Child Welfare Act of 1978 gave jurisdiction of child welfare cases to tribal rather than state courts, thus placing tighter controls on practices such as the adoption of Native American children by non-Native American families.

Still, Native Americans have a more distinctly different cultural heritage than most other ethnic minorities, and the struggle to simultaneously preserve this heritage and integrate with the rest of society has taken its toll. For example, poverty on some rural reservations is as pervasive and severe as anywhere in the country, and little progress has been made in improving economic conditions in these areas. Also, alcoholism rates, especially among adult males living on reservations, remain high. One recent report estimated the annual age-adjusted alcoholism mortality rate among Native Americans at 26.1 per 100,000 population in 1985 (U.S. Department of Health and Human Services 1990). This figure is less than half the rate of twelve years earlier, but it is still four times higher than that for the general population, and it remains an indication of the difficulty faced by Native Americans in adjusting to life in two different worlds.

Hispanics are one of the fastest growing ethnic populations in the country, yet they remain a diverse group with a wide array of backgrounds, problems, and goals. Overall, they tend to be younger than the population as a whole, mostly urban, and concentrated in the southwestern border states of California, Arizona, New Mexico, and Texas, where they comprised from 16 percent to 37 percent of the population in 1980 (Estrada 1987). Immigration from Mexico and Central

America during the 1980s increased this concentration, but compounded many of the problems facing this group. Among these problems are high rates of school dropout and pervasive language barriers. These related concerns have been the source of considerable controversy. For example, in recent years both California and Arizona voters passed "English-only" initiatives designed to restrict official use of Spanish in areas such as public education and voting. The expressed goal of this movement is to force Spanish speakers to learn English and thus integrate more fully into society. Critics charge that it has had the opposite effect, especially among children who have greater difficulty in school because they must learn in an unfamiliar language.

In recent years, considerable public attention has been directed toward the educational achievements of Asian American youngsters, who, for example, have led all other ethnic groups in standardized test scores and rates of college completion (U.S. Department of Education 1988). Unfortunately, this success has sometimes masked problems facing other Asian Americans, particularly Southeast Asian immigrants whose numbers have increased rapidly in the past twenty years. Many of these people are refugees from regional wars who arrived penniless and without other family members. Once here, they had to cope with "(1) the great disparity between their culture and American society, (2) the lack of an already established ethnic community to help them adjust, and (3) the poor economic conditions in this country at the time of their arrival" (Kitano 1987, 168). As a result, they are now struggling to overcome lingering problems of poverty, poor housing, and racial discrimination.

A combination of factors has helped to ease the isolation of and institutional discrimination toward gay men and lesbian women. One factor has been research results providing evidence that homosexuality is a basic and possibly genetically transmitted trait in many people. These results have reduced some of the fear and misunderstanding of gays and lesbians on the part of heterosexuals. However, of greater importance has been political activism on the part of both gays and lesbians. Lesbian women, for example, were an integral part of the Women's Movement and have both contributed to and benefitted from its achievements. Marotta (1981) notes that many gay males were inspired by the work of black civil rights leaders in the 1950s and 1960s, and this helped lead to the formation of organizations such as the Gay Liberation Front. These organizations have been pointedly visible in their advocacy and lobbying efforts, and have helped many men accept and acknowledge their affectional preferences. In addition, gay and lesbian activism has led to the repeal of antihomosexual laws and the passage of ordinances against discrimination based on sexual orientation.

On the other hand, lobbying efforts by gay and lesbian groups have generally been more successful at the local level than at the state and national levels. For example, members of the armed forces remain under the threat of immediate dismissal for identifying themselves as homosexuals. Moreover, gays and lesbians are still targets for individual acts of discrimination and violence, and in most states they remain subject to arrest and prosecution for consensual sexual behavior. Finally, the AIDS epidemic has struck a devastating blow to the gay male community, and hysterical fear of the disease has compounded the problem of discrimination experienced by all homosexuals.

Finally, women's advancement in recent years has been marked by both progress and disappointment. One of the most important gains was the development of women's groups such as the National Organization of Women (NOW), which was organized in the mid-1960s. NOW and other organizations formed the core of the Women's Movement, which has had considerable success in calling attention to institutional sexism present in employment, government policy, and even in language. These efforts helped produce tangible gains, such as the narrowing of the difference in earnings between men and women. However, as of 1985, women on average still earned only 64 percent as much as men (U.S. Bureau of the Census 1987). A significant defeat was the failure of the Equal Rights Amendment, intended to be an important protection against gender-based discrimination. Unfortunately, the amendment drew vociferous opposition by other women's groups who felt that it would undermine traditional roles. In 1982, it failed due to lack of ratification by a sufficient number of states. Its downfall serves to illustrate that sexual stereotyping exists on the part of both men and women, and its elimination will require continued efforts on a societywide basis.

Overall, though public acts of discrimination were increasingly condemned during and after the 1960s, prejudicial attitudes toward women and sexual and ethnic minorities remain. In addition, many overtly discriminatory laws were altered, but blatant discrimination often simply gave way to more subtle forms. For example, with respect to attitudes toward racial and ethnic differences, Austin (1988) cites a 1986 study by Shuman, Steeh, and Bobo indicating that "while racial equality is supported in principle, negative attitudes toward governmental economic initiatives explicitly intended to redress the consequences of past racial discrimination are, in fact, widespread throughout the United States" (p. 58).

Health and human service programs often reflect the status quo because they address the symptoms of oppression rather than the causes. Professionals frequently assume they know the causes of oppression, and hence the needs of consumers, rather than asking the people they serve. During recent decades, however, efforts such as the social movements and citizen participation activities described above have taken initial steps to address the needs of special populations in a more comprehensive and consumer-involved manner. Still, the task for practitioners remains that of finding interventions that are sensitive to the needs of these populations (Kettner et al. 1985).

THE IMPORTANCE OF CHANGE

The development of social work macro practice has been accompanied by a number of changes over the years. In fact, change is one of the few constants in modern life. Nevertheless, change is not always seen as desirable or favorable, and resistance to change occurs as individuals, groups, and organizations attempt to hold on to the familiar. Brager and Holloway (1978) define three types of change that affect health and human service providers:

People-focused change

Technological change

Structural change

People-focused change centers on alterations in values, knowledge, and skills. Because it involves the values that underlie our attitudes and perceptions, people-focused change is often very difficult. Yet, in dealing with trends such as oppression, social workers are often faced with the need to change people's values, knowledge, and skills.

Technological change refers to alterations in the process of service delivery, those activities and procedures that guide policy and program implementation. The contemporary high tech explosion directly relates to this type of change, and it clearly has important ramifications for the provision of human services, though it also stretches the practitioner's ability to utilize up-to-date methods.

Since the days when COS staffers and settlement house workers demanded training to become more systematic in how they approached individuals, groups, and communities, professional technologies have changed. Today we see the development of large organizations with computerized management information systems. However, we are still challenged to apply new technologies in a humane way so that clients are not depersonalized in the process.

Structural change deals with how units within a system relate to one another. Reprivatization of services represents this type of change, in that it has the potential to fundamentally alter the process of meeting the needs of disadvantaged persons in society. However, its success requires a thorough reexamination of public-private relationships at the community, state, and national levels.

The mounting tension between individualism and the collective good becomes an overriding trend that requires reaching a balance in order to create a competent community. Competent communities are ones that provide mutual support regardless of who is in need. This raises professional questions. Should macro practitioners react to trends, attempting to respond as spontaneous changes occur within the environment? Or should they seize opportunities to plan community changes to address human need by selecting and utilizing the available tools? We believe that if the practitioner chooses a planned change perspective, he or she must be equipped with knowledge and values in order to cope with the inevitable dilemmas that will arise. Chapter 3 will focus on the knowledge and value base of professional macro practice.

SUMMARY

The need for social workers to be able to understand and practice in macro systems is based on both the history of the social work profession and the society in which it evolved. The effects of immigration, industrialization, and rapid population growth led to a concentration of peoples in large urban areas, where, for the first time, modern institutional structures (e.g., highly specialized organizations) began to arise. So, too, did modern problems of urban poverty, alienation, loss of a sense of community, and others. The types of service that developed to address these problems were affected by new ideologies. Social Darwinism led to assistance that was often paternalistic and judgmental, but this was tempered by liberalism and even radical ideologies that led to much more proactive helping efforts.

The traditions of the COS agencies, with their emphasis on case-level practice, and the settlement houses, with their more community-oriented efforts, led to a dualistic professional model that continues today. Within this model, social workers must be able to perceive their clients not only as individuals with personal problems; they must also understand clients as members of larger, community systems, and they must be prepared to intervene at the community level as well.

Moreover, social workers themselves typically work within large, complex organizations, and the actions of these organizations also has much to do with how well social workers can do their jobs. For example, these organizations are tending to become more bureaucratized, meaning that they may be more efficient, but they may also be more rigid and less focused on client interests. Other organizational trends such as privatization, and computerization also present both risks and opportunities for the social workers practicing within them. Understanding these trends and acquiring skills in bringing about planned change within organizations are the best means for reducing the risks and maximizing the opportunities.

A critical point in this chapter was that a meaningful understanding of the development of modern macro systems and of the social work profession cannot be gained in the absence of an awareness of the history of oppressed groups within society. A key point is that macro systems can both overcome or exacerbate institutionalized oppression, depending on how they are structured. For example, protections supposedly guaranteed to African Americans and Latinos through the Emancipation Proclamation and the Treaty of Guadalupe Hidalgo were undermined by other economic and legal policies that effectively continued the oppression. Complex urban, industrial communities produced vast wealth during the last century, but this was not always shared by ethnic minorities segregated (formally or informally) in ghettos or on reservations. Highly bureaucratized organizations became very efficient at processing individual clients in standardized ways, but they did not reliably advance in their ability to meet specific individual needs or to avoid practices that institutionally discriminate against particular groups.

Traditional debates about whether social workers should pursue casework, group work, or community organization seem less important in light of these realities. Macro systems pervade all types of social work practice, and the ability to recognize and redirect their influence is critical to all social workers, regardless of their primary role. The next issue to be addressed is how social workers involve themselves in macro practice in ways that are both informed and rooted in professional ethics. These issues are covered in the discussion in Chapter 3 concerning the knowledge and value base of macro practice.

REFERENCES

Abramovitz, M. (1991) Putting an end to doublespeak about race, gender, and poverty: An annotated glossary for social workers. *Social Work, 36*(5): 380–84.

Austin, D. M. (1983) The Flexner myth and the history of social work. *Social Service Review, 57*(3): 357–77.

Austin, D. M. (1988) *The political economy of human service program.* Greenwich, CT: JAI Press.

Axinn, J., and H. Levin. (1992) *Social welfare: A history of the American response to need* (3rd ed.). New York: Longman.

Beane, S. (1989) Indian child welfare social policy history. In E. Gonzalez-Santin, ed., *Defining entry-level competencies for public child welfare workers serving Indian communities.* Tempe, AZ: School of Social Work, Arizona State University.

Bogue, D. J. (1985) *The population of the United States.* New York: Free Press.

Brager, G., and S. Holloway. (1978) *Changing human service organizations: Politics and practice.* New York: Free Press.

Brieland, D. (1990) The Hull-House tradition and the contemporary social worker: Was Jane Addams really a social worker? *Social Work, 35*(2): 134–38.

Chambers, C. A. (1985) The historical role of the voluntary sector. In G. A. Tobin, ed., *Social planning and human service delivery in the voluntary sector* (pp. 3–28). Westport, CT: Greenwood Press.

Chambers, C. A. (1986) Women in the creation of the profession of social work. *Social Service Review, 60*(1): 3–33.

Children's Defense Fund. (1990) *S.O.S. America: A Children's Defense Fund budget.* Washington, DC: Author.

Estrada, L. F. (1987) Hispanics. *Encyclopedia of social work* (18th ed., 1: 732–39). Silver Spring, MD: National Association of Social Workers.

Fabricant, M. (1985) The industrialization of social work practice. *Social Work, 30*(5): 389–95.

Garvin, C. D., and F. M. Cox. (1987) A history of community organizing since the Civil War with special references to oppressed communities. In F. M. Cox et al. eds., *Strategies of community organization* (4th ed., 26–63). Itasca, IL: F. E. Peacock.

Gibson, G. (1987) Mexican Americans. *Encyclopedia of social work* (18th ed., 2: 135–48). Silver Spring, MD: National Association of Social Workers.

Ginsberg, L. H. (1988) Data processing and social work management. In P. R. Keys and L. H. Ginsberg, eds., *New management in human services.* Silver Spring, MD: National Association of Social Workers.

Jansson, B. S. (1988) *The reluctant welfare state.* Belmont, CA: Wadsworth.

Kettner, P. M., J. M. Daley, and A. W. Nichols. (1985) *Initiating change in organizations and communities.* Monterey, CA: Brooks/Cole.

Kettner, P. M., and L. L. Martin. (1987) *Purchase of service contracting.* Newbury Park, CA: Sage.

Kitano, H. H. L. (1987) Asian Americans. *Encyclopedia of social work* (18th ed., 1: 156–71). Silver Spring, MD: National Association of Social Workers.

Leiby, J. (1987) History of social welfare. *Encyclopedia of social work* (18th ed., 1: 755–77). Silver Spring, MD: National Association of Social Workers.

Lewis, H. (1978) Management in the nonprofit social service organization. In S. Slavin, ed., *Social administration: The management of the social services.* New York: Council on Social Work Education.

Marotta, T. (1981) *The politics of homosexuality.* Boston: Houghton Mifflin.

McMurtry, S. L., F. E. Netting, and P. M. Kettner. How nonprofits adapt to a stringent environment. *Nonprofit Management and Leadership, 1*(3): 235–52.

NASW Standards for the Classification of Social Work: Copyright 1981, National Association of Social Workers, Inc.

Netting, F. E., S. L. McMurtry, P. M. Kettner, and S. Jones-McClintic. (1990) Privatization and its impact on nonprofit service providers. *Nonprofit and Voluntary Sector Quarterly, 19*(1): 33–46.

Patti, R. J. (1987) Managing for service effectiveness in social welfare: Toward a performance model. *Administration in Social Work, 11*(3/4): 7–21.

Peterson, P. E., and J. D. Greenstone. (1977) The mobilization of low-income communities through community action. In R. H. Haveman, ed., *A decade of federal antipoverty programs: achievements, failures, and lessons.* New York: Academic Press.

Pruger, R. (1973) The good bureaucrat. *Social Work, 18*(4): 26–32.

Reisch, M., and S. Wenocur. (1986) The future of community organization in social work: Social activism and the politics of profession building. *Social Service Review, 60*(1): 70–93.

Szasz, T. S. (1965) Legal and moral aspects of homosexuality. In J. Marmor, ed., *Sexual inversion: The multiple roots of homosexuality.* New York: Basic Books.

Trattner, W. I. (1989) *From poor law to welfare state: A history of social welfare in America* (4th ed.). New York: Free Press.

U.S. Bureau of the Census. (1987) *Statistical abstract of the United States.* Washington, DC: U.S. Government Printing Office.

U.S. Congress. (1964) *Act to Mobilize the Human and Financial Resources of the Nation to Combat Poverty in the United States,* 88-452, 88th Congress, 2nd Session.

U.S. Department of Education. (1988) *Digest of educational statistics, 1988.* Washington, DC: National Center for Educational Statistics.

U.S. Department of Health and Human Services. (1990) *Seventh Special Report to the U.S. Congress on Alcoholism and Health from the Secretary of the Department of Health and Human Services.* Rockville, MD: National Institute on Alcohol Abuse and Alcoholism.

Wagner, D. (1989) Radical movements in the social services: A theoretical framework. *Social Service Review, 63*(2): 264–84.

Warren, R. L. (1978) *The community in America* (3rd ed.). Chicago: Rand McNally.

CHAPTER **3**

The Knowledge and Value Base of Macro Practice

Overview

INTRODUCTION

In Chapter 1, we presented the kinds of situations that confront social work practitioners on a daily basis. These situations illustrate the philosophical and value dilemmas, as well as the contradictions, that social workers must face. In Chapter 2, we reviewed both the history of social work and of macro practice. These reviews should help to illuminate the great need for macro-level social work intervention.

In this chapter, we will begin to examine the knowledge base and the value base for macro practice. This is a complex and extensive undertaking and cannot be comprehensively covered in a single chapter. Therefore, we will establish a framework or context for examining macro-practice knowledge and values, but we will continue with knowledge and value themes throughout the remainder of the book.

If one intends to pursue macro social work practice, one needs a knowledge base, a value system, and a practice model. The knowledge base begins with an understanding of the arenas in which one practices. For the macro practitioner, this means understanding communities and organizations. In this chapter, we will explore the functions of communities and organizations, and discuss why social workers need to understand these arenas of practice in order to be effective practitioners. Then we will examine the value base of macro practice and the resulting ethical dilemmas faced by professionals.

A more advanced level of knowledge, beyond a generic understanding of organizations and communities, focuses on the specific community or organization to be changed in some way. For a community-level change effort, this requires an orderly, systematic study designed to produce a thorough understanding of the relevant factors that define that community. The format for this study and analysis will be covered in Chapter 4. Community change also requires an understanding of the human service system in the community. A framework for data collection and analysis of community human service systems will be covered in Chapter 5.

If the focus or target of a change effort is an organization, it is important that the macro practitioner first be able to analyze and understand organizations and organizational behavior. This content will be covered in Chapter 6. Second, there are factors unique to human service organizations that must be understood and addressed. This content will be addressed in Chapter 7.

Finally, the knowledge and values that underlie macro-practice intervention must be applied to a planned change effort. This effort proceeds within a problem-solving framework in which the macro practitioner coordinates and orchestrates collective movement toward specified outcomes. These procedures will comprise the practice model outlined in Chapters 8, 9, and 10.

We will present this process as though it is linear—that is, as though one could begin at point A and proceed logically and systematically through to point Z. In practice, this is almost never the case. Because people's lives are affected, a situation may need to be resolved immediately before moving backward into a planned long-term solution. Because funding from multiple sources may be involved, a change may have to meet budgeting deadlines. Because macro practitioners are also direct-service workers, supervisors, or managers, regular duties may limit the time available to devote to initiating and following through on macro-level changes.

Nevertheless, despite all the potential barriers and complications, effective macro-level changes are implemented every day because of the efforts of social workers who recognize the need for change. Community and organizational problems are often challenging and complex. Sometimes they are almost overwhelming at the outset, but when carefully considered and persistent efforts are applied, the problems may be surprisingly amenable to change.

THE KNOWLEDGE BASE OF MACRO PRACTICE

Communities and organizations are entities with which most people are familiar because they have lived in at least one community and have interacted with many organizations. However, "living in" or "interacting with" does not necessarily mean that they understand these systems. Thus, the first part of the knowledge base of macro practice to be addressed will be the fundamentals of understanding communities and organizations.

Understanding Communities

Community has been defined by Warren (1978) as "that combination of social units and systems that perform the major social functions" relevant to meeting people's needs on a local level (p. 9). Community, then, means the organization of social activities that affords people access to what is necessary for day-to-day living. Generally we think of social units as beginning with the domestic unit, extending to the neighborhood or to the voluntary association, and on to the larger community. Community may have no specific boundaries, but is significant because it performs five important functions that Warren lists as:

1. production, distribution, consumption
2. socialization
3. social control
4. social participation
5. mutual support

Production, distribution, and consumption functions are community activities designed to meet people's material needs, including the most basic requirements of food, clothing, shelter, and the like. While there may have been a time when a family could produce all it consumed, those times are long since past. People today are interdependent for such basic needs as food, clothing, shelter, medical care, sanitation, employment, transportation, recreation, and other goods and services. The generally accepted medium of exchange for these goods and services is money. Money, therefore, becomes an important factor in defining the limits of consumption, and comes into consideration in most, if not all, community change efforts.

A second function of community is *socialization* to the prevailing norms, traditions, and values of those with whom people interact. Young people growing up in severely deprived communities will develop value perspectives different from those growing up in affluent communities, for example. Socialization guides attitudinal development, and these attitudes and perceptions influence how people view themselves, others, and their interpersonal rights and responsibilities. To understand an individual or a population, it is important to understand the norms, traditions, and values of the community or communities in which he or she has been socialized.

Social control is the process by which community members ensure compliance with norms and values by establishing laws, rules, and regulations, and by ensuring their enforcement. Social control is a function performed by institutions representing various sectors such as government, education, religion, and social services. Many social workers serve in practice settings in which they constantly strive to achieve a balance between their dual roles as helpers and agents of social control. Schools, correctional institutions, probation and parole offices, and employment and training programs are just a few examples of such settings.

Other settings and programs deal with more subtle forms of control such as patterns of service distribution and eligibility criteria that govern access to resources on the part of vulnerable groups. For example, case managers often balance the redistribution of services with the constraints of limited resources. Sensitivity to these restrictions may spur the practitioner to work toward change, only to discover that key policymakers prefer to restrain recipients of aid rather than provide the level of assistance really needed to combat the identified problem. Recognizing how social control is manifested in social welfare policies, programs, organizations, and communities can be disillusioning, but is necessary for understanding the structure and process of service delivery.

Social participation includes interaction with others in community groups, associations, and organizations. Communities provide an outlet for people to express their social needs and interests as well as opportunities to build natural helping and support networks. Few people can survive without some form of social outlet, even when physiological needs are met. Some find this outlet through local churches, some in civic organizations, and some in informal neighborhood groups. Understanding the patterns of social participation for a target population is helpful in assessing the extent to which a community is meeting the needs of its members.

Mutual support is the function that families, friends, neighbors, volunteers, and professionals carry out in communities when they care for the sick, the unemployed, and the distressed. Most helping professions developed in response to the inability of other social institutions (i.e., domestic units, churches, civic organizations) to meet the mutual-support needs of community members. As society grew more complex and the supportive capacity of traditional institutions such as families and neighbors was increasingly strained, professions were established to address the resulting unmet needs.

These five functions, according to Warren (1978), define the purpose of a community. If all functions were performed in a given community in a manner that met the needs of all its members—that is, if all consumption, socialization, social control, social participation, and mutual support needs were met in a healthy, positive and constructive manner—then the existing natural structures of that community would represent all the resources needed to nurture and care for its members.

However, such an ideal community is rarely found. Some religious communities in rural areas have been able to fulfill most of these functions in a way that precluded the need for intervention and change, but these are clearly exceptions. It is far more common to find that these functions are carried out in a way that falls short of meeting the needs of at least some community members. There may be inadequate resources for distribution and consumption, or they may be distributed unevenly. Socialization may be to a set of values not in the best interest of some community members. The social control function may not operate in a fair and evenhanded manner for all. Social participation opportunities may be severely limited for some. Mutual support functions may be undermined by a dominant value system that places a premium on rugged individualism. In short, communities can be considered "healthy" or "unhealthy," or "competent" or "incompetent," based on their ability to meet community needs, and this may be particularly true for oppressed target populations within their boundaries.

Understanding Organizations

Many of the social problems we face today (i.e., drug abuse, street-gang violence, teen pregnancy, elder abuse) occur in the context of community life and must, therefore, be addressed at the community level. However, some problems that social workers and clients encounter, emerge because of organizational constraints and barriers. These problems must be addressed through knowledge about the functions of organizations and through an understanding of the barriers that human service organizations often inadvertently erect that interfere with good-quality services to clients.

Nearly any collectivity of individuals may be considered an organization, and even informal groupings of individuals may jointly carry out certain tasks. For our purposes, however, the focus is on more clearly delineated groups that conform to Daft's definition of organizations as "social entities that are goal-directed, deliberately structured activity systems with an identifiable boundary" (1983, 8).

Over the 150 years in which we have transformed ourselves into a society of large, complex communities, we have become, to an ever greater extent, an organizational society. Prior to the industrial revolution, most individuals lived in agrarian settings in which they were personally responsible for meeting most of their basic needs. People built their own houses, drew their own water, grew their own food, and made their own clothes. In modern times, most of these needs are met by organizations: supermarkets, restaurants, department stores, municipal utilities, construction companies, schools, and social welfare institutions. Communities provide the superstructure within which these myriad organizations interact, but it is the organizations themselves that actually carry out most essential community functions. Sociologist Talcott Parsons notes: ". . . the development of organizations is the principal mechanism by which, in a highly differentiated society, it is possible to 'get things done,' to achieve goals beyond the reach of the individual" (1960, 41).

Human service organizations are ". . . the vast array of formal organizations that have as their stated purpose enhancement of the social, emotional, physical, and/or intellectual well-being of some component of the population" (Brager & Holloway 1978, 2). In the same way that supermarkets have developed as highly organized systems to meet subsistence needs once addressed through family farms, human service organizations have developed to meet higher-order needs, some of which have only recently been recognized. For example, in the previous century there were few if any organizations existing to provide services such as child and adult protection, day care, or psychotherapy because the society had not yet reached a point to stimulate their development.

Human Service Organizations and Their Constituencies. In an analysis of human service organizations and their interactions with their communities, Martin (1980) focuses on the way in which different levels of a typical, bureaucratically structured service agency are linked with, and thus respond to, specific constituencies in the environment. As illustrated in Figure 3.1, the structure of most agencies includes five major levels. In the order of their importance for decision making within the organization, the levels are: (1) directors and senior administrators, (2) middle managers, (3) direct service providers, (4) support and maintenance staff, and (5) individual clients. External to the organization but exerting influence on its actions are a variety of constituencies grouped according to their positions or interests.

Several features of the model are worthy of note. First, as indicated by the curved arrows connecting each level of the organization, decisions made at one level of the hierarchy flow downward through subsequent levels. The effects of the decisions also move only one direction. There are no important lines of communication from lower to upper levels. Clients, who occupy the bottom step of the hierarchy, thus have the least input into, and the least control over, the operation of the organization that is responsible for meeting their service needs. Note, too, that the model depicts clients in a sort of limbo, neither internal nor completely external to the organization. This reflects the precarious position in which clients often find themselves. Because they are not fully a part of the organization they tend to be excluded from decision making, yet, because they are not viewed as a distinct external constituency, they have less ability to influence the organization from the outside.

This is a considerably different role than that played by consumers in relation to commercial organizations. There, vast resources and efforts are devoted to pleasing the consumer and attracting demand for the purchase of products and services.

What this means is that, unlike commercial firms, human service agencies do not necessarily have to please their clients. Since clients often do not pay for their services, the question of whether or not they are satisfied with them is often perceived as irrelevant to whether the agency will continue to receive resources necessary for its survival. This is not to imply that human service organizations arbitrarily eliminate client input from all decision making. There are many human service agencies that have advisory councils and community-based boards that include consumer membership. Since the 1960s, when the War on Poverty programs developed mechanisms for citizen and consumer participation, many organizations have continued these practices.

However, the point is that the organizational dynamics in many human service agencies are such that quality service provision can become secondary to meeting standards imposed by funding sources. Since funding sources themselves

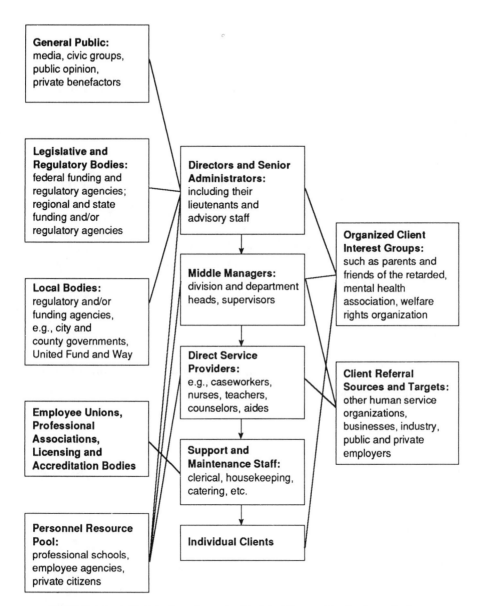

FIGURE 3.1 A Multiple Constituencies Model of Human Service Organizations

SOURCE: Patricia Martin Yancy. Multiple constituencies, dominant societal values, and the human service administrator. *Administration in Social Work,* 4(2), Haworth Press, 1980.

are often distant from direct contact with service recipients, these standards may also have little to do with the needs of clients. This situation is often described as a conflict between *efficiency* (the degree to which an agency makes optimal use of its resources) and *effectiveness* (the degree to which its services meet the needs of clients). Patti (1988) describes this conflict:

The manner in which an agency is managed is likely to be considered more important than the results it achieves. This can and frequently does lead to an anomalous situation in which the agency is "well" managed, but has little demonstrable impact on the clientele it serves. (p. 8)

For example, a metropolitan agency provides shelter services to homeless women and their children. Many of the women come from abusive relationships and desire to use the shelter as a place to stay until they can find a job that will allow them to live independently. However, in order to be able to compete successfully for a job, they must be able to leave their children at the shelter, travel to different parts of the city, and sometimes spend lengthy periods of time filling out forms and waiting to be interviewed. The agency, on the other hand, has a rule that children cannot be left alone by the mother. To do so would require having a formal day-care setting, and the agency is unwilling to face the regulatory and liability issues necessary to provide such a setting. The result is that most women at the shelter who have young children are not able to find jobs, thus when the thirty-day limit on stays at the shelter runs out, they must simply move to another shelter, return to the abusing spouse, or face life on the streets. The irony is that each woman's thirty-day stay may be recorded as a successful completion of service on the agency's records.

Scenarios such as these happen all too often, and they are particularly characteristic of bureaucratically structured organizations, which embody a rationalized, regulation-bound approach to agency operations. As Sosin (1979) concludes: "Bureaucracies are formally rational in that they follow sets of rules well. But they are substantively irrational because these rules often do substantive damage" (p. 400).

The Functions of Organizations.   Organizations can be analyzed from a number of perspectives. For those interested in organizational change, Miles (1975) identifies five functions of organizations that can be viewed as possible points at which change can be introduced:

1. Direction and leadership
2. Organizational structure and job design
3. Selection, training, appraisal and development
4. Communication and control
5. Motivation and reward systems

Direction and leadership refers to the ways in which policies and decisions are made, and to the leadership style of top-level administrators. Decisions can be made unilaterally and passed down, or they can be reached through dialogue and negotiation with those affected. Supervision can be close and detailed, or individuals can be permitted self-direction in the pursuit of agreed-upon objectives. Direction and leadership greatly influence organizations and can affect the quality of work life for employees and the quality of services to clients.

Organizational structure and job design define the manner in which the organization and its programs are structured and the way workloads are assigned.

A highly bureaucratic organization follows a rigid hierarchy with each person reporting to a superior, all the way up through the chain of command. A more flexible structure might use loosely linked, self-paced teams grouped around a product or service. Job designs can be highly specialized or loosely defined. These factors can affect the way clients get into service, who they relate to in the process, and the nature of the services they receive.

One of an organization's most valuable resources is its employees. *Selection, training, appraisal, and development* are the personnel processes that have to do with recruiting, hiring, evaluating, and developing staff. Organizations can choose to select and train people who fit a narrowly defined description, or they can attempt to balance the needs of the organization with the abilities and interests of the individual. Evaluations can be based on a very specific set of criteria, or they can be joint appraisals shared by superior and subordinate focused on progress toward previously agreed-upon objectives. Performance evaluations become significant to client services in that they tend to express what behaviors are most highly valued by the organization.

Other functions of organizations that affect both quality of work life and client services are *communication and control.* As pointed out earlier, communication systems can be oriented primarily toward downward flows of orders and instructions and upward flows of reports. In other systems, there can be a thorough sharing of information with all operating units, with everyone having access to data necessary to their performance. Control systems can collect and disseminate data in one direction, or they can provide for feedback loops that allow operating units to immediately appraise and adjust their own performance.

Finally, *motivation and reward systems* can be built around such factors as longevity and loyalty, or they can focus primary emphasis on performance. There can be a unilateral determination of standards for rewards or there can be peer establishment of the types of achievements that should be rewarded.

These functions of organizations are not intended to be exhaustive as much as they are intended to identify points at which changes can be made. In analyzing an organization, one should tend to look for consistency. For example, if workers are expected to be responsive to the full range of client needs, they must have the authority and resources to provide comprehensive services. If they are expected to specialize, services need to be structured so that other needs can be met by other specialists. Whatever the structure, staff must be rewarded for excellent performance in the tasks identified in their job descriptions rather than simply for loyalty and longevity. These are the types of factors one would look for in analyzing and attempting to understand an organization.

Organizational change can be a difficult and painfully slow process because of organizational rigidity, leadership that is not committed to serving clients in need, and many other factors. As with community change, we believe that a professionally assisted change effort approached in a deliberate and systematic manner offers the optimum opportunity for achieving change objectives. We also believe that community and organization change occurs within the context of multiple, and often conflictual, value systems.

THE VALUE BASE OF MACRO PRACTICE

Lengthy lists of characteristics have been proposed to describe what constitutes a profession. Gustafson (1982) identifies three principal characteristics common to all professions: (1) people-oriented purpose, (2) an extensive knowledge base, and (3) mechanisms of control.

First, professions "exist to meet the needs of others" within the larger community (Gustafson 1982, 508). Professions are therefore client-oriented and conform to a set of values that encapsulate the community good that is to be served. Activities that are designed only to serve the political or economic needs of powerful community members, even though they may be carried out by skilled individuals, do not qualify as professional endeavors.

Second, professions require mastery of a large body of technical knowledge, concepts, and theories that the professional is responsible for applying in real-world settings. We have briefly discussed the functions of communities and organizations as an introduction to the knowledge base required for social work macro practice. Professional judgment derives from the ability to take this knowledge and skillfully apply it in a workable manner. Gustafson argues that professional practitioners prefer guidelines rather than rules because guidelines offer direction rather than rigid formulation. They allow professionals to exercise discretion and to use their judgment. However, professionals also carry enormous responsibility because what they decide and how they act will directly affect not just their clients but also the multiple constituencies previously discussed.

Gustafson's third characteristic of professions is that they place many social controls on professional activities. In social work, these controls include the accreditation activities carried out by the Council on Social Work Education (CSWE) to insure the quality and consistency of degree programs in social work; the sanctioning capacity of the National Association of Social Workers (NASW); the NASW Code of Ethics, which provides basic value guidelines through which professional judgment is applied; and the credentialing and licensing requirements in various states. In short, there are many mechanisms for overseeing what occurs under the guise of professional practice.

All three characteristics of professions are riddled with values. Since professional practice implies the intent to work with people, the diversity of these clients and colleagues will assure contact with multiple and competing value systems. The knowledge base that informs practice is developed by persons and groups with diverse views, and students must learn to critically analyze this information, rejecting some views and using others. Lastly, controls such as codes of ethics are heavily value-laden. In fact, it can be argued that social work values cannot be separated from theory and practice (Vigilante 1974).

Because codes of ethics serve as guidelines for professional practice, it is imperative that students know the content and the limitations of written codes. The boxed text opposite provides a summary of the major principles contained in the NASW Code of Ethics.

The NASW Code of Ethics is intended to introduce a perspective that drives practitioners' thinking, that establishes criteria for selecting goals, and that influences

NASW Code of Ethics Summary of Major Principles

I. The Social Worker's Conduct and Comportment as a Social Worker

    A. *Propriety.* The social worker should maintain high standards of personal conduct in the capacity or identity as social worker.

    B. *Competence and Professional Development.* The social worker should strive to become and remain proficient in professional practice and the performance of professional functions.

    C. *Service.* The social worker should regard as primary the service obligation to the social work profession.

    D. *Integrity.* The social worker should act in accordance with the highest standards of professional integrity.

    E. *Scholarship and Research.* The social worker engaged in study and research should be guided by the conventions of scholarly inquiry.

II. The Social Worker's Ethical Responsibility to Clients

    F. *Primacy of Clients' Interests.* The social worker's primary responsibility is to clients.

    G. *Rights and Prerogatives of Clients.* The social worker should make every effort to foster maximum self-determination on the part of clients.

    H. *Confidentiality and Privacy.* The social worker should respect the privacy of clients and hold in confidence all information obtained in the course of professional service.

    I. *Fees.* When setting fees, the social worker should ensure that they are fair, reasonable, considerate, and commensurate with the service performed and with due regard for the clients' ability to pay.

III. The Social Worker's Ethical Responsibility to Colleagues

    J. *Respect, Fairness, and Courtesy.* The social worker should treat colleagues with respect, courtesy, fairness, and good faith.

    K. *Dealing with Colleagues' Clients.* The social worker has the responsibility to relate to the clients of colleagues with full professional consideration.

IV. The Social Worker's Ethical Responsibility to Employers and Employing Organization

    L. *Commitments to Employing Organization.* The social worker should adhere to commitments made to the employing organization.

V. The Social Worker's Ethical Responsibility to the Social Work Profession

    M. *Maintaining the Integrity of the Profession.* The social worker should uphold and advance the values, ethics, knowledge, and mission of the profession.

    N. *Community Service.* The social worker should assist the profession in making social services available to the general public.

    O. *Development of Knowledge.* The social worker should take responsibility for identifying, developing, and fully utilizing knowledge for professional practice.

VI. The Social Worker's Ethical Responsibility to Society

    P. *Promoting the General Welfare.* The social worker should promote the general welfare of society.

how information is interpreted and understood. Regardless of which role the social worker plays—whether it is community organizer, political lobbyist or direct practitioner—these professional actions are not value-free. What is believed to be important to ask, how the answers to these questions are interpreted, and what actions are taken in response are all influenced by values. This is the case, whether or not the practitioner openly acknowledges it. Essentially, social work values serve as the overarching ideology within which practitioners perform their roles (Collins 1986).

Collins suggests that the value with the greatest consensus among members of the social work profession is "the vision of the unique individual with inherent dignity, sharing common needs with all others" (1986, 216). This value underscores the concept of human interdependence. The human condition is viewed as part of a dynamic, interactive, open system in which the person is part of the environment. The person-in-environment perspective that derives from this overriding value is the essence of social work practice. Collins also points out that the person-in-environment perspective is compatible with the person-is-political perspective inherent in feminist thought. Both reflect the interaction of what occurs in both micro and macro roles and the significance of their integration in social work practice.

The person-in-environment perspective gives social work a unique approach to intervention. Because the client exists within a larger community, the practitioner cannot ignore the larger reasons for why the client may have a problem. It is just as likely that the environment needs to change as it is that the client needs to change. It is also possible that many persons will be adversely affected if environmental change does not occur.

Similarly, the person-is-political perspective underscores the belief that individuals cannot be viewed separate from the larger society. The actions, and even the inactions, of individuals influence those around them and may have broad implications for others within an organization or community. Bricker-Jenkins and Hooyman (1986) explain:

> . . . just as no "private realities" exist apart from political processes, there are no private solutions. Given that we are interconnected and the sum of our individual actions create the social order, we are thereby responsible to each other for our actions. Accordingly, failure to act is to act; likewise, failure to work to transform social and political realities is to support the status quo. (p. 14)

The NASW Code of Ethics specifies one's commitment to individual clients. For the practitioner, this often poses a dilemma. There are many instances in which it is difficult to determine just who the client is, or more precisely who the client is not. It may be equally difficult to decide how many people will be affected by the situation.

Reid and Billups (1986) discuss a situation in which a social work student became an intern in a guardianship project. An infant child was born to a mildly retarded couple and child welfare authorities initiated proceedings to terminate parental rights. Having been trained to view the client in the context of his or her environment, the student attempted to include the parents in discussions about the child's future. The student's supervisor argued that the project's commitment was solely to the child. Certainly the child was a client, but the student argued that the parents were clients as well.

Another example arose in a congregate housing facility for low-income elderly. The administrator began receiving complaints about a resident who wandered the hallways and seemed confused. The residents argued that the individual should be placed in a nursing home where restraints would be provided. The administrator faced a basic dilemma; the confused resident was a client, as were the complaining residents. The administrator knew the confused resident very well. This person was able to perform basic activities of daily living, had caused no harm to anyone, and was an avid hiker. To restrict this individual's movements would be excessively cruel. Those residents who complained were very fearful of aging and their ageism was reflected in the emotion with which they wanted to get this resident out of sight so that there would be no reminder of what could happen to them. The code of ethics does not specify which client comes first, only that the social worker's primary commitment is to the client.

Ethical Dilemmas

Although values tell us what is important, ethics are the operationalization of values or the behavior that occurs in carrying out those values. The code of ethics, therefore, reflects the values of social work, but its intent is to provide direction for what actually happens in social work practice.

In many situations, social work practice presents ethical dilemmas, which implies that one is faced with a situation that necessitates a choice between equally important values. The student in the guardian ad litem project valued the child's right to a safe and secure environment, but also valued the parents' rights to have a say in their child's future. The retirement community administrator valued the freedom of the wandering resident, but also valued the importance of being responsive to the larger resident community. Inherent in both situations were dilemmas. A choice between equally important values had to be made where there was no easy, or obviously right and wrong, solution.

Although a potentially unlimited number of value conflicts can arise, Kapp (1987) offers three ethical principles that may be used to assist in analyzing macro-practice decision making:

Autonomy
Beneficence
Justice

Autonomy is based on self-determination and freedom. It implies that each person should have the right to make his or her own life choices. Concepts such as empowerment are built on the principle of autonomy, implying that power or control over one's life means seizing the opportunity to make one's own decisions. As an example, the pro-choice proponents in the abortion controversy advocate for autonomy, a woman's right to choose. This stance conflicts with a number of religious codes arguing the immorality of abortion and stating that the right of the unborn child must be considered as well. Although autonomy may be perceived as individualistic and therefore more relevant to direct practice situations, one has only to be involved in the heated debate over abortion to realize the macro-practice implications of this basic ethical principle.

Beneficence is a second ethical principle that is based on the concept of doing good for others. This principle is probably a primary motivator for those professionals who work in health and human service settings. It is their hope that they will find ways to assist others in making life more meaningful. The problem is that beneficence can slide into paternalism in which decisions are made according to what is seen as the client's best interest rather than according to the client's expressed wishes. This presents a conflict between the principles of beneficence and autonomy.

A classic case occurred several years ago when a seventy-two-year-old woman was hospitalized for frostbite. Her physician concluded that amputation of her leg was necessary to save her life, but the older woman refused. Believing that a competent, rational person would choose life over death, the state brought suit to declare her legally incompetent so that surgery could be performed. Her situation quickly deteriorated, however, and the dangers associated with surgery became too great. Shortly thereafter, she died (Wilson & Netting 1986). Originally, this situation was a client-level conflict between autonomy and beneficence—a struggle between a professional and a client. It quickly escalated, however, into a macro problem involving hospital social workers, adult protective service workers, and the state's legal system. Although self-determination is viewed as sacrosanct by the social work profession, there was disagreement within the field regarding whether to allow this woman to die or to save her life by forcing her to have surgery.

Justice is a complex ethical principle. Ideally, justice is achieved when there is a fair distribution of society's resources and benefits so that every individual receives a deserved portion. Social work is in the business of distributing and redistributing resources, whether they are as tangible as money and jobs or as intangible as status and stigma. Undergirding the distribution of resources in our society is a value consideration that influences the enactment of laws, the enforcement of regulations, and the frameworks used in making policy decisions.

Reid and Billups (1986) tell us that the code of ethics instructs social workers to "promote social justice" and to insure that "persons have access to resources," but justice is never operationalized. "What is missing from the NASW code is a construction of ethics that goes beyond human relations and personal 'righteousness,' but is genuinely 'social'—allowing a more systematic consideration of the effects of social work intervention" (p. 7).

Macro practitioners frequently face justice-related dilemmas. Justice considerations pose the question, "Is this fair?" and social work practice is deeply embedded in asking questions of fairness. The following questions are based on several posed by Reid and Billups (1986) to assist social work students in analyzing situations involving distributional ethics and fairness.

1. Will the intervention (e.g., program or policy) change the distribution of resources?
2. What resources will be distributed through the intervention?
3. Who has control over the resources to be distributed?
4. How will redistribution of these resources affect the total supply?
5. What will this redistribution mean to the current or future welfare of the persons receiving these resources?
6. Who will be indirectly affected (e.g., community members, other client groups, organizational actors, etc.) by this distribution?
7. Are these resources considered "rights" or "privileges"?

The situation of the student in the guardian ad litem project discussed by Reid and Billups (1986) has similar ramifications. To the infant, autonomy is meaningless. Beneficence is essential in situations where the client cannot speak or advocate for him or herself. But what of justice? The social work student argued that fairness was not served if the parents were not consulted. In this situation, "one must consider the moral basis of the child's claims upon the resources of parents and others, including the State. Likewise, the legitimacy of the parents in claiming the personal resources of the child must be considered" (pp. 14–15).

Concerns about justice become exacerbated when clients cannot pay for services. As long as clients can pay, professional decision making may not conflict with the larger society because resources do not have to be redistributed. Conceivably, as long as clients can pay for professional services, professions can operate within the market economy. Private practice and fee-for-service agencies conform to this model. Quality care is exchanged for economic resources, often in the form of third-party payments. The key to this model is that the client has access to the resources or has insurance coverage.

This model breaks down, however, when clients cannot pay. Most social work clients are in the situations they are in because resources are not available. AIDS patients may find themselves unable to pay for care at the same time their needs increase because they are fired from their jobs when news about their disease becomes known. An older individual could avoid institutional care by hiring an in-home caregiver. However, despite having accumulated considerable savings during his or her lifetime, medical expenses incurred during a spouse's terminal illness now leave insufficient funds to meet personal needs. A minority youth who has grown up in poverty knows exactly what it means when the model breaks down. A broken model has been a way of life, and there are no expectations of, nor reasons to strive for, a better standard of living.

The reality we face in our society is that our health and human service systems are often driven by considerations of whether resources are available to pay for (or to subsidize) the services clients need. If resources are not available, the AIDS patients and the older individual may be forced to impoverish themselves before ending up in public institutions, and the minority youth may continue to be trapped in a cycle of inadequate education, health care, housing, and job opportunities. In a resource-driven, rather than a client-driven system, social workers may have difficulty maintaining a vision of the compassionate community in which mutual support is provided to all those in need. These justice-related dilemmas face social workers because the profession is enmeshed in issues of redistribution.

Balancing autonomy, beneficence and justice demands an analytical approach to decision making and intervention. Inevitably, the macro practitioner will face ethical dilemmas that go beyond the bounds of the code of ethics. This requires that he or she have a strong professional identity.

PROFESSIONAL IDENTITY

Professional identity, according to Gustafson (1982), is built on the sense of calling that draws individual social workers to professional practice. "A profession without a calling lacks moral and humane roots, loses human sensitivity, and restricts the vision of the purposes of human good that are served" (p. 501). Quality of motivation and an in-depth vision of the ends to be served are the distinguishing characteristics that make a profession a calling (Gustafson 1982).

Quality of motivation indicates that the social worker becomes part of the profession because of a deep sense of commitment. This commitment may emanate from a variety of basic principles. One social worker may feel that empowerment of oppressed persons is the primary goal. This speaks to the importance of autonomy in promoting respect for civil rights, individual control over one's life, and freedom of choice. Another individual may enter the field of social work because of a basic belief that there is a moral obligation toward beneficence—to relieve the suffering and pain of persons who are vulnerable to the insensitivities within their communities or within society as a whole. Still another person may see the injustice in society and want to contribute to changing that injustice through redistributing resources to those in need. Regardless of the individual's motivation, a person is "called" to a profession by a sense of moral obligation and concern. Therefore, one's practice is more than a job or a vocation, it is a commitment that goes beyond one's self to serve the collective good.

An in-depth vision of "what could be" also characterizes professional identity. Certainly, each practitioner will have a vision of what the social work profession can be. The vision may be as broad as a higher quality of life for all and a better society, and may never be achieved as fully as one would like. But it is the beacon upon which the practitioner sets his or her sights. These individual visions may come together into a shared professional perspective, based on the overriding values in which social work is grounded. However, practitioners cannot take for granted that their vision is shared by their colleagues. Moving toward a shared vision is an evolutionary process that is ongoing and probably never completed.

Gustafson (1982) suggests that one major barrier to this shared vision is specialization within the profession. As the social work profession has developed (and as human service organizations have become larger and more bureaucratized), multiple specialties have emerged. For example, it is not uncommon to have social workers describe themselves as psychiatric social workers, geriatric specialists, child welfare workers, etc. These specialties denote the target populations with whom these practitioners work. Just as common are terms such as medical social worker or behavioral health specialist, indicating a setting in which these professionals are employed. Terms such as *planner, community organizer,* and *group worker* describe actual functions performed by social workers. Specialization can contribute to tunnel vision, in which one begins to focus on specific areas of expertise to the exclusion of broader concerns. The task is to maintain a broader vision, amid specialization within the profession.

A second barrier is bureaucratization. As professional organizations have developed and grown, as settings in which social workers function have become multipurpose and have diversified their programs, and as communities have established numerous mechanisms that structure interaction amid units within those communities, it is easy to lose one's professional sense of the broader vision. Sometimes there are so many impediments to instituting change in an organization or community that the change agent becomes frustrated.

Fabricant (1985) discusses the *industrialization* of social work practice, particularly in large public welfare agencies. In his discussion, he argues that social work is losing its aspects of *craft.* A craft implies that the person responsible for beginning the professional task sticks with it until the end. For example, if a social worker provides intake for the client, that same social worker assesses the client, contracts with the client regarding a care plan, and continues to work with the client until the goals of that plan are achieved. This provides both the worker and the client with a sense of continuity, with ownership of the entire process, and with a shared understanding of what the outcome is to be.

As our health and human service delivery systems have become increasingly complex, as new actors enter the arenas, and as professionals specialize, it becomes rare for the practitioner to see an intervention from beginning to end. As tasks become more standardized and routinized, social workers may feel bound by rules rather than directed by flexible guidelines that facilitate discretion and judgment. These changes can jeopardize the maintenance of a professional vision that transcends individual organizations and communities.

Amid these barriers, we believe that professional vision is built on a commitment to perform the function of mutual support within a society that does not always perform this function well and at times actually denies mutual support to oppressed populations. The achievement of this function serves as an integrating force for social workers as well as their interactions with other helping professionals. Competent performance of this function is built on a set of values that serve as an overriding ideology.

The challenge is to work toward the development of comprehensive, effectiveness-based health and human service systems within local communities. This often requires the practitioner to understand situations without accepting "what is," to analyze dilemmas with the full realization that an ethical response is a choice among values, to envision competent and compassionate alternatives to what currently exists, and to skillfully use a macro practice model to change "what is" to "what could be."

SUMMARY

The knowledge base of macro practice must begin with an understanding of both communities and organizations. In this chapter, we defined communities as combinations of local systems that carry out five major community functions. These include *production, distribution, and consumption* of material needs, *socialization* to community norms, *social control* that brings about adherence to these norms, *social participation* through which individual involvement in the community is developed and maintained, and *mutual support* of community members in need by other community members. Healthy versus unhealthy communities can be distinguished by analyzing how well these functions are carried out.

Organizations, which we differentiate from loosely linked groups, are characterized by distinct boundaries and structured activities designed to achieve particular goals. Modern communities may be understood as complex networks of organizations whose specialized goals involve one or more of the five basic community functions. Human service organizations, within which most social workers operate, have specific goals of enhancing the well-being of all or certain members of society. In this context they may be involved in any of the first four community functions, but their particular province is to serve the mutual support function.

In a community context, however, human service organizations must respond to a wide array of constituencies, ranging from funding sources, to regulatory bodies, to the "general public." Sensitivity to these constituencies is often based on their relative importance to the organization, thus sources of funds and other resources have the greatest influence. Clients, who often do not directly pay for the services they receive, may have very little influence on organizational decision making. This is where the role of macro practitioners becomes critical, as it is their job to effect change in these organizations so as to ensure that client services remain effective.

The value base of social work is summarized most succinctly in the NASW Code of Ethics, which embodies the profession's orientation to practice. One part of this orientation that most clearly distinguishes social work is the person-in-environment perspective, through which individuals are understood not only in terms of their personal traits but also in the context of their family, community, and other systems in their environment. This perspective means that social workers must be prepared to intervene at the macro as well as the micro level, because clients' problems may reside more in their environments than in themselves.

Intervening at any level, however, presents ethical dilemmas that must be faced by the practitioner. In many cases no right or wrong answer is present, and the appropriate course of action is not at all clear. In such cases, the practitioner's job can be facilitated by analyzing the situation in terms of three basic, though sometimes conflicting, ethical principles. *Autonomy* refers to the value we ascribe to an individual's right of self-determination. *Beneficence* refers to the value of helping others, and *justice* relates to the value of a fair distribution of resources across members of society. As macro practitioners we may find that our job is one of balancing these values. In micro practice, for example, we must often temper our desire to help (and our notions of how best to solve a client's problem) with a recognition of the client's need for personal autonomy. From a macro-practice perspective, social justice considerations may demand that we focus not on individual helping but on attempts to alter macro systems that fail to distribute resources in a fair manner.

Working through these dilemmas aids in the development of a professional identity that incorporates both micro- and macro-practice aspects. Just as the profession must be built on social workers who are committed to making a difference in the lives of individual clients, these same workers must also be committed to making a difference in the systems within which clients live and upon which they depend.

Part II, which follows, will expand on the knowledge and value base begun in this chapter by addressing communities as targets of macro-level change. Chapter 4 will provide a framework for understanding and analyzing communities as macro systems, after which Chapter 5 will focus more specific attention on the human service systems within communities.

REFERENCES

Brager, G., and S. Holloway. (1978) *Changing human service organizations: Politics and practice.* New York: Free Press.

Bricker-Jenkins, M., and N. R. Hooyman. (1986) *Not for women only.* Silver Spring, MD: National Association of Social Workers.

Collins, B. G. (1986) Defining feminist social work. *Social Work, 31*(3): 214–19.

Daft, R. L. (1983) *Organizational theory and design.* St. Paul, MN: West.

Fabricant, M. (1985) The industrialization of social work practice. *Social Work, 30*(5): 389–95.

Gustafson, J. M. (1982) Professions as "callings." *Social Service Review, 56*(4): 501–15.

Kapp, M. B. (1987) Interprofessional relationships in geriatrics: Ethical and legal considerations. *The Gerontologist, 27*(5): 547–52.

Martin, P. Y. (1980) Multiple constituencies, dominant societal values, and the human service administrator. *Administration in Social Work, 4*(2): 15–27.

Miles, R. E. (1975) *Theories of management: Implications for organizational behavior and development.* New York: McGraw-Hill.

Parsons, T. (1960) *Structure and process in modern societies.* Glencoe, IL: Free Press.

Patti, R. J. (1988) Managing for service effectiveness in social welfare: Toward a performance model. *Administration in Social Work, 11*(3/4): 7–21.

Reid, P. N., and J. O. Billups. (1986) Distributional ethics and social work education. *Journal of Social Work Education, 22*(1): 6–17.

Sosin, M. (1979) Social welfare and organizational society. *Social Service Review, 53*(3): 392–405.

Vigilante, J. (1974) Between values and science: Education for the profession during a moral crisis. *Journal of Education for Social Work, 10*: 107–15.

Warren, R. L. (1978) *The community in America* (3rd ed.). Chicago: Rand McNally.

Wilson, C. C., and F. E. Netting. (1986) Ethical issues in long-term care for the elderly. *Health Values, 10*(4): 3–12.

PART II

The Community as the Target of Change

In Part I, we discussed social work macro practice from value and historical perspectives. We also began the process of building a knowledge base about communities and organizations—the two principal macro systems with which social workers must interact. In Part II, we will discuss the process of assessing communities, first from the perspective of understanding the community itself, and second, from the perspective of assessing the adequacy of the community's human service system as it relates to populations in need.

CHAPTER 4

Understanding Communities and Community Social Problems

INTRODUCTION

Setting out to understand a community is a major undertaking. Often long-time residents will comment, "I've lived here for forty years and I still don't understand this town!" How, then, can a student or practitioner hope to understand something as complex as a community, much less propose ways to change it?

First, it should be made clear that there is no single accepted, orderly, systematic method that allows one to understand all the elements that go into making up a community. Understanding, for the macro practitioner, means gathering as much data and information as possible in a narrowly focused area of interest or concern, and making the best informed decisions the information will allow.

There are three reasons why macro practitioners need a systematic approach to conceptualizing a community and its social problems. First, the person-in-environment view is critical to professional social work practice. The community in which one lives has a lot to do with who that person is, the problems he or she faces, and the resources available to deal with these problems. Professional social work prescriptions may not be feasible or realistic without an understanding of these community influences. The framework presented here for understanding community is designed to assist in conceptualizing the environment within which clients experience hope and draw strength, as well as face oppression and frustration.

Second, community-level macro change requires an understanding of the history and development of a community as well as an analysis of its current status. Without this knowledge, the practitioner has a limited grasp of the breadth and depth of values, attitudes, and traditions, and their significance in either maintaining the status quo or allowing for change.

Third, communities constantly change. Individuals and groups move into power, economic structures change, sources of funding change, and citizens' roles change. A framework for understanding community can be helpful in recognizing and interpreting these changes.

A FRAMEWORK FOR CONCEPTUALIZING COMMUNITY

A first step toward understanding community is creating a framework that will help in comparing elements in one community to elements in another. Some communities are larger than others, some have different ethnic makeups, some are wealthier than others.

In searching for a framework to help understand community, we turn to Warren (1978). In his classic, *The Community in America,* Warren proposes that communities can be better understood if selected community variables are analyzed. Based on these variables, we have identified nine tasks that comprise a four-step framework to be used in conceptualizing and understanding a community. In subsequent chapters, we will present methods for planning changes based on this understanding. This framework is shown in Table 4.1.

Focus A: Identifying Target Populations

Many approaches to community analysis propose that the community be understood in its totality to the greatest extent possible before intervention is planned. We propose, instead, that the definition of community be narrowed

TABLE 4.1   The Community Encounter Framework

Focus	Task
A. Identifying the Target Population	1. Understand characteristics of target-population members
B. Determining Community Characteristics	2. Identify community boundaries 3. Profile social problems 4. Understand dominant values
C. Recognizing Differences	5. Identify formal and covert mechanisms of oppression 6. Identify evidence of discrimination
D. Identifying Structure	7. Recognize locations of power 8. Determine resource availability 9. Identify patterns of resource control and service delivery

by first selecting a target population, and that the community be understood from the perspective of the concerns and needs of that population. The target population is defined as those individuals, families, and/or groups who are experiencing a problem or need, and for whose benefit some type of community change is being considered.

The choice of a particular target population is a choice of values. In every community there are multiple groups with varying needs. Therefore, the social worker must realize that in focusing on one target population, he or she is making a choice to examine the community from a specific perspective. It will be important, then, to go back and look at the community again from the perspective of more than one target population so that a richer understanding can develop. For example, existing reports on community issues and populations may predetermine what target group the practitioner will serve, with only limited opportunity to familiarize oneself with other community needs and concerns.

We suggest that a community be analyzed and understood from this limited perspective because (1) practically speaking, people who become involved in community change are generally people with full-time jobs, and it is not unusual that macro-level intervention responsibilities are added to those jobs; and (2) there is a limit to the amount of information that can be used in macro-level interventions. In short, we don't disagree with those who suggest that, in the ideal, everything possible should be known and understood about a community. We are simply suggesting that, with limited time and resources, responsible change efforts can be initiated by narrowing the parameters of community analysis.

Identifying a population in need can, in itself, be complex. None of us is a part of only one community. Community can be defined in terms of ethnicity (e.g., the Latino community), religion (e.g., the Jewish community), commitment to a position (e.g., the pro-choice community), profession (e.g., the social work community), avocational interest (e.g., recreational and sports enthusiasts), and many other designations. Each of us, in fact, would be more realistically defined as a part of many different communities at once.

We recognize that there are differences in urban and rural communities and that this approach may be difficult in a rural community where members of the target population are geographically dispersed. We also caution the reader not to assume that the target population can be disengaged or isolated from the larger community, even though one may focus on the target population in order to manage this complex undertaking. In fact, members of the target population may already feel isolated from the larger community. Certainly, we do not want to reinforce this isolationism. Brager, et al. (1987), view communities as being:

> composed of people who have relationships that are systematic, interactive, and interdependent. These relationships are based on shared history, mutual expectations, predictable roles, values, norms, and patterns of status differentiation. These relationships are part of what constitutes individual identity; these relationships may be neutral or positive or negative; they may involve low to high degrees of reciprocity and alienation. (p. 33)

Viewed graphically, a community would look like a series of overlapping circles. As an individual, any person from a community, pictured graphically, might look like a circle subdivided into many different reference groups, as illustrated in Figure 4.1.

By beginning with a population in need, we are suggesting that a person attempting to understand a community first identify the population of focus. This begins a narrowing-down process. Initial definitions of population can be broad, with the understanding that the more precise the definition selected, the more feasible a full understanding of the community context for this population.

For example, issues surrounding alcoholism prompt a concern for macro-level change, the population of focus for a particular community analysis could be "people with alcohol problems who live in Riverdale County" or "ethnic minority women alcoholics who have been convicted of driving while intoxicated within the past two years in Riverdale County." One is more inclusive, the other more focused. It is probably advisable, at this early stage, that a broader definition be adopted, with an understanding that it will become more precise as a clearer understanding of needed change emerges.

Once a population has been identified and the definition appropriately narrowed, all other dimensions of the community are explored and examined from the perspective of that population. For each dimension to be explored, we will identify a task intended to bring focus to the collection of data and information. We will next focus on questions about the population. Finally, we will propose some questions about a community that will aid in understanding each dimension, and in comparing it to other communities. Although this framework contains a number of tasks, the process of analyzing any community requires the social worker to go back and forth, returning to refine previous tasks as new information is gathered. The social worker is urged to use the framework as an interactive guide rather than a rigid formula for approaching community.

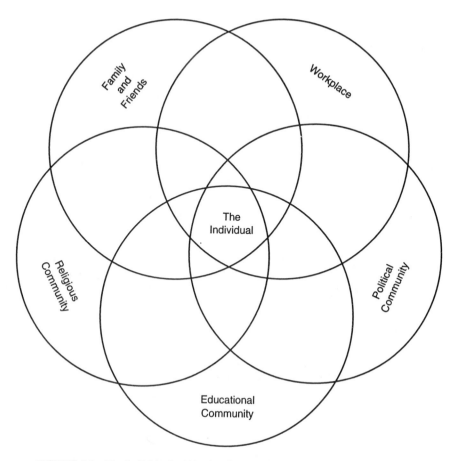

FIGURE 4.1 The Individual within the Community

Task 1: Understand Characteristics of Target-Population Members.
Questions to be asked:

- What is known about the history of the target population in this community?
- How many persons comprise the target population and what are their characteristics?
- How do persons in the target population perceive their needs?
- How do persons in the target population perceive their community and its responsiveness to their needs?

In their book on community organization, Brager, et al. (1987), remind us that:

Demographic differences [do not] exhaust the variations among subgroups of the poor. Although attitudinal differences are more difficult to define and identify, a wide diversity of world views exists even within demographically homogenous populations. Thus, some poor are more alienated than others, some more upwardly aspiring, and some angrier. Where they fall on these dimensions has a bearing on how they will respond to particular efforts to involve them in organizing projects. (p. 60)

It is precisely these shades of difference about the target population that the macro practitioner is attempting to understand. The study usually begins with an examination of available demographic data. Basic to any understanding is analysis of socioeconomic status, age, race, and gender by census tract. It is important to identify areas of poverty and high need, and to determine whether the target population is heavily concentrated in these areas or spread across an entire county.

In addition to gathering statistics, it is also important to talk with people who understand its history, as perceived by the target population. Bellah, et al. (1985), explain why this is important:

> A community is a group of people who are socially interdependent, who participate together in discussion and decision-making, and who share certain practices that both define the community and are nurtured by it. Such a community is not quickly formed. It almost always has a history and so is also a community of memory, defined in part by its past and its memory of its past. (p. 313)

Examining the characteristics of the target population and identifying where they are located, together with gathering information from the perspective of people in the target population, completes the first step in the community encounter.

The following questions can be helpful in collecting and using data and information:

1. What are the key demographic characteristics of the target population and how do they compare to the demographic profile of the various political subdivisions (e.g. city, county, state, whichever is relevant) within which the community is located? Key demographic characteristics should include at least socioeconomic status variables, race, gender, and age, by census tract.
2. Generally, how do people in this target population (and others close to them) perceive their concerns, problems, issues, and/or needs? Do they tend to see them in terms of a need for empowerment and freedom from oppression? In terms of access to opportunity and removal of barriers? In terms of a need for resources, protection, or services?
3. Generally how do people in this target population perceive the community's responsiveness to their concerns, problems, issues, and/or needs?

Focus B: Determining Community Characteristics

Size is an important characteristic of a community, and can be assessed in a number of ways. Size can be calculated in terms of the amount of space covered, by the number of people living within its boundaries, or both. It is an important

characteristic for the macro practitioner because geographical boundaries established for macro-level interventions can range from neighborhood to county and
even larger. Clearly the size of the community as defined will affect the nature
of the macro-level analysis, and ultimately the intervention.

Task 2: Identify Community Boundaries.   Questions to be asked:

- What are the geographical boundaries within which intervention on
  behalf of the target population will occur?
- Where are members of the target population located within the
  geographical boundaries?
- What physical barriers exist for the target population?
- How compatible are jurisdictional boundaries of health and human
  service programs that serve the target population?

Space is the distance or area covered by a community. It is one dimension
of a community's size. Focusing on space allows the practitioner to establish
manageable boundaries. If resources are available to focus on the entire city or
county, then these may be appropriate boundaries in that instance. If, however,
the effort is to be undertaken by a small committee of volunteers who have limited
time and resources available, then one may decide to focus the encounter on a limited
part of the city where there appears to be the greatest need for intervention.

Establishing boundaries for macro-level intervention, therefore, is initially
done by focusing on a target population and, secondly, is further refined by
selecting a geographical boundary. For most macro-level interventions we
recommend beginning one's understanding of community by limiting boundaries
to county or its equivalent, and focusing down from that level to more limited
boundaries if appropriate. This is in no way intended to indicate that intervention
at state, regional, or national levels is not appropriate. It is simply to recognize
that, for the vast majority of interventions, a level of county or smaller will be
most relevant.

Figure 4.2 illustrates the boundary-setting process. Knowing that one cannot
address all target population needs within large arenas, the encounter focuses
on the target population within a manageable portion of the broader community.
This becomes the focus of the macro-level intervention.

A community may be a small section of the inner city or a fairly large expanse
encompassing scattered farms in a rural area. For example, community as space
is applicable to barrios in which groups of Hispanic people reside within a larger
metropolitan area. Spacial concepts of community are also relevant in less
population-dense areas but may be more difficult to determine. This was pointed
out by a Navajo social worker who explained how difficult it was to determine
spacial boundaries on a reservation. There were no street systems, property information or signs indicating county lines, or well-defined human service areas.

Another characteristic important in understanding community as space is
jurisdictional units established by various government agencies for planning and

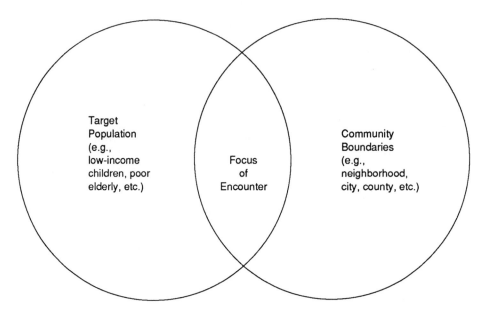

FIGURE 4.2   Setting Parameters for the Community Encounter

service provision purposes (e.g., school districts or mental health catchment areas). Because the macro practitioner's focus is typically limited to a designated geographical area, mapping jurisdictional units that overlap can be important and useful. For example, a change agent may be working with people in a particular county to establish a prenatal health care campaign for pregnant teens, only to discover that he or she is dealing with representatives from county and multiple city governments. Establishing who is responsible within what geographical domain can be extremely important politically. Similarly, the practitioner hired by a mental health clinic may find that the clinic's geographical boundaries overlap parts of three school districts, requiring letters of agreement from multiple school boards. It pays to know the geographical parameters of various institutional units within the community of focus.

A third characteristic related to space and helpful in understanding target populations is service accessibility. If health and human service organizations are scattered across a broad area where public transportation is limited, consumers may find that they are simply not able to make use of existing services. Centrally located multiservice centers, on the other hand, may make problems much more manageable.

To gain a better understanding of community as space, it may be helpful to attempt to answer the following questions:

1. Is the target population highly concentrated or scattered throughout identified community boundaries?
2. What jurisdictional boundaries overlap within the community?
3. How accessible are services for the target population?

Task 3: Profile Social Problems.   Questions to be asked:

- What are the major social problems affecting the target population within this community?
- Are there subgroups of the target population that are experiencing major social problems?
- What data is available on the identified social problems and how is available data used within the community?
- Who collects the data, and is this an ongoing process?

Macro-level interventions tend to be conceptualized and organized around a selected population and a specific problem they are experiencing. For example, a social worker might discover a lack of child-care options for teen parents who wish to return to school, or an increasing problem of malnutrition among isolated elderly, or a community made up primarily of African Americans and Latinos who believe their requests are not receiving a fair hearing by the city council.

This is not to indicate, however, that any target population experiences only one problem at any one time. If one is to understand a target population, we propose an understanding of as much as possible about the social problems they experience. Do people in this population tend to have limited or adequate financial resources? Are transportation options limited? Is unemployment a problem? How widespread is drug or alcohol abuse?

Understanding social problems helps in two ways: (1) it enables the macro practitioner to appreciate the full range of difficulties experienced by the target population, thereby helping to prioritize needs, and (2) it should help in proposing more realistic solutions. For example, sometimes a transportation need must be addressed before a service can be offered.

Social problems are negatively labeled conditions recognized by community residents. Identified social problems will vary by community and by target population. Sometimes there are conditions that exist that have not been labeled as problems. It may be the social worker's task to bring these conditions to the attention of people in power so that they are recognized as social problems. This is not always easy because community residents may have a great deal invested in denying that there is a problem.

The purpose of establishing a profile is to understand conditions affecting the target population. This requires both direct contact and library research. Direct contact with people who can articulate the problems and needs of the target population gives the practitioner a first-person interpretation of issues. Library research adds theoretical knowledge about identified social problems, as well as practice and research findings based on the experiences of others with the same or similar populations and problems.

We cannot emphasize strongly enough the importance of original, authoritative sources in understanding a target population. Populations must be understood in terms of their diversity. In family practice, for example, the meaning of family—of husband-wife relationships, of parent-child relationships, of aging grandparent roles in the family—may differ from one culture to the next. Similarly, the ways in which members of the gay and lesbian community define family may depart radically from traditional community values. A target population will not be adequately understood if these potentially widely divergent views are not taken into consideration.

Once major social problems defined by community members have been identified, one can begin to determine their incidence and prevalence. "Incidence refers to the actual occurrence of a phenomenon during a period." For example, fifteen students may have been arrested for drug use in the local high school in the most recent academic year. "Prevalence refers to the number of cases or instances of a phenomenon existing in a community group at a given time" (Kettner et al. 1985, 72). For example, current estimates indicate that drug use among teenagers is as high as 50 percent.

Social indicator data may be helpful in gaining a broad overview of social problems at the national, regional, state, and local levels. In this way, the community's social problems can be comparatively assessed. Other professionals in the community, or at the county or state levels, can also be valuable sources of information. They may have firsthand experience with the target population, or their organizations may have conducted surveys or collected statistics of specific social problems. The local public, college, or university library may also provide many documents valuable in understanding local problems and needs.

Pursuing answers to the following questions will aid in understanding the major social problems experienced by the target population:

1. What data sources are available to aid in understanding a community's social problems?
2. What are the major social problems affecting the target population as perceived by their spokespersons?
3. To what extent are they interconnected? Must some be solved before others can be addressed?

Task 4: Understand Dominant Values.   Questions to be asked:

- What cultural values, traditions, or beliefs are important to the target population?
- What are the predominant values that affect the target population within the community?
- What groups and individuals espouse these values and who opposes them?
- What are the value conflicts surrounding the target population?

Another variable to be considered in attempting to understand a community is values. Values are strongly held beliefs, and community values are those beliefs that are strongly held by persons who make up the community. These values are often reinforced by the associations and organizations with which community residents affiliate.

The idea of shared values requires refinement in today's changing world. At one time, communities without divisions of labor (e.g., farming communities) were more likely to have shared value systems. As people specialized, community members had limited understanding of what other persons in the community did for a living. In addition, differentiation of interests and associations occurred as society shifted from primary (face-to-face groups such as families and neighbors) to secondary groups (more formalized groups and organizations). Local associations became chapters of national organizations, tying their members into an extracommunity network (Warren 1978). Technological advances increased extracommunity ties. For example, telephones, fax machines, and computers expanded community boundaries. Technology made it possible to maintain contact with others who were geographically dispersed. Given these changes, one must take care not to assume a single, common, shared value system in contemporary communities. Also, the social worker must not assume that members of the target population have equal access to these advances in technology.

Depending on the selected target population, practitioners will find a host of value perspectives. For example, if the target population consists of people with AIDS, some persons in the community will feel strongly that they deserve the best possible care and comfort, while others will react in fear, not wanting people with AIDS in their local acute and long-term care facilities. Similarly, if the target population is pregnant teens, value conflicts may arise between community residents who believe that teens should be given contraceptive information and those who believe that this information only encourages sexual activity.

Jansson (1988) states that "value clarification lies at the heart of social welfare" (p. 6). He identifies five moral issues that drive decision making. Applied to the target population within a local community, these questions arise:

Should the target population receive services and on what terms?

For what needs and problems is the community responsible and what target population needs should receive priority?

What strategies should be used to address specific target population problems?

Should the community give preferential assistance or treatment to the target population?

Should the community use its resources to address target population needs?

These five value-clarification questions may be answered differently depending on the population targeted within the community. This series of questions implies that some populations may be valued more than others, that some may be perceived as deserving and others as undeserving. Whereas there may be an outcry to treat drug-addicted infants, their addicted mothers may be treated with disdain. Whereas homeless families may be perceived as "down on their luck," homeless alcoholics may be seen as "bringing this upon themselves."

Depending on the target population group, there may be subgroups within the larger whole that are viewed differently. Recognition of the importance of diversity will lead the macro practitioner to check carefully the values of each ethnic or racial group affected, the possible different perspectives of men and women in the target population, and the perspectives of representatives of gay and lesbian groups, if they are affected by the change. It is far wiser to take the time to be inclusive of a wide range of values than to find out, too late, that a change effort is not working because differing perspectives were overlooked. Change agents should go into this values-clarification exercise understanding that they may not always like what is discovered about community values, but struggling with value conflicts will give the change agent some understanding of how much the community is committed to addressing the needs of the target population.

As one begins to form an understanding of major community value perspectives, one must take care to recognize the fit (or lack of fit) between target population perspectives and dominant community perspectives. Are target population perspectives taken into consideration when decisions are made that affect them? Recognizing value differences and power discrepancies is an important part of the community analysis process.

Answering the following questions may help in understanding community values and the potential for conflict:

1. How do people in and close to the target population perceive the etiology of their current problems?
2. What are alternative perspectives on the etiology of these current problems?
3. Which perspectives are held by community leaders?
4. How widespread is the support for target population perspectives?
5. How do people in this community feel about giving and receiving help?
6. What are the predominant shared perspectives in this community on inclusion of the target population in decisions that affect them?

Focus C: Recognizing Differences

Up to this point we have examined two areas of focus relevant to understanding communities: identifying a target population and determining community characteristics. We turn now to a third area of focus: recognizing differences. No matter what target population one identifies, there will be differences between this population and other groups within the community. There will even be differences within the target population. Potential differences include culture, race, ethnicity, gender, age, and a host of other factors.

The "dynamics of difference" (Cross et al. 1989, 20) may involve cross-cultural exchanges where groups with diverse histories and values interact. There is always room for misunderstanding and misinterpretation when this occurs. "Both will bring culturally-prescribed patterns of communication, etiquette, and problem-solving. Both may bring stereotypes or underlying feelings about serving or being served by someone who is 'different'" (Cross et al. 1989, 20). For example, professionals who serve the elderly may rationalize why they do not serve many Hispanic clients by stereotyping Hispanic families as taking care of their own, and therefore needing few formal services. This oversimplification may ignore the fact that one-fourth of the Hispanic families in a local community are poor, and caring for an older family member is a tremendous financial burden. It also ignores the fact that not all Hispanic elderly have family members residing within the community.

Differences may be subtle or taken for granted, yet they may influence the way in which members of the target population communicate with one another and with other groups. Feminist writers encourage the recognition of gender differences in psychological development (Gilligan 1982), in interpreting the world (Belenky et al. 1986), and in communication (Tannen 1990). Tannen's research indicates that men and women speak in "genderlects" that comprise a "cross cultural communication" (p. 18). For example, a male social worker was assessing a community's responsiveness to single mothers with young children. He attended several support groups for the target population and was frustrated that none of the discussion ended in a consensus on what they wanted from the larger community. He assessed part of the problem as an unwillingness on the part of the target population to face their problems and to work on solutions. The women in the support group, however, felt that this was an opportunity to process their thoughts and feelings; they did not view the group as a place to resolve problems for immediate resolution. The group was a place to make connections and to achieve intimacy.

Task 5: Identify Formal and Covert Mechanisms of Oppression. Questions to be asked:

- What differences are observed among members of the target population?
- What differences are observed between members of the target population and other groups within the community?
- How are target population differences viewed by the larger community?
- In what way is the target population oppressed because of these differences?
- What target population strengths can be identified and how might these strengths contribute to empowerment?

Oppression is "the social act of placing severe restrictions on a group or institution. Typically, a government or political organization that is in power places these restrictions formally or covertly on oppressed groups so that they may be exploited and less able to compete with other social groups" (Barker 1987, 112). Oppression focuses on differences, the assumption being that some group is lesser than, not as good as, or less worthy than others.

Differences, however, do not have to imply that one way is better than another. Differences simply tell us that there are a variety of ways to view the world, to believe, and to behave. What we are suggesting is that the social worker view differences as potential strengths within the target population. For example, in the women's group described earlier, the social worker was frustrated because the group members were not solving their problems. What the practitioner failed to see was that this community had a forum in which single mothers could share their most intimate thoughts and could find unqualified social support. These support systems were a foundation on which additional services could be built.

Areas around which oppression often occurs are gender, race, ethnicity, sexual orientation, age, and ability. Depending on the target population, all of the resulting *isms,* or selected ones, may be relevant. In many cases, the target population may be defined as persons affected by one of the "isms."

Sexism is discrimination based on attitudes and assumptions about gender. Often these attitudes become barriers to community participation even though they are subtle and difficult to identify. They exist in the values, norms, and traditions of a society to be translated into local community activities. For example, as children are socialized in their educational and familial roles, they are given messages regarding what are considered appropriate male and female roles. Bricker-Jenkins and Hooyman (1986) propose that patriarchy within the community be examined. They suggest that the recording of history and the establishment of myths that set direction for succeeding generations are parts of a patriarchal system in which experiences of women tend to be devalued as subordinate to those of their male colleagues.

The devaluation of the homemaker role may also be an important form of sexism. Many women feel compelled to enter the workplace, not so much by economic pressures, but by societal pressures. So much of one's identity is derived from work, yet, women's housework, volunteering, childbearing, and rearing are not considered economically productive (Waring 1988).

Access to employment and services may, in some instances, limit opportunities for women. For example, women may be limited to homemaker roles because work opportunities are not readily available close to home. Lack of services such as day care and transportation may limit access to employment. Inadequate transportation systems within the community may require women to transport children, limiting their abilities to be engaged in some types of employment as well as other pursuits in which they may have an interest (Fellin 1987). Groups such as the displaced homemakers' network or public offices that deal with equal employment opportunity complaints may be able to help in understanding gender-based practices that affect the target population.

Clearly the most serious type of oppression against women is violence. Statistics on violence against women and resources to deal with this problem are available from such organizations as women's support groups, women's centers, or shelters for battered women.

Racism is stereotyping and generalizing about people based on the physiological characteristics of their racial group. Ethnic groups share a common language, customs, history, culture, race, religion, or origin. *Ethnocentrism* implies that one's ethnic group is superior to others (Barker 1987).

The terms *ghetto* and *barrio* are important in understanding racial and ethnic communities. Choldin (1985) defines ghetto as a "bounded geographical residential area in which a defined racial or ethnic group is forced to live" (p. 236). Barrio describes neighborhoods with large proportions of Hispanic people. Within the ghetto and barrio, residents develop their own culturally driven interactions and ways of looking at the larger society. In many large cities, ethnic communities are named according to the group that occupies that portion of the city—the Polish community, for example (Fellin 1987).

Barrera, et al. (1972), view the barrio as an internal colony. "To be colonized means to be affected in every aspect of one's life: political, economic, social, cultural, and psychological" (p. 467). The internal colony is based on four interrelated concepts: (1) forced entry, (2) cultural impact, (3) external administration, and (4) racism.

Forced entry implies that the colonized group has no choice in being a part of the dominant society. Because of this involuntary process, the cultural impact of the dominant culture transforms and destroys indigenous values and the ways of responding. External administration speaks to the management of the colonized group by the dominant group, based on a racist perspective that assumes the superiority of the managers. Barrera, et al., reject the possibility of assimilation into the larger society because they believe that trading the Chicano culture for the dominant society would result in a bland, consumer-oriented replacement of a rich tradition.

The target population may encompass one or more racial or ethnic groups. Information on such factors as rates of employment, educational achievement, and socioeconomic status within these subgroups is important to understanding effects of institutional racism. Involvement of ethnic minority people from the target population in decision-making roles is an important indicator of sensitivity to ethnic and cultural issues. Service to ethnic minority people in the target population proportionate to their numbers in the community is another.

Homophobia is a term used to describe irrational fears held by people toward others who have a same-sex affectional preference. Homophobia, in the extreme, has taken the form of "gay bashing," a practice of physically beating gay men. In other forms, homophobia results in job discrimination, ridicule, and ostracizing. Like all prejudices (literally, "pre-judgments"), homophobia blinds those afflicted with it to individual qualities of lesbian women and gay men and causes them to be perceived only in the context of their sexual orientation.

Ageism is stereotyping and generalizing about people because of their age, and *ableism* is discrimination against those who are not considered physically or functionally able to perform as well as others.

Although older persons are often perceived as being too physically or mentally challenged to engage in ongoing community activities, only 5 percent of those persons over sixty-five are institutionalized, and an additional 12 percent need some in-home care (Rabin & Stockton 1987, 156). Clearly, however, the vast majority are capable of self-sufficiency and productive lives, yet, they may be excluded from employment and from playing an important role in the community because of perceptions about their abilities. The same treatment is often experienced by people of any age who have physical or functional limitations.

If age or ability are relevant to understanding the target population, statistics on the numbers and age ranges of those persons in the community should be compiled. How many are considered frail elderly? How many are physically challenged and what types of disabilities are documented? Is there adequate access to services that engage these persons in active community roles—transportation and outreach, for example? Are there support services (e.g., nutrition programs, homemaker, respite) that sustain these persons and their caregivers?

Gathering data in response to the following questions will help in understanding the impact of discrimination on selected subpopulations of the target population:

1. What percentage of the target population is ethnic minority, women, gay or lesbian, aged, or physically challenged?
2. What do available data and information indicate about quality of life factors as they affect ethnic minorities as compared to the nonminority community? Women as compared to men? Homosexual or bisexual as compared to heterosexual? Elderly or disabled as compared to younger or abled persons?
3. To what extent are the perspectives of minorities, women, gays and lesbians, aged, and disabled sought in decisions affecting the target population?

Task 6: Identify Evidence of Discrimination. Questions to be asked:

- Are there barriers that inhibit the target population from becoming fully integrated into the community?
- What forms of discrimination are experienced by the target population within the community?

Identifying value conflicts is critical to recognizing oppression and discrimination. Values may be based on prejudices, those pre-judgements that community residents have about the target group that are not grounded in systematic evidence. The issue of systematic evidence is one that needs to be treated with a great deal of care and sensitivity. Many people still believe that every individual essentially controls his or her own destiny, and that hard work and persistence will overcome any barrier or limitation. This belief is reinforced when severely handicapped people accomplish incredible physical feats or severely deprived people make it to the top.

These accomplishments become evidence for local, state, and national leaders that those who need help are simply not trying hard enough. People who hold this belief look at what they consider to be systematic evidence, and deny that their beliefs are prejudices. What is overlooked here, however, is generations of differential treatment that have made it difficult for minorities, women, disabled people, and others to have equal access to economic resources and self-sufficiency. So, for example, when a job is available and a homeless person chooses not to take it, one person will see that as evidence that he is lazy while another will recognize it as a response to a lifetime of hopeless, discouraging, dead-end jobs. For some, the pain of life on the street is less than the pain of hopelessness in their share of the workplace.

Prejudices are intimately tied to values and may affect how a person feels. Discrimination is acting out those prejudices. These actions can be observed in the differences in quality of life between the target population and the rest of the community.

For example, existing data indicates that, "most of the elderly poor are female (72 percent) and either black (40 percent) or Hispanic (26 percent) . . . To be old, female, nonwhite, and living alone is to bear the heaviest burden of all. An astonishing 55 percent of that multimarked contingent lives *below* the poverty level" (Margolis 1990, 10). This is the type of evidence that points to generations of blocked opportunities, discrimination, and neglect. Serious damage occurs to the fabric of the country, and, therefore, to the fabric of its communities, when any group of people is discriminated against as a whole, when an individual is treated only as a member of a group, and when individual differences are disregarded. To many who are victims of this attitude, the message is that it doesn't matter how hard they work, how honest and law-abiding they are, or how well they play by the rules; they can never escape discrimination and oppression because they are lifetime members of the group.

Recognizing discriminatory behavior is important in assessing the community. These questions may assist in the process:

1. What barriers have been identified that inhibit the target population from being a part of the larger community?
2. What community groups, organizations, rules, procedures, or policies discriminate for or against the target population?

Focus D: Identifying Structure

The fourth area of focus in the pursuit of understanding a community is structure. Its purpose is to ground the macro practitioner in recognizing the distribution of power, the provision and allocation of resources, and the patterns of service distribution that affect the target population within the community.

Task 7: Recognize Locations of Power. Questions to be asked:

- What are the primary sources of funding (both local and extracommunity) for health and human services designed for the target population within the community?
- Are there strong leaders within the segment of the health and human service community that serves the target population?
- What type of community power structure influences the service delivery network designed for the target population?

Originally, primary groups, composed of families, friends, and neighbors, performed the functions necessary for community survival. Gradually, business and government have assumed many of these functions. The most obvious change occurred during the New Deal era in the mid-1930s when government reluctantly responded to the social welfare needs of a postdepression society. At that time, the balance between public and private service provision shifted, with public dollars taking over an increasing share of human service funding.

Urbanization and industrialization have greatly affected the social, political, and economic structures of this country. One of the major areas of impact, noted by Warren (1978), was the separation of one's working life from one's home life. Because of this change, people who hold power change, depending on the way in which a community is defined.

As local and extracommunity ties have expanded, so has bureaucratization and its accompanying impersonalization. Bureaucratic structures are usually adopted by government, business, and voluntary organizations as size increases. Funding patterns can lead to power brokers external to the community. Major sources of funding for local service efforts imply the ability to influence and direct provider decisions in regard to target population needs. For example, the specialized volunteer-run, community-based agency that once served the neighborhood may have been transformed into a multiservice agency with a paid staff of many. This means that there may be a number of leaders within the health and human service system, all representing different sectors of the economy. In addition, the larger multiservice organization may have multiple funding sources including federal, state, and local government funds, United Way, private contributions, and fees. Each source must be satisfied that its expectations are being met.

Viewing the community from a power perspective requires identifying the formal and informal leaders within a community. It also means examining their effectiveness in making achievements. Assessing the political climate requires reading the local newspaper and talking with local community leaders to determine top priority issues competing for funding. If a legislative change is needed, it is necessary to identify who may be willing to take the lead on issues affecting the target population.

Community power has been viewed from three perspectives: (1) an elitist structure, (2) a pluralist structure, and (3) an amorphous structure. An elitist approach assumes that a small number of people have disproportionate power in various community sectors. A pluralist perspective implies that as issues change, various interest groups and shifting coalitions arise. This perspective may be increasing as more special interest groups develop within the local community. The amorphous structure implies no persistent pattern of power relationships within the community (Meenaghan et al. 1982).

Gaining a growing understanding of the community's power dynamics will enable the practitioner to evaluate the community on these questions:

1. Who are the major community leaders who will respond to concerns of the target population?
2. Who are the major community leaders who will oppose requests from the target population?

3. What public and private resources are available to deal with target population needs?
4. What individuals or groups control the resources required to bring about needed changes for the target population?

Task 8: Determine Resource Availability.   Questions to be asked:

- What are the existing community agencies and groups currently seen as major service providers to the target population?
- What are the major funding sources for services to the target population?
- What nonmonetary resources are needed and available?

Also related to community structure is the issue of available resources. Communities can be described as resource rich or resource poor when it comes to providing for the needs of the target population. While it is important to consider resources in connection with power, it is also important to compile information on resources so that appropriate sources will be targeted in pursuit of community change.

There are many types of resources to consider. Resources may be very tangible, such as a welfare check, or highly symbolic, such as caring or social support. Resources can be grouped into six categories: love, status, information, money, goods, and services (Specht 1986). Most early community encounters will focus heavily upon the more concrete resources that are exchanged (money, goods, and services) because tangible resources are easier to define and observe. However, as the professional becomes more actively engaged in community practice, there will be increasing opportunities to learn about those more symbolic exchanges (love, status, and information) that are equally important to members of the target population.

Resources may be available from a number of different domains. King and Mayers (1984) have developed guidelines for community assessment designed for use in analyzing community resources for minority elderly. Their framework, presented in the box on p. 86, is a tool that may be helpful in examining community resources for selected target populations. It suggests that, in assessing community resources available to a particular population, a number of domains be explored (e.g., health, welfare, education). Within each domain, questions of policy, practice, eligibility, location, and participation must be addressed in order to determine how available each resource is to the target population.

For example, if the target population is low-income children, resources to be explored would include child welfare services, day-care services, the educational system, and others. How effective are these systems in meeting the needs of the community's children and satisfying the expectations of the community? If the target population is low-income families, a thorough analysis would require exploration of those services designed to meet basic needs of food, clothing, shelter, and health care.

Guidelines for Community Assessment

1. Target Population Groups
   a. Age distribution
   b. Socioeconomic, ethnic and religious characteristics
   c. Organizational and political affiliations
2. Health Resources (hospitals; district health centers; dental, mental health, and other specialized out-patient clinics, etc.)
   a. Service policies, practices and limitations
   b. Admission practices (eligibility and waiting list)
   c. Distance from community
3. Welfare Resources (human services, food stamps, senior citizens' centers)
   a. Service policies, practices, limitations
   b. Admission practices (eligibility, waiting lists, drop-out after intake, short-term services, etc.)
   c. Distance from community
4. Educational Resources (public schools, community and four-year colleges, other educational institutions)
   a. Admission policies, practices, limitations
   b. Program offerings
   c. Fees and payment procedures
   d. Locations
5. Housing Resources (public and private)
   a. Condition of housing stock
   b. Availability of housing units
   c. Public housing policies affecting senior citizens
   d. Tenant involvement in policy determination
6. Recreational Facilities (public and private)
   a. Senior centers
   b. Parks, clubs, sporting outlets
   c. Special services for older people
7. Additional Resources
   a. Courts and criminal justice systems
   b. Consumer affairs and citizen protection advocates (public and private non-profit)

SOURCE: John S. McNeil, and Shirley Wesley King, *Guidelines for Developing Mental Health and Minority Aging Curriculum with a Focus on Self-help Groups.* January 1984.

The major focus of the macro practitioner, however, will in most instances be the formal health and human service network that serves the target population. Formal government service systems, as currently designed in most communities in the nineties, however, operate in close cooperation with a whole network of community organizations. For example, a child and family agency may provide counseling funded by local government, child welfare services under contract with state government, federally funded congregate meals, and home-delivered meals through private contributions, and a grant from a religious denomination.

Having examined the resources available to the target population, those involved in community analysis should attempt to address the following questions:

1. What resources are available from the following systems:

   - Health
   - Welfare
   - Education
   - Housing
   - Recreation
   - Employment
   - Business
   - Others

2. What factors affect how the target population accesses and utilizes resources within the community?

Task 9: Identify Patterns of Resource Control and Service Delivery. Questions to be asked:

- What groups and associations advocate for and provide assistance to the target population?
- How is resource distribution to the target population influenced by interaction within the community?
- How is resource distribution to the target population influenced by extracommunity forces?

In 1954, the urban renewal program acknowledged the importance of participation by those persons affected by change within the community. Administrative regulations required that citizen participation be incorporated into planning in order to legitimize change efforts and to change citizen attitudes. During the 1960s, citizen participation took on new meaning. The War on Poverty programs were some of the first to mandate that consumer groups should have a voice in planning. Agencies created by the Community Action Program (CAP) were fundamental in including the poor in community decision making. Attempts to phase out CAP agencies under the Nixon administration failed because constituents had become too strong and CAP agencies were closely aligned with local government. These poverty programs institutionalized citizen participation as a legitimate means of involving community people in those mutual aid exchanges initiated by the federal government (Burke 1968). In recent years, requirements for participation have weakened or disappeared along with the traditional poverty programs. Depending on the target population, the practitioner may find varying degrees of citizen participation efforts influencing patterns of service distribution within the community.

When assessing patterns and levels of participation, it is important that the macro practitioner distinguish between citizen and consumer-client participation.

There are many citizens who, for reasons of altruism and conviction, are committed to fight for the rights of the poor and oppressed. They bring a certain perspective to the discussion, and make a contribution to constructive change in communities. However, it should not be assumed that interested citizen advocates represent the same perspective as those persons directly affected by the problem. Representatives of the target population should, whenever possible, be sought out to represent themselves in their own words; it should not be left to professionals and other concerned citizens to speak for them.

When dealing with the question of control over service availability to a target population, there can be both intracommunity and extracommunity sources of control. In practice, external and internal patterned interactions tend to develop as community units work together (Fellin 1987). Examples of extracommunity sources of control are state and federal government funding of community-based health clinics. Resources are typically allocated through contracts that include regulations and expectations. Various human service agencies within the local community, then, interact with these extracommunity public entities. Relationships internal to a community have an important part in linking community subsystems together. Organizations with similar interests often form loosely knit federations to accomplish certain functions where there are common interests. For example, several women's groups may form a coalition to establish a battered women's shelter.

Warren (1978) discusses the extracommunity and the increasing systemic relationships with the larger society. Not only are there horizontal relationships that tie one to local informal and formal groups and organizations within the community, there are also numerous vertical ties that transcend geographical boundaries. Local community autonomy may be reduced as extracommunity forces influence what one does and how one thinks. The importance of extra-community forces on the target population within the local community must be considered in order to understand service distribution patterns. On the other hand, extracommunity forces may actually strengthen communities by providing more options and additional resources.

How powerful the controlling entities become in a community often depends on the extent of citizen participation. Burke (1968) describes five citizen participation roles:

1. Review and comment
2. Consultation
3. Advisory
4. Shared decision making
5. Controlled decision making

One role is to review proposals for change within communities. This review process may be carried out in committee meetings, through requests for feedback from selected individuals, or through public hearings. It is a very limited role, and comments may or may not be incorporated. Consultation involves giving opinions on the change when asked. An advisory role usually involves a formal ongoing mechanism such as a United Way advisory council or planning committee, the purpose of which is to react to all factors affecting the target population. While advisory committees do not have the power of policy boards, they can have a strong voice because of their access to decision makers. Shared decision making is clearly a stronger role than advising, and places citizens and consumers in roles where they can, in collaboration with community leaders and professionals, affect decisions. Finally, controlled decision making places citizens and consumers in positions of control over decisions such as policy statements, review boards or membership on boards of directors. These types of positions allow for the greatest amount of control by citizens and consumers. For example, a consumer who serves on the governing board of a family service agency may convince other board members that quality day-care services for single mothers should be a top agency priority.

One cannot assume that citizen participation automatically goes hand in hand with changes practitioners initiate within the community. The concept of citizen participation is essential to democracy, but it will often involve groups who disagree with one another. Just as citizens may comprise the local board of planned parenthood, there are citizens who believe that some of the services offered by this agency are morally wrong. Whenever interested citizens and consumers participate in community activities, these types of clashes in perspective should be expected.

A review of the following questions will be helpful in assessing control and citizen participation in a community:

1. What organizations internal to the community exercise control over decision making for services to the target population?
2. What organizations external to the community exercise control?
3. What limits are placed on services to the target population, and who establishes these limits?
4. What roles do citizens and consumers play in the control of services to the target population?

SUMMARY

We began this chapter by discussing three reasons why macro practitioners need a framework for assessing communities. First, macro practice requires one to view the person-in-environment. In this chapter, the community in which the target population functions comprises the environment. Second, communities change and professionals need a framework for understanding these changes. We have discussed nine tasks that must be completed in order to determine how the target population is served within the community. Third, macro-level change requires an understanding of the history and development of a community as well as an analysis of its current status.

The community encounter provides one method of analyzing what has occurred and is occurring within the designated arena. Skilled macro practice requires (1) focused and precise data collection, (2) analysis of historical trends, and (3) a thorough understanding of qualitative elements that reflect human experiences, interactions, and relationships.

REFERENCES

Barker, R. L. (1987) *The social work dictionary*. Silver Spring, MD: National Association of Social Workers.

Belenky, M. F., B. M. Clinchy, N. R. Goldberger, and J. M. Tarule. (1986) *Women's ways of knowing*. New York: Basic Books.

Bellah, R. N., R. Madsen, W. M. Sullivan, A. Swidler, and S. M. Tipton. (1985) *Habits of the heart: Individualism and commitment in American life*. New York: Harper & Row.

Barrera, M., C. Munoz, and C. Ornelas. (1972) The barrio as an internal colony. *Urban Affairs Annual Review, 6*: 480–98.

Brager, G., H. Specht, and J. L. Torczyner. (1987) *Community organizing*. New York: Columbia University Press.

Bricker-Jenkins, M., and Nancy R. Hooyman, eds. (1986) *Not for women only*. Silver Spring, MD: National Association of Social Workers.

Burke, E. M. (1968) Citizen participation strategies. *Journal of the American Institute of Planners, 34*(5): 293.

Choldin, H. M. (1985) *Cities and suburbs*. New York: McGraw-Hill.

Cross, T. L., B. J. Bazron, K. W. Dennis, and M. R. Isaacs. (1989) *Towards a culturally competent system of care*. Washington, DC: Georgetown University Child Development Center.

Fellin, P. (1987) *The community and the social worker*. Itasca, IL: Peacock.

Gilligan, C. (1982) *In a different voice*. Cambridge, MS: Harvard University Press.

Jansson, B. S. (1988) *The reluctant welfare state: A history of American social welfare policies*. Belmont, CA: Wadsworth.

Kettner, P. M., J. M. Daley, and A. W. Nichols. (1985) *Initiating change in organizations and communities*. Monterey, CA: Brooks/Cole.

King, S. W. and R. S. Mayers. (1984) A course syllabus on developing self-help groups among minority elderly. In J. S. McNeil and S. W. King, eds., *Guidelines for developing mental health and minority aging curriculum with a focus on self-help groups*. Publication supported by National Institute of Mental Health Grant #MH 15944-04.

Margolis, R. J. (1990) *Risking old age in America*. Boulder, CO: Westview Press.

Meenaghan, T., R. O. Washington, and R. M. Ryan. (1982) *Macro practice in the human services*. New York: Free Press.

Rabin, D. L. and P. Stockton. (1987) Long-term care for the elderly: A factbook. Oxford, England: Oxford University Press.

Specht, H. (1986) Social support, social networks, social exchange, and social work practice. *Social Service Review, 60*(2): 218–40.

Tannen, D. (1990) *You just don't understand*. New York: William Morrow.

Waring, M. (1988) *If women counted*. San Francisco: Harper & Row.

Warren, R. L. (1978) *The community in America* (3rd ed.). Chicago: Rand McNally.

Framework for Conceptualizing Community

FOCUS A: IDENTIFYING TARGET POPULATIONS

Task 1: Understand Characteristics of Target-Population Members

- What is known about the history of the target population in this community?
- How many persons comprise the target population and what are their characteristics?
- How do persons in the target population perceive their needs?
- How do persons in the target population perceive their community and its responsiveness to their needs?

FOCUS B: DETERMINING COMMUNITY CHARACTERISTICS

Task 2: Identify Community Boundaries

- What are the geographical boundaries within which intervention on behalf of the target population will occur?
- Where are members of the target population located within the geographical boundaries?
- What physical barriers exist for the target population?
- How compatible are jurisdictional boundaries of health and human service programs that serve the target population?

Task 3: Profile Social Problems

- What are the major social problems affecting the target population within this community?
- Are there subgroups of the target population that are experiencing major social problems?
- What data is available on the identified social problems and how is available data used within the community?
- Who collects the data, and is this an ongoing process?

Task 4: Understand Dominant Values

- What cultural values, traditions, or beliefs are important to the target population?
- What are the predominant values that affect the target population within the community?
- What groups and individuals espouse these values and who opposes them?
- What are the value conflicts surrounding the target population?

FOCUS C: RECOGNIZING DIFFERENCES

Task 5: Identify Formal and Covert Mechanisms of Oppression

- What differences are observed among members of the target population?
- What differences are observed between members of the target population and other groups within the community?
- How are target population differences viewed by the larger community?
- In what way is the target population oppressed because of these differences?
- What target population strengths can be identified and how might these strengths contribute to empowerment?

Task 6: Identify Evidence of Discrimination

- Are there barriers that inhibit the target population from becoming fully integrated into the community?
- What forms of discrimination are experienced by the target population within the community?

FOCUS D: IDENTIFYING STRUCTURE

Task 7: Recognize Locations of Power

- What are the primary sources of funding (both local and extracommunity) for health and human services designed for the target population within the community?
- Are there strong leaders within the segment of the health and human service community that serves the target population?
- What type of community power structure influences the service delivery network designed for the target population?

Task 8: Determine Resource Availability

- What are the existing community agencies and groups currently seen as major service providers to the target population?
- What are the major funding sources for services to the target population?
- What nonmonetary resources are needed and available?

Task 9: Identify Patterns of Resource Control and Service Delivery

- What groups and associations advocate for and provide assistance to the target population?
- How is resource distribution to the target population influenced by interaction within the community?
- How is resource distribution to the target population influenced by extra-community forces?

CHAPTER 5

Understanding a Community Human Service System

INTRODUCTION

In any situation where an assessment is called for, whether it be an assessment of an individual, a family, or an entire community, it is helpful to use a framework. A framework aids in identifying each of the variables to be examined, just as was done in the previous chapter. Few such analytical frameworks are available for assessing local community human service systems. In this chapter, we will propose a conceptual approach intended to permit a student or practitioner to examine a constellation of services within a given locale to determine adequacy of existing resources to deal with current or projected levels of need.

While we will use the term human service *system* to describe the focus of the assessment, we caution students and practitioners not to place too much emphasis or credence in the term "system." There is rarely a master plan. Human service systems are generally made up of loosely related or unrelated client-serving programs operating under a variety of auspices, rather than clearly planned parts that come together into a comprehensive whole. We will attempt to present a framework for assessing the extent to which this network of existing resources is capable of meeting need.

A FRAMEWORK FOR ANALYZING COMMUNITY HUMAN SERVICE SYSTEMS

We approach the assessment of a community's existing human service system with several assumptions: (1) that an entire human service system in most communities is too complex to analyze as a whole, and therefore services must be assessed for a specified target population, (2) that a community's human service system should be assessed and evaluated in relation to the extent to which it meets the needs of its people, and (3) that the needs of the people in a community should be examined not only in terms of individual need, but also in terms of collective need.

Following these assumptions, we propose a framework for analyzing and evaluating a community's human service system. The tasks that comprise this framework are shown in Table 5.1.

Focus A: Understanding Need

Task 1: Identify the Target Population.   Questions to be asked:

- What target populations are identified within the community, and how are they categorized?
- What target population will be the focus of this assessment?
- What priority is given to the needs of the target population in this community?

People who are identified as being in a target population are consumers of services, and ideally the services provided are designed to meet their needs. However, it is important to recognize that people's needs are always changing. This requires a human service system that has flexbility to respond to changing needs. Gonzalez, et al. (1991), remind us that even cultural identity changes. "One can always expect to find both change and diversity within any community. In fact, even a community that appears to represent one culture or cultural group will actually be quite mixed, demonstrating a range of behaviors and beliefs that

TABLE 5.1 Framework for Assessing Community Human Service Systems

Focus	Tasks
A. Understanding Need	1. Identify the target population
	2. Define a continuum of need
	3. Assess target population needs
	4. Identify collective community needs
B. Identifying Auspice or Sponsoring Organizations	5. Examine informal service-delivery units
	6. Examine mediating service-delivery units
	7. Examine formal service-delivery units
C. Determining Systemic Competence	8. Determine linkages between units

are common to that culture'' (p. 2). Because the characteristics of community residents vary, there may be subgroups that require special attention. For example, if a community has a high proportion of retirees, one can expect that many of the services will address the needs of older people. If services are not available, the delivery system may not be adequately addressing community needs.

For the sake of discussion, consider the following seven target populations. They are frequently used for planning purposes, and funding tends to be clustered around these categories:

Children

Youth

Families

Older adults

Adults

Developmentally challenged

Physically challenged

Obviously, these groups are neither exhaustive nor mutually exclusive. In addition, they do not specify the many subgroups that fall within each category. For example, if the target population is children, it is important to recognize that children come from families of all socioeconomic statuses, racial and ethnic groups, and locations within a community.

Although we have identified seven categories of people who may have common characteristics and needs, individual communities will have their own definitions of target populations. How does the community categorize client groups for planning purposes? Local and regional planning agencies, United Ways, community councils, and associations of agencies often produce agreed-upon classification schemes for data collection and planning purposes. Regardless of existing categories, it is ultimately the task of the individual or group conducting the community assessment to define the target population.

Task 2: Define a Continuum of Need.   Question to be asked:

- How can target population needs be conceptualized so that a determination can be made about the extent to which they are (or are not) being met?

Need is a concept that has been defined in a number of ways. Meenaghan, et al. (1982), define need as "any identifiable condition that limits a person as an individual or a family member in meeting his or her full potential" (p. 168). They go on to identify four ways in which needs are quantified:

1. the need represents an identified social, economic, or health-related problem of individuals and/or families;
2. the problem affects categories of individuals (or families) with similar characteristics;
3. persons affected may be located in a defined geographic area; and
4. the identified problem may be directly addressed by some current or future service that may be provided by an organization or individual (p. 168).

Abraham Maslow developed a hierarchical framework for understanding lower- and higher-level needs. Maslow's hierarchy of needs moves from the most basic survival or physiological needs to the next higher level of safety and security needs, to social or belonging needs, to esteem or ego needs, and finally to the highest level of self-actualization needs, as depicted in Figure 5.1.

Maslow hypothesized that lower-level needs must be addressed before an individual can move on to the next level. At any point that a lower-level need is not being met, one regresses down the hierarchy to satisfy that unmet need. Lower-level needs usually require a more immediate response, thus having high urgency.

This framework can be useful in rank ordering and assessing the needs of a target population and using this understanding of needs to assess adequacy of services. The assessment task is one of defining more specifically the problems faced by the target population at each level and identifying the extent of met and unmet need in relation to each problem. For example, for the target population of the elderly, problems can be defined as follows:

Survival Needs
Some elderly are malnourished;

some elderly are not able to meet their daily personal needs/perform basic activities of daily living;

some elderly have no place to live, etc.

Safety and Security Needs
Some elderly are abused;

some elderly are neglected;

some elderly are victims of crime, etc.

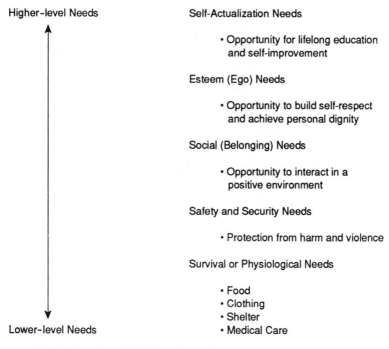

FIGURE 5.1   Maslow's Hierarchy of Needs

Table 5.2 illustrates an approach to identifying needs and resources for widows aged eighty-five-plus living alone in the hypothetical community of West Kingston.

Table 5.2 allows the practitioner to use the hierarchy of needs concept to assess what services are available within the local community. By categorizing these services according to Maslow's framework, priority services that address the survival or safety and security needs of this vulnerable target population can be identified. Whereas medical and personal care services appear to be available in this community, transportation and in-home services are very limited if they exist at all. For elderly widows living alone in West Kingston, therefore, a crisis would most likely be handled in an institutional setting because there would be limited services available to them in their home environments. Similarly, if they required a more sheltered environment, a variety of housing options would not be available in West Kingston. The hierarchy of needs framework, therefore, allows the practitioner to identify needs in order of urgency as well as potential gaps in available services for the target population.

Pantoja and Perry (1992) view the "nature of the human person [and] his/her dimensions and the needs these create" (p. 229) in discussing a community development perspective. They begin, as does Maslow, with basic biological needs such as food, rest, and medicine. They then discuss the need for love and belonging (a second level of biological need); for groups and relationships, particularly in times of emergency (social); for self-expression through symbols

TABLE 5.2   Community Service Identification

	Widows Aged 85 + Living Alone in West Kingston	
Type of Need	Services Typically Designed to Meet Need	Services Available in This Community
Self-actualization Needs	Education Programs Volunteer Opportunities	Available at Kingston Senior Center
Esteem Needs	Support Groups Psychosocial Counseling Mental Health Centers	Two support groups Mental health center has limited services
Social Needs	Recreational and Social Groups Senior Centers Home Visitors	One senior center
Safety and Security Needs	Emergency Response System Adult Family Homes Congregate Care Facilities Senior Housing Continuing Care Retirement Communities Wellness Clinics Telephone Contact	No emergency system Three unlicensed homes One congregate facility No senior housing No retirement community Public health department has wellness clinic Church runs telephone reassurance program
Survival Needs	Home Delivered Meals Senior Discounts Mobile Meals Transportation Homemaker Home Health Personal Care Medical Care	Limited delivered meals program Twenty mobile meals slots No bus system, one senior van available One licensed homemaker program No home health provider Two licensed personal care agencies One community hospital and one nursing home

such as art and language (cultural); for learning from the past (historical); for the use of power (political); for viewing the past, present and future through action, words and movement (creative/spiritual); and for explanations that connect what happens in one's world through investigation and experimentation (intellectual).

Task 3: Assess Target Population Needs.   Question to be asked:

- What are feasible and appropriate ways in which to find out how many people are in need in each of the areas identified as relevant to this target population?

Eight general methods of approaching a needs assessment have been discussed in the literature. They include (1) *general population surveys,* which consist of interviews with a sample of community residents; (2) *target population surveys* that interview members of a select group; (3) *service provider surveys,* which interview those groups and organizations that serve the target population within the community; (4) *key informant surveys* that focus on knowledgeable and influential community residents; (5) *secondary data analysis* of existing statistics on the target population; (6) review of *social indicators* such as income or occupational levels of the target population; (7) administrative or managerial *record review;* and (8) review of *information from other agencies* (Meenaghan et al. 1982).

The preferred approach in assessing need for a particular population is to use existing data. Original data collection is expensive and time-consuming, and is usually beyond the scope of the macro practitioner unless a particular change effort has widespread community and financial backing. Table 5.3 summarizes the advantages and disadvantages using each approach.

Ideally, the macro practitioner would like to know (1) the number of people in the target population who are experiencing each problem, and (2) the number of people that can be served using existing resources. The first number minus the second number presents the community's unmet need. Unmet need, inadequately met need, or inappropriately met need are frequently the focus of macro-level change efforts.

With special population groups that require multiple services, classification schemes are often based on the concept of a continuum of care. A continuum

TABLE 5.3 Needs Assessment Methods: Advantages and Disadvantages

Method	Description	Advantages	Disadvantages
General Population Surveys	Interviews with community residents	Provides broad overview of needs	Requires great time and expense
Target Population Surveys	Interviews with a select group	Obtains data directly from target	Often difficult to locate survey respondents, is time-consuming and costly
Service Provider Surveys	Interviews with providers that service target population	Gives perspective from those who serve the target group	Providers may be professionally biased
Key Informant Surveys	Interviews with knowledgeable/influential residents	Provides a community leaders' perspective	Community leaders may represent power structure, but may not represent target
Secondary Data Analysis	Analyzing existing data	Data is already collected and usually accessible	Analysis is restricted by what data was collected
Social Indicators	Reviews of data such as income, age, occupation	Data is available and provides broad overview of community	Indicators do not provide detailed information
Record Review	Review administrative/ managerial documentation	Provides insights into major issues and concerns	Is subjective and may be difficult to access
Information from Other Agencies	Review any other data from county, state, local agencies	May provide new information not available elsewhere	May be difficult to locate

TABLE 5.4   Continuum of Long-Term Care Services by Category

In-home Services	
Outreach	Homemaker and Chore Services
Information and Referral	Household Repair Services
Comprehensive Geriatric Assessment	Personal Care
Emergency Response System	Home Delivered Meals
Companionship/Friendly Visiting	Home Health
Telephone Reassurance	In-Home High Technology Therapy
Caregiver Respite Services	Hospice
Community-based Services	
Case Management	Adult Care Homes
Transportation	Shared Housing
Senior Centers	Congregate Housing
Senior Discount Programs	Wellness and Health Promotion Clinics
Recreational Activities	Geriatric Assessment Clinics
Caregiver Support Groups	Physician Services
Self-help Groups	Adult Day Care
Counseling	Mental Health Clinics
Foster Homes	Outpatient Clinics
Institutional Services	
Alcohol and Drug Treatment	Swing Beds
Rehabilitation	Skilled Nursing Care
Psychiatric Care	Extended Care

of care consists of a broad menu of services from which items can be selected to address the specific needs of certain individuals or groups. Conceivably, each menu will vary based on what is needed for the target population served. Table 5.4 provides one method of classifying continuum of care services for those persons requiring long-term care.

Task 4: Identify Collective Community Needs.   Questions to be asked:

- Are there needs in this community that require something other than a human service response?
- What data supports the existence of these needs?
- How are these needs expressed by the people of this community?

While understanding need and examining community responses to each level are important steps in conceptualizing a hierarchy, this is not enough. Need is an elusive, complex concept that must be understood from a variety of perspectives.

At the simplest level are needs experienced by individuals that require some type of response: a hungry person needs food; an unemployed person needs a job. If there are resources to meet these needs, the needy person is matched up with the resources and the need is met.

What we have discussed thus far is really individual need experienced by many people. When one person is hungry, it is an individual problem. When hundreds of people are hungry and the community is not prepared to feed them, it becomes a social problem. When needs clearly outstrip resources, it is a communitywide problem and may require a human service response. More food banks, more homeless shelters, and more employment training services may be needed. It is important to note, however, that just because social workers believe that a community should respond to a problem does not mean that this belief will be shared by everyone in that community.

There is yet another perspective on need that should be understood by the macro practitioner. It is a need that requires something other than a human service response. It may even require some fundamental redesign of structures and systems. As discussed in the previous chapter, structure and power are important variables for community analysis. When a whole community suffers from inferior housing, transportation, or schools, or from an inadequate economic base, these problems may be more than simply individual problems on a large scale. They should be understood as collective needs.

It is an assumption in the social work field that communities need adequately functioning basic systems to achieve at least a minimally acceptable quality of life. They need an economic base that will produce jobs and income. They need affordable housing, adequate transportation, sound community health practices, protection from disease, good quality and relevant education for their children, protection from harm and violence, and freedom to pursue obligations and interests without fear. When these conditions are absent, a service response (more money, more resources of any kind) may provide temporary relief without dealing with fundamental structural problems.

The long-term need may be for collective empowerment, a collective sense of dignity, full participation in decisions that affect the lives of people in the community, self-direction, and self-control. Assessing collective need requires an understanding of the history and development of the community, an ability to compare economic data and social problem data to other surrounding communities, and a sensitivity to the needs and aspirations of those who live in the community. Collective need may also need to be addressed at another level such as the state legislature or U.S. Congress. The focus can remain on the local community where actions can be taken, but the point of intervention may be outside the community.

When collective need for empowerment, participation, control and other such factors is identified or expressed, the role of the macro practitioner is different from the role taken when the need is for a human service response. These roles will be discussed in Part IV (Chapters 8 through 10).

Focus B: Identifying Auspice or Sponsoring Organizations

In assessing and understanding a community's human service system, it is important to examine the sponsoring unit or organization. Table 5.5 identifies the types of units that should be considered when assessing service provision in a community.

TABLE 5.5   Units Within the Health and Human Service Delivery System

Informal Units

Household Units
Neighborhood/Groups

Mediating Units

Self-help Groups
Voluntary Associations

Formal Units

Nonprofit Agencies
Public Agencies
For-profit Agencies

These units, taken together, comprise the total health and human service delivery system within the community, each operating interdependently. A given community, depending on availability of resources, may emphasize the provision of services through one set of units more than another. For example, in a resource-poor community, reliance on informal units may be a necessity until publicly funded formal services can be obtained. However, in all communities, elements of informal, mediating, and formal service units will be found. The astute practitioner will carefully assess all avenues of service delivery for the target population.

Task 5: Examine Informal Service-Delivery Units.   Questions to be asked:

- What informal units would typically assist the target population within a local community?
- What importance does the household unit have to the target population within this community?
- What importance do natural support systems or social networks have to the target population within this community?
- What informal units are actively engaged in service delivery to the target population within this community?
- Are race, ethnicity, or gender factors in the provision of informal services and support?

Informal units are those that are not publicly incorporated as legal entities to deliver health and human services. Often, these units have not been recognized for their importance in the service delivery system, whereas they in fact perform a vast assortment of mutual support tasks. They include the household unit, and natural support systems and social networks.

Household Units.   The household unit consists of those persons who reside within a common dwelling, whether they consider themselves families, significant others, friends, partners, or roommates. "The concept of the family is roughly equivalent to the household, but in recent decades more and more people have lived together in dwelling units without being related, making household a more broadly useful term'' (Smith 1991, 138). Service provision in this unit generally takes the form of caregiving and tends to fall heavily on women in our society. The potential for caregiver burden or strain suggests that mutual support provided by the informal system may require assistance from others within the community. Respite services are often needed in the interest of sustaining the physical and mental well-being of the caregiver.

In assessing the extent of service provided in household units within a given community, one should look for indicators of what is happening within private dwellings for the target population. For example, are identified caregivers within the community overburdened? Is there an identified need for respite services for caregivers of the physically disabled, developmentally disabled, elderly, and/or young children? Are requests for live-ins and shared housing increasing? Answers to these and related questions will aid in the process of assessing the domestic dwelling as a service-delivery unit.

Of particular concern is identifying the importance of the household unit for the target population. For example, if the target population consists of frail widows living alone, the household unit does not contain others who can assist. Not only are caregivers not available, but formerly active older women may suddenly find themselves alone after years of providing care to children and spouses. On the other hand, target populations such as inner-city children, who often live in crowded households where privacy is limited and tension is high, may draw support from siblings, peers, and parents. Respite for single mothers may be difficult to locate; poverty may have reduced opportunities and life choices. Yet the household unit can be a critical source of support for these children, fragile as it may be. Recognizing the household unit as a source of community strength and developing services to support this unit can produce a double benefit in strengthening families and reducing the need for other support services.

Natural Support Systems and Social Networks. Often, an unstructured, informal approach to mutual support will evolve as natural or social support systems develop. Most people are part of social networks, but this in itself does not constitute a natural support system. A natural support system, according to McIntyre (1986), exists when resources have actually been exchanged.

The existence of natural support systems have been recognized for years. Recent studies and an emphasis on informal support have prompted a more intense examination, particularly among minority and aging populations (Specht 1986).

Because networks do not have established boundaries and depend upon interaction between informal individuals and groups, they are likely to extend beyond the local community. Mutual support tasks may be provided by geographically dispersed, as well as geographically close, network members. Dispersed networks will depend upon linkages such as transportation systems and telephones, and may, therefore, be vulnerable in times of crisis. Balgopal (1988) explains the importance of social networks:

> Social networks such as kin, friends, neighbors, and coworkers are suppor-
> tive environmental resources that function as important instruments of help,

especially during times of crisis. Social networks provide emotional resources and strength for meeting the need of human relatedness, recognition, and affirmation. They also serve as mutual aid systems for the exchange of resources such as money, emotional support, housing, and child care. Well-developed social networks often consciously and purposefully serve as helpers to families in crisis, making it unnecessary for these families to resort to institutionalized services through publicly and privately supported health and welfare agencies. The concept of a family's social network emphasizes the idea of the family with multiple affiliations, some of which overlap and some of which do not, as well as the idea of the family as an active selector, manipulator, and creator of its environment. (p. 18)

Within the local community there are indicators of the extent of informal neighborhood groups and support systems. Neighborhood associations, child-care exchanges, and neighbor-to-neighbor interaction are all indicators of the extent of support available within this unit.

The significance of natural support systems and social networks will depend on the target population. Networks that advocate for and provide ongoing support for the target population should be identified as a part of the human service system.

Task 6: *Examine Mediating Service-Delivery Units.*   Questions to be asked:

- What mediating units would typically assist the target population within a local community?
- What self-help groups are available to the target population within this community?
- What voluntary associations have members from, or take an interest in, the target population within this community?
- What mediating units are actively engaged in service delivery to the target population within this community?

Self-help Groups.   Self-help groups are one of the fastest growing elements of community support. They have been formed to deal with a variety of personal and social problems and needs including bereavement and loss, depression, parenting, and many other issues. A number of self-help groups (probably the best known being Alcoholics Anonymous) have formed national and international chapters and are recognized vehicles of service delivery.

Hutcheson and Dominguez (1986) acknowledge the importance of ethnic self-help groups in their research on Hispanics. Because language and cultural barriers can confront ethnic populations, self-help groups assist in maintaining community identity and involvement.

Self-help groups are often viewed as being compatible with a feminist perspective as well. Such groups are directed at widows, women who have been exploited or abused, and caregivers. Mutual support provided through self-help groups may assist in protecting the mental and physical health of caregivers.

Depending on the target population identified, self-help groups may be more or less important. For example, groups that already have access to the service system and its resources may find them less necessary, while populations that are struggling to have their needs recognized may find them extremely helpful in supporting their efforts.

Voluntary Associations.   Voluntary associations often serve as a bridge between the informal and formal components of a human service system. Voluntary association is defined as "a structured group whose members have united for the purpose of advancing an interest or achieving some social purpose. Theirs is a clear aim toward a chosen form of 'social betterment' " (Van Til 1988, 8). Community groups such as neighborhood associations or local churches fall within this category. Similar to self-help groups, voluntary associations vary in their degree of formalization. Since they are membership groups, a dues structure will often be in place. Therefore, their boundaries become more clearly defined than informal groups in terms of those who are paying members and those who are not.

Voluntary associations have several characteristics. Members share a sense of community, which provides a collective identity. Social status may be enhanced by membership; social control may be exercised over members. A function of the association may be to enhance the well-being of its members in a supportive manner. If the association is strong, it may serve as a powerful force to non-members. This influence may be positive or negative (Williams & Williams 1984). For example, associations such as the Ku Klux Klan are powerful yet destructive forces within certain communities.

Voluntary associations are a study in inclusiveness as well as exclusiveness. Williams and Williams (1984) discuss the importance of the black church in the development and growth of mutual aid societies. Historically, many mainstream activities beyond the church were closed to blacks who migrated to urban centers. "Blacks organized voluntary associations in the church in such forms as sick and burial societies, economic self-help groups, mission societies, and various secret and fraternal orders" (Williams & Williams 1984, 21). Voluntary associations within the black church became an adaptive mechanism to deal with discrimination. Numerous studies report higher participation rates of blacks in voluntary associations than for any other groups (Florin et al. 1986). In fact, ethnic minorities, lesbians and gays, and other oppressed groups may generally use informal and mediating units to a larger degree than other populations. Neighborhood groups, self-help groups, and voluntary associations serve as means of mutual support, as a place for clarifying perspectives, and as a focal point for action. In some cases these activities lead to recognition and wider support, and to improved access to the existing formal units of human service delivery in a community.

In assessing available services for a target population, it is important that the macro practitioner identify voluntary associations. Churches, unions, and professional groups are all potential sources of support for the target population. They may not be listed in human service directories, yet they may be the first source to which some people turn when in need.

Task 7: Examine Formal Service-Delivery Units.   Questions to be asked:

- What nonprofit agencies deliver services to the target population within this community?
- What public agencies deliver services to the target population within this community?
- What for-profit agencies deliver services to the target population within this community?
- Are there differences in service delivery across formal units that appear to be based on race or ethnicity, gender, affectional preference, disability, or age?

In this section, we are concerned with formal vehicles of health and human service delivery. Although these service providers are interconnected in numerous ways, we shall examine them according to three types of auspice:

Nonprofit (voluntary)
Public (governmental)
For-profit (commercial)

Nonprofit Agencies.   As voluntary associations become more formalized, they may become incorporated as nonprofit agencies, recognized as publicly chartered tax-free organizations (Van Til 1988). There are many types of nonprofit agencies, but here we will focus on nonprofit human service agencies, defined by Kramer (1981) as: "those [organizations] that are essentially bureaucratic in structure, governed by an elected volunteer board of directors, [and] employing professional or volunteer staff to provide a continuing human service to a clientele in the community" (p. 9).

Nonprofit agencies are formal vehicles of health and human service delivery. They are often viewed traditionally within local communities as the agency of choice—a voluntary initiative that targets a specialized clientele. This traditional view is based on the early welfare system in this country which arose from a profusion of agencies sponsored by various religious and secular groups.

Today, health services represents 51 percent of the operating expenditures within the nonprofit sector (Hodgkinson & Weitzman 1989, 22). Health services primarily includes hospitals, nursing and personal-care facilities, and outpatient care and allied services. The 1982 Census of Service Industries indicated that there were 52,571 nonprofit human service organizations in the United States (U.S. Department of Commerce 1984). Although expenditures within this sector had risen until the early 1980s, federal budget cuts caused some declines in growth. Many agencies reacted to budget cuts by increasing their revenues from dues, fees and charges (Hodgkinson & Weitzman 1986, 111). Therefore, nonprofit agencies often charge fees and have expanded over the years through the infusion of government funds.

Nonprofit agencies provide many different services within local communities. While all nonprofit agencies using government funding serve clients without regard to race or gender, there is a growing trend toward agencies designed to serve the special needs of ethnic minority communities and families, women who are victims of discrimination and/or violence, and other groups underserved by more traditional agencies. The macro practitioner should identify which nonprofit agencies serve the target population and whether they have particular service emphases.

Public Agencies.   The public sector consists of federal, state, regional, county and city government entities. When the mutual support function is performed by government, it is referred to as social welfare. The United States social welfare system has been described as a "patchwork quilt" which "does not represent a coordinated, comprehensive, integrated, and nonredundant series of social welfare services; instead, it is a helter-skelter mix of programs and policies that defy a systematic understanding of the welfare state" (Karger & Stoesz 1990, 167).

By the time federal programs are operationalized within the local community, they have usually gone through several levels of bureaucracy. Depending on the structure, which will vary by program type, there may be several extracommunity levels through which dollars have flowed. There may be regional as well as state mandates, rules, regulations, and procedures that instruct local providers regarding what they can and cannot do. Local decision making and autonomy will vary depending on the policies that drive a particular program. In short, extracommunity sources have a definite influence on the local delivery of public services.

In assessing a community's human service system, it is important to gain knowledge about policies and programs that affect the target population. For example, working with the elderly means that one must be familiar with the Older Americans Act. Familiarity with the Older Americans Act tells us that there is a designated state unit on aging in every state and a network of area agencies on aging (AAAs). Every state must have a three- to five-year plan for services to the elderly, and each AAA must have a more localized plan. Therefore, every community within the United States will be included in a plan that addresses the needs of the elderly. Experience suggests that this does not mean that every community *meets* the needs of their elderly members. Resources will be limited, and actually carrying out the plan will include the use of Older Americans Act dollars, in partnership with other public and private initiatives. In addition, many communities have waiting lists for services, and state commitments to carrying out the objectives of the federal legislation vary.

If one's target population is single mothers receiving Aid to Families with Dependent Children (AFDC), the social worker will need to know that states vary in what income is counted against benefits received. States also establish their own needs standard for families in that state. Therefore, although AFDC is a large public assistance program developed at the federal level, state-level decisions influence the benefits families receive. To be effective, the social worker will need to understand how federal and state governments interact and how community attitudes toward AFDC recipients influence clients.

In assessing the distribution of public resources across an entire community, including the funding of social service programs, it is important once again to examine community practices from the perspective of special populations.

Voluntary associations often serve as advocates for their members and have had varying degrees of success in influencing the allocation of resources. In many communities the elderly have been highly successful in these efforts, but attention to the needs of children varies. Ethnic minority groups have exercised increasing political power over the last few decades, but still find, in many communities, that their interests and needs are considered a low priority. Lesbian and gay groups have increasingly taken up causes such as funding for AIDS research, and have participated in the political arena to influence allocation of resources, but they still face widespread discrimination.

Understanding the political system within the community is a challenge. In the United States, jurisdiction over health and human service programs is "distributed across municipal, county, state, and federal governments, in addition to specialized governmental units such as school districts, housing authorities, and regional and metropolitan governments" (Brager et al. 1987, 20).

Assessing the public sector requires stamina. Not only are there federal statutes, regulations, administrative rules, and funding formulae to contend with, but there are state and local laws and funding procedures to identify. Professional colleagues, however, can provide perspectives on types of services and whether government is truly addressing the needs of the target population. For example, for macro practitioners working in a public housing development, social workers in other developments will be helpful in interpreting how regulations assist as well as constrain their efforts. Locating colleagues in similar settings is important to developing a professional support system to aid in coping with public policies, procedures, and rules.

For-profit Agencies.   In the past, the for-profit or commercial sector assumed a lesser role in providing mutual support within the community than either the nonprofit or public sector. However, this does not discount the role corporate foundations have played in funding programs that benefit local communities or the many corporations that have provided employee benefits addressing health, human service, and retirement needs. Indeed, a growing number of social workers are involved in the corporate workplace through employee assistance programs (EAPs). These programs have developed as corporations realize that productive employees are those who are supported in all aspects of their lives (Abramovitz & Epstein 1983). In an aging society, some large corporations have created elder-care support networks for employees caring for aged parents.

In the last decade, the actual delivery of health and human services has been increasingly carried out by for-profit corporations. For example, the majority of nursing homes are now for-profit organizations (Margolis 1990, 154). According to Gronbjerg (1987), the entry of proprietary or for-profit organizations into any given service area is marked by a cooling effect on the relationship between the public and nonprofit sectors. Because proprietary organizations tend to dominate within the economy, patterns of interaction shift.

These shifting patterns were first noticed in the health care arena, when proprietary hospitals began competing with traditional nonprofit providers.

Marmor, et al. (1987), explain this shift in terms of a life-cycle model involving these steps:

A new service is developed by nonprofits;

the service is broadly accepted;

use in the proprietary sector increases;

policymakers become concerned about those unable to pay for this service.

First, a new service is developed through technical or social innovation. Typically, these efforts are initiated by nonprofits because new services are normally expensive and require subsidization from private or public sources. Second, once the service is well-received, broad acceptance follows. Third, interest from the proprietary sector is sparked and proprietary organizations enter the arena, competing with the nonprofit providers. In efforts to keep up with the competition, nonprofit providers begin behaving much like their for-profit competitors. Last, policymakers become concerned about those persons who cannot pay for the service because both for-profit and nonprofit organizations are competing for those who can pay. If the service is important enough, the public sector will finance the poor and uninsured, "which in turn tends to reduce the importance of charitable provision of care by private nonprofit agencies" (p. 229). Inevitably, some consumers fall into the gaps—not being able to purchase the service themselves, but not qualifying under the strict eligibility criteria set for public subsidy. This life-cycle model reflects patterns identified in the health care field, as proprietary corporations have begun competing with nonprofits in the community.

Public financing of health care through private mechanisms was only the beginning. Stoesz (1988) tells us more:

By the 1980s, human service corporations had established prominence in child care, ambulatory health care, substance abuse and psychiatric care, home care, and life care. Increasingly, proprietary firms obtained funds for facilities through commercial loans or sales of stock and met ongoing costs by charging fees to individuals, companies, and nongovernmental third parties. Insofar as resources for human service corporations were not provided by the state, firms were free to function independently of the government. (pp. 54–5)

As profit-making corporations bid for public contracts, competition with nonprofit organizations increases. Ten years ago our discussion of the health and human service systems would have focused almost entirely on the government and nonprofit sectors and their partnership. Today, as we approach the twenty-first century, the term *mixed economy,* including government, nonprofit, and for-profit services is clearly a more accurate description.

Given the complexity of the formal service delivery system, the purpose of this assessment is to gain a better understanding of what organizations are providing services to the target population in this community. Having a general idea of what nonprofit, public, and for-profit agencies are available leads to an examination of how they work together.

Focus C: Determining Systemic Competence

Knowing what agencies are available does not go far enough. It is important for the macro practitioner to know whether or not those agencies actually work together so that target groups do not fall through gaps in the service-delivery system. The next two tasks in the assessment process thus examine the linkages that are evident to the practitioner and require a judgment as to whether these interacting units truly comprise a system that is responsive to multiple needs.

Task 8: Determine Linkages Between Units.   Questions to be asked:

- How are the various types of service units generally connected within a community?
- What are the established linkages between units that serve the target population within *this* community?
- Where are linkages between service units obviously needed, but not currently established?
- Are the interests of ethnic minorities and women represented in the network established through linkages between units?

If there are multiple agencies with overlapping relationships and numerous types of services, is there a glue that holds the community delivery system together? Certainly there may be competition among units, but there will also be connections. Just as the individual is embedded in a social network, so are the group and organizational units within the community. These relational patterns may change over time.

Tobin et al. (1986), identify five levels of interaction between human service agencies within the community. Table 5.6 provides an overview of their inter-actional types.

Communication.   Communication can be formal or informal. Information and referral exemplifies formal communication that occurs between units on a daily basis. Communication designed to increase interagency information and under-standing may be enhanced through the use of brochures, pamphlets and media. Informal communication occurs between units as groups meet to discuss community issues or staff members talk about their programs at conferences. Although communication is assumed, breakdowns in the delivery system often occur because this process of sharing information between units is not nurtured. Frequently, written agreements are developed as a reminder of the importance of constant communication as staff changes within organizations and new groups are formed within the community.

Cooperation.   Cooperation occurs when units within the community agree to work toward similar goals. A local private child day-care center may work closely with a public human service agency. Both want to provide supports for single

TABLE 5.6   Five Levels of Interaction Leading to Improved Programming

Level of Interaction	Type of Interaction
Communication	Verbal, written, or other forms of communication limited to sharing information or ideas between organizations. Includes consultation.
Cooperation	Two or more separate organizations plan and implement independent programs, but all work toward similar, nonconflicting goals. The organizations share information but act on it independently. Organizations advertise for each other and try to avoid unnecessary duplication of services.
Coordination	Two or more separate organizations work together to plan programs and ensure that they interact smoothly and avoid conflict, waste, and unnecessary duplication of services. Organizations share information, advertise for each other, and make referrals to each other.
Collaboration	Two or more separate organizations join together to provide a single program or service. Each organization maintains its own identity but resources are jointly shared.
Confederation	Two or more organizations merge to provide programs or services. None of the participating organizations maintains a separate identity or separate resources.

SOURCE: *Enabling the Elderly:* by Sheldon S. Tobin, James W. Ellor, and Susan Anderson-Ray. *Chart 9.1 Five Levels of Interaction Leading to Improved Programming,* p. 149, State University of New York Press, 1986.

mothers with young children, yet these units provide different resources. Social workers at the day-care center meet with staff at the human service agency once a month to discuss common concerns and to maintain a sense of continuity for mothers who are clients of both agencies. If the target population is single mothers, the practitioner needs to know that these linkages are established.

Corporate volunteerism represents a cooperative linkage between the for-profit and nonprofit sectors. The Levi Strauss Company provides an example. In communities throughout the United States in which Levi Strauss factories are located, there are community involvement teams. In one southeastern city, the company encouraged its employees to become actively involved with a multi-county nonprofit home aide service for the elderly and physically handicapped. Employees donated time to painting and repairing the homes of older shut-ins, as well as providing friendly visits to the agency's clients. If the target population is older widows, the social worker needs to know that the corporate sector is willing to address client needs.

The concept of corporate volunteerism is manifested in a number of ways. A business may subsidize their employees by giving them release time to do community service work. Other companies will loan employees to human service agencies for a specified period of time so that the expertise required for a project can be provided at no cost to the agency. As employees near retirement, the for-profit sector often provides preretirement training in which postretirement volunteer opportunities are presented. In this way, the for-profit sector actually performs a recruitment function for the nonprofit service delivery system.

The interchange between the for-profit and nonprofit sectors also occurs in the form of corporate cash and in-kind contributions. Computer manufacturers may donate hardware to a local service agency, assisting in computerizing its information system. Restaurants may donate food to homeless shelters. A local for-profit nursing home may open its doors to older community residents who live alone in a large metropolitan area during a time of anxiety over a crime wave. In this community, what cooperative efforts exist between service units within different sectors that focus on the target population's needs? Are ethnicity, gender, or affectional preference factors that need to be taken into consideration in assessing service system interactions? Are any of these interests left out when they should be included?

Coordination.   Coordination implies a concerted effort to work together. Often separate units will draft agreements, outlining ways in which coordination will occur.

In a continuum of care system that attempts to address the needs of such populations as older persons, those with disabilities, or AIDS victims within the community, coordination is necessary. As consumers exit the acute care hospital, discharge planners work to develop a care plan. This requires knowledge of and close coordination with local service providers. Service plans often include a package to support the client's needs—mobile meals, visiting nurses, and home-maker services. Depending on the level of disability and length of time expected for recovery, this service plan may make the difference between returning home or convalescing in a long-term care facility. Extensive coordination is required.

The growth of case management within local communities reflects the need for interunit oversight as consumers receive services from multiple units. Case management programs attempt to provide a coordination function so that service delivery flows across informal and formal providers of care. Where there are case managers serving the target population it is useful to learn how they view the relationships between service units that serve the target population and where they see gaps.

Collaboration.   Collaboration implies the concept of a joint venture. Joint ventures are agreements in which two or more units within the community agree to set up a new program or service. This usually occurs when no one separate unit within the community is able or willing to establish the new venture alone.

For example, a local senior citizens center identified the need for repair services for many of its participants. Because older persons tend to own older homes, repairs were often needed. The center did not have the resources to begin this program alone, but by working with a community action agency within the community, a home repair service was sponsored jointly by the center and the agency. Eventually, the home repair service became a separate unit, incorporated as a nonprofit organization.

Coalition building is another form of collaboration. A coalition is a loosely developed association of constituent groups and organizations, each of whose primary identification is outside the coalition. For example, state coalitions have been formed as part of the National Health Care Campaign. Community organizations, voluntary associations, public agencies, and interested individuals have joined forces to work toward a common goal—health care for all citizens. In coming together, a new voluntary association is formed. Even though the diverse members of this coalition represent various interests across community units, their collaboration on health care concerns provides a strong and focused network for change. In some communities, agencies created to serve the needs of a special population collaborate to assess need, to examine the fit between needs and services, and to present a united front and a stronger voice in pursuing funding for programs.

Albrecht and Brewer (1990) call for change agents within communities to move beyond coalition building, which is often temporary, and toward building alliances. The "concept of alliance as a new level of commitment that is longer-standing, deeper, and built upon more trusting political relationships" requires asking questions such as: "Who sets the agenda? What are the power differentials? What different skills do we bring to the table? What different visions of social change do we have? And what different leadership styles do we use and do we value?" (p. 4)

In this community, what coalitions are focused on target population needs? How active are coalitions in advocating for change? Are there joint ventures (new programs) developed by two or more service units? Are there coalitions that are moving toward building long-term alliances?

Confederation.   Units within the community may actually merge, often when one or both units becomes unable to function autonomously. A horizontal merger occurs, for example, when two mental health centers consolidate into a single organization. A vertical merger occurs when a hospital absorbs a home health provider. A conglomerate merger occurs when units within the community form a confederation of multiple smaller units under a large umbrella agency. These actions are generally limited to nongovernmental agencies.

Agency interaction inevitably involves competition and conflict. Change agents learn to cope with competition and conflict on a regular basis. These types of interactions will be discussed in Part III.

SUMMARY

In this chapter, we have endeavored to present a means for assessing a community's human service system. The assessment process begins with the definition of a target population, whose needs must then be conceptualized in a hierarchy according to their urgency. Following this, the human service response is explored and collective needs are considered. Sources of help are then addressed, including informal sources such as households and social networks and mediating sources such as self-help groups and voluntary associations. Formal sources of services include nonprofit, public, and for-profit providers, and both the nature and orientation of services may differ in important ways across these auspices. Determining the competence of these systems in combining to meet needs in an effective way is the final consideration.

Overall, the above steps may be approached as a series of general questions to be applied to the task of assessing community services in a community. These include:

1. Is the community generally sensitive to the needs of the target population?
2. Are target population needs adequately assessed in this community?
3. Is there a "continuum of care" concept or framework that guides service planning and funding for target population needs?
4. How adequate is funding to meet target population needs in the community?
5. Are services appropriately located for target group accessibility?
6. What is the degree of cooperation, collaboration, and competition in providing services to the target population?
7. What gaps in services and problems affecting the target population have been identified in the process of conducting this assessment?
8. How does the race or ethnicity, gender, or sexual orientation of the target population, or some people in the population, affect the need for and provision of services?

Based on data and information accumulated in the process of assessing a community's human service system, the macro practitioner must finally exercise professional judgment in evaluating the adequacy of resources devoted to the target population within the community. If the assessment has been thorough and productive, the practitioner will have gained enough understanding of what occurs within the community to identify and begin assessing needed change on behalf of the target population.

REFERENCES

Abramovitz, M., and I. Epstein. (1983) The politics of privatization: Industrial social work and private enterprise. *Urban and Social Change Review, 16*(1): 13–9.

Albrecht, L., and R. M. Brewer. (1990) *Bridges of power: Women's multicultural alliances.* Philadelphia, PA: New Society Publications.

Balgopal, P. R. (1988) Social networks and Asian Indian families. In Jacobs, C., and D. D. Bowles, eds., *Ethnicity and race: Critical concepts in social work* (pp. 18–33). Silver Spring, MD: National Association of Social Workers.

Brager, G., H. Specht, and J. L. Torczyner. (1987) *Community organizing.* New York: Columbia University Press.

Florin, P., E. Jones, and A. Wandersman. (1986) Black participation in voluntary associations. *Journal of Voluntary Action Research, 15*(1): 65–86.

Gonzalez, V. M., J. T. Gonzalez, V. Freeman, and B. Howard-Pitney. (1991) *Health promotion in diverse cultural communities.* Palo Alto, CA: Health Promotion Resource Center.

Gronbjerg, K. (1987) Patterns of institutional relations in the welfare state: Public mandates and the nonprofit sector. *Journal of Voluntary Action Research, 16*: 64–80.

Hodgkinson, V., and M. S. Weitzman. (1986) *Dimensions of the independent sector* (2nd ed.). Washington, DC: The Independent Sector.

Hodgkinson, V., and M. S. Weitzman. (1989) *Dimensions of the independent sector* (3rd ed.). Washington, DC: The Independent Sector.

Hutcheson, J. D., and L. H. Dominguez. (1986) Ethnic self-help organizations in non-barrio settings: Community identity and voluntary action. *Journal of Voluntary Action Research, 15*(4): 13–22.

Karger, H. J., and D. Stoesz. (1990) *American social welfare policy*. New York: Longman.

Kramer, R. M. (1981) *Voluntary agencies in the welfare state*. Berkeley, CA: University of California Press.

Margolis, R. J. (1990) *Risking old age in America*. Boulder, CO: Westview Press.

Marmor, T. R., M. Schlesinger, and R. W. Smithey. (1987) Nonprofit organizations and health care. In Powell, W. W., ed., *The nonprofit sector* (pp. 221–39). New Haven, CT: Yale University Press.

McIntyre, E. L. G. (1986) Social networks: Potential for practice. *Social Work, 31*(6): 421–26.

Meenaghan, T. M., R. O. Washington, and R. M. Ryan. (1982) *Macro practice in the human services*. New York: Free Press.

Pantoja, A., and W. Perry. (1992) Community development and restoration: A perspective. In Rivera, F. G., and J. L. Erlich, eds., *Community organizing in a diverse society* (pp. 223–49). Boston, MA: Allyn and Bacon.

Smith, D. H. (1991) Four sectors or five? Retaining the member-benefit Sector. *Nonprofit and Voluntary Sector Quarterly, 20*(2): 137–50.

Specht, H. (1986) Social support, social networks, social exchange, and social work practice. *Social Service Review, 60*(2): 218–40.

Stoesz, D. (1988) Human service corporations and the welfare state. *Society, 25*(5): 53–8.

Tobin, S. S., J. W. Ellor, and S. Anderson-Ray. (1986) *Enabling the elderly: Religious institutions within the community service system*. New York: State University of New York Press.

U.S. Department of Commerce, Bureau of the Census. (1984) *1982 Census of Service Industries*. Washington, DC: Government Printing Office.

Van Til, J. (1988) *Mapping the third sector: Voluntarism in a changing social economy*. New York: The Foundation Center.

Williams, C., and H. B. Williams. (1984) Contemporary voluntary associations in the urban black church: The development and growth of mutual aid societies. *Journal of Voluntary Action Research, 13*(4): 19–30.

Framework for Analyzing Community Human Service Systems

FOCUS A: UNDERSTANDING NEED

Task 1: Identify the Target Population

- What target populations are identified within the community, and how are they categorized?
- What target population will be the focus of this assessment?
- What priority is given to the needs of the target population in this community?

Task 2: Define a Continuum of Need

- How can target population needs be conceptualized so that a determination can be made about the extent to which they are (or are not) being met?

Task 3: Assess Target Population Needs

- What are feasible and appropriate ways in which to find out how many people are in need in each of the areas identified as relevant to this target population?

Task 4: Identify Collective Community Needs

- Are there needs in this community that require something other than a human service response?
- What data supports the existence of these needs?
- How are these needs expressed by the people of this community?

FOCUS B: IDENTIFYING AUSPICE OR SPONSORING ORGANIZATIONS

Task 5: Examine Informal Service-Delivery Units

- What informal units would typically assist the target population within a local community?
- What importance does the household unit have to the target population within this community?
- What importance do natural support and social networks have to the target population within this community?

- What informal units are actively engaged in service delivery to the target population within this community?
- Are race, ethnicity, or gender factors in the provision of informal services and support?

Task 6: Examine Mediating Service-Delivery Units

- What mediating units would typically assist the target population within a local community?
- What self-help groups are available to the target population within this community?
- What voluntary associations have members from, or take an interest in, the target population within this community?
- What mediating units are actively engaged in service delivery to the target population within this community?

Task 7: Examine Formal Service-Delivery Units

- What nonprofit agencies deliver services to the target population within this community?
- What public agencies deliver services to the target population within this community?
- What for-profit agencies deliver services to the target population within this community?
- Are there differences in service delivery across formal units that appear to be based on race or ethnicity, gender, affectional preference, disability, or age?

FOCUS C: DETERMINING SYSTEMIC COMPETENCE

Task 8: Determine Linkages between Units

- How are the various types of service units generally connected within a community?
- What are the established linkages between units that serve the target population within *this* community?
- Where are linkages between service units obviously needed, but not currently established?
- Are the interests of ethnic minorities and women represented in the network established through linkages between units?

PART III

The Organization as the Target of Change

Part II addressed communities as the focus of planned change. Communities are important arenas of practice for social workers because they have such a major influence on the lives of clients and they establish a context within which human service organizations function. In Part III, we will discuss organizations as another important form of macro system in which social workers operate. Chapter 6 begins with a review of the considerable theoretical literature that exists concerning organizations. This review is intended to promote an understanding of how and why organizations function the way they do. Chapter 7 focuses specifically on human service organizations and attempts to identify the major areas in which organizational problems have been identified and solutions proposed.

CHAPTER 6
Understanding and Analyzing Organizations

INTRODUCTION

Organizations are a fundamental part of our everyday lives. We join them, learn in them, worship in them, and obtain from them most of the goods and services necessary to meet our basic needs. Most of us also work in them, and places of work consume large portions of our time, energy, and commitment. In most organizations other than the workplace, we have a consumer-provider relationship. This means that we have other options to turn to if the relationship is not satisfactory. The place of work, however, represents a different type of relationship that is not as easily terminated, since people depend on income from work for their livelihood. Furthermore, if a human service organization is functioning in a manner that is disrespectful or detrimental to clients, the professional social worker has an obligation to try to change those practices and not simply walk away in favor of a more attractive work environment. Organizations that do not function well often provide poor-quality services to clients and, at the same time, contribute to burnout on the part of their staff. Conversely, the provision of high-quality services can be helpful to clients, energizing to staff, and a constant source of renewal to the organization.

It is not unusual for organizations to stagnate over time, to lose sight of mission and goals, and to provide a very mediocre level of service to clients. Sometimes this happens because of the sheer size of the organization, sometimes because of the complexity of its mission, sometimes because of inadequate resources, or because of a combination of these and other factors. But just as organizations can lose a sense of mission and direction, so, too, can they regain it. We believe that the path to renewal begins with an understanding of the organization itself—its history, its underlying theoretical principles and assumptions, and the etiology of its current problems. The major focus of this chapter will be on understanding organizations from a theoretical perspective.

Defining Organizations

Organizations are defined here as collectivities of individuals gathered together to serve a particular purpose. The key word in this definition is *purpose*. As Parsons (1960) notes, "*primacy of orientation to the attainment of a specific goal* is . . . the defining characteristic of an organization which distinguishes it from other types of social systems" (p. 17).

The kinds of goals that people may organize themselves to achieve span the full range of human needs, from obtaining basic necessities to achieving growth of the self. Goals may focus on production and profitability, as is usually the case in profit-making enterprises. Or, as in human service agencies, the goal may be to improve the quality of life of persons outside the organization. In each case, the organization exists because, as a collective, it makes possible the accomplishment of tasks that could be completed either not as well or not at all by a single individual.

As we discussed in Chapter 2, today's society has been made possible in large measure by the rise of an "organizationalized" social structure. This point is expressed well by Etzioni (1964) in the introduction to his classic book on modern organizations:

> Ours is an organizational society. We are born in organizations, educated by organizations, and most of us spend much of our lives working for organizations. We spend much of our leisure time paying, playing, and praying in organizations. Most of us will die in an organization, and when the time comes for burial, the largest organization of all—the state—must grant official permission. (p. 1)

The ubiquity of organizations is certainly true in human services as well. As social workers, our roles within, interactions with, and attempts to manipulate organizations define much of what we do. Clients often come to us seeking help because they are not able to obtain help from organizations that are critical to their survival or quality of life. In turn, the resources we attempt to gain for these clients usually come from still other organizations. For example, consider the basic social work function of case management that was mentioned in Chapter 5. Barker (1987) defines case management as:

> [a] procedure to coordinate all the helping activities on behalf of a client or group of clients. The procedure makes it possible for many workers in the agency, or different agencies, to coordinate their efforts to serve a given client through professional teamwork. . . . Case management may involve monitoring the progress of a client whose needs require the services of many different professionals, agencies, health care facilities, and human service programs. (p. 20)

Thus, social work practice, beginning with this fundamental role, requires considerable effort spanning many different agencies and service systems. Social workers with little or no idea of how organizations operate, how they interact, or how they can be influenced and changed from both outside and inside are likely to be severely limited in their effectiveness.

The purpose of this chapter is to provide an introduction to organizations as societal units that social workers must both work in and work with in order to do their jobs. Our review will by no means be complete, as there exists a prodigious body of theory and research on organizations that is far beyond the scope of this book. Instead, we will present a brief review of the most important schools of thought concerning organizations, including a brief review of the main tenets of each school, and the strengths and weaknesses of each.

Distinguishing Organizational Theories

In our discussion, we will examine ways of understanding organizations that have been proposed by various theorists, proceeding in a roughly chronological order. An important distinction that we will make will be between *descriptive* and *prescriptive* schools of thought. Descriptive approaches are intended to provide a means of analyzing organizations in terms of certain characteristics or procedures. They often reflect a sociological approach to organizations, which has as its goal the understanding of organizations as social phenomena. In contrast, prescriptive approaches are designed specifically as "how-to" guides, and their goal is to help build better organizations. Not surprisingly, since managers usually play important roles in deciding how to build and operate an organization, most prescriptive organization theories are part of the literature on management and leadership.

Table 6.1 illustrates other distinctions between various schools of thought about organizations that will be covered. These distinctions are shown partly in terms of key concepts associated with each school. Also illustrated are distinctions relating to whether each particular theory approaches organizations as *open systems* or *closed systems*. Open-system perspectives are concerned

TABLE 6.1   Comparative Dimensions of Key Organizational Theories

	Dimension	
Theory (Theorist)	**Key Concepts**	**Conception of Organization in Environment**
Bureaucracy (Weber)	Structure Hierarchy	Closed System
Scientific and Universalistic Management (Taylor; Fayol)	Efficiency Measurement	Closed
Human Relations (Mayo)	Informal structure Social rewards	Closed
Management by Objectives (Drucker)	Setting goals and objectives	Closed
Organizational Goals (Michels, Selznick)	Goal displacement Natural systems	Closed
Decision Making (Simon; March)	Bounded rationality Satisficing	Closed
Open Systems (Katz and Kahn)	Systems theory Inputs/outputs	Open
Contingency Theory (Burns and Stalker; Morse and Lorsch; Thompson)	Environmental constraints Task environment	(Varies)
Power and Politics (Pfeffer; Wamsley and Zald)	Political economy	Open
Organizational Culture (Schein)	Artifacts, values, beliefs	Closed
Theory Z (Ouchi)	Quality control in process and outcome	Closed
"In Search of Excellence" (Peters and Waterman)	Consumer/Quality orientation	Open
Managing Diversity (Thomas)	Empowerment of employees	Open

with how organizations are influenced by interactions with their environments, while closed-system approaches are more concerned with internal structures and processes.

BUREAUCRACY AND ORGANIZATIONAL STRUCTURE

Organizational structure refers to the way relationships are constituted among persons within an organization. As we discussed earlier, one of the advantages of organizations is that individuals working in concert can often accomplish much more than the same number of individuals working independently. The reason for this is the coordination of organizational members' activities such that the work of each enhances that of the others. Organizational structure is the means by which this coordination is achieved.

Even in informal task groups, members usually do not all attempt to do the same activities. Instead, they divide among themselves the responsibilities for diverse tasks. Members also have varying skills and interests, and the process of dividing up specific tasks usually takes this into account. Finally, to insure that each person's activities are both appropriate to reaching the goal and supportive of other members' efforts, at least one individual in the organization usually takes on a management role. These aspects of organizational functioning, including task specialization, matching of person and position, and leadership, are among a group of structural characteristics that are common to virtually all organizations and that provide a means by which they may be analyzed and understood.

The most important conceptual work on organizational structure remains that of German sociologist Max Weber. Weber coined the term *bureaucracy* and applied it to a particular form of organization. The bureaucracy is an *ideal type,* meaning that it is a pure conceptual construct, and it is unlikely that any organization fits perfectly with all the characteristics of a bureaucracy. The bureaucracy typifies descriptive organizational theories in that it provides a model against which organizations can be compared, after which they can be described in terms of the extent to which they fit this model. It is also important to note that Weber did not conceptualize the bureaucracy as some sort of goal toward which organizations should strive. Instead, he designed it as a theoretical tool to assist in understanding organizational structure.

The characteristics of a bureaucracy are:

1. Limited areas of command and responsibility attached to each position within the organization.
2. Hierarchical authority structure with control and responsibility concentrated at the top of the hierarchy.
3. Central system of file collections summarizing the activities of the organization.
4. High degree of specialization based on expert training.
5. Activity demanding the full working capacity of the member, that is, full-time staff and the job as a career.
6. Definite outlined rules of procedure for rational coordination of activities.

7. Impersonality of relationships between organizational members.
8. Recruitment of officials on the basis of ability and technical knowledge.
9. Distinct separation of private and public lives and positions of members.
10. Promotion by seniority. (Summarized by Rogers 1975, from Weber 1947.)

Weber was interested in this organizational model because he believed it reflected a change in the values of society as a whole. Indeed, his work began with a more general concern about the way power is legitimized in social relations—why people consent to do the will of others. Power exercised on a consensual basis is termed authority, of which there are three different forms:

1. *Traditional authority:* the right to govern bestowed on kings, emperors, popes, and other patrimonial leaders. This type of authority rests in the ruler's claim to historic or ancestral rights of control.
2. *Charismatic authority:* dominance exercised by an individual through extraordinary personal heroism, piety, fanaticism, martial skill, or other traits. Systems based on this type of authority tend to be unstable and transitional.
3. *Rational/legal authority:* power assigned on the basis of the ability to achieve instrumental goals. This type of authority derives from the legitimacy given to rational rules and processes and from authoritativeness rather than authoritananism.

Bureaucracies are the embodiment of rational/legal authority, and the fact that they have become the dominant organizational model reflects societal movement away from systems based on traditional or charismatic authority.

Strengths and Weaknesses.   Bureaucratic organization is designed to bring about the accomplishment of specific instrumental tasks, and its focus is on maximizing the *efficiency* with which this is done. Weber argues: "The decisive reason for the advance of bureaucracy has always been its purely technical superiority over any other form of organization. The fully developed bureaucratic mechanism compares with other organizations exactly as does the machine with the non-mechanical modes of production" (1946, 214).

As the bureaucracy evolved, this technical superiority helped to bring about the industrial revolution and the immense growth in size and complexity of manufacturing, distribution, and other commercial firms. It also furthered the rise of vast governmental institutions, ranging from the military to a broad range of public welfare organizations responsible for income maintenance, child welfare, mental health, corrections, and other services. In particular, bureaucratic organization helped these institutions carry out their tasks in greater quantity than was possible before. Consider the number of people served by governmental organizations providing AFDC benefits, Food Stamps, or Social Security payments. These agencies are not simply larger than the social welfare organizations that preceded them; they are clearly more bureaucratic in their organization.

In some ways, the practice of social work functions in a manner consistent with certain characteristics of bureaucracy. For example, the profession tends to support a high degree of specialization based on professional training and practice expertise. Assigning individuals to specific jobs and organizational levels on the basis of this expertise is also considered a part of good practice. Social workers support full-time employment and professional careers, and in most human service organizations the accumulation of experience and expertise is rewarded by favoring the most senior persons for promotion. Finally, the profession subscribes to the belief that people's abilities on the job should count for more than who they know or how well-liked they are, and fame or fortune outside the organization should not count for more than their competence on the job. In other words, though we don't often think of it in such terms (and though we may argue vehemently that social workers should not be "bureaucratic"), social workers and the organizations they typically work in are like many others in modern society in their adherence to the above principles.

However, bureaucratic agencies often conjure up images of vast, impersonal, monolithic organizations that are anything but efficient. They and other organizations go out of their way to avoid being described as *bureaucracies,* and this term has become one that in everyday usage is almost unfailingly negative. Why is this so? Weber certainly didn't believe the bureaucracy was a model for poor organization, and research has shown that bureaucratic organization and structure can indeed contribute to greater productivity and efficiency.

The answer is complex and important. As the bureaucracy has become more prevalent, it has shown both its good and bad sides. For example, the machinelike qualities to which Weber calls attention may be consummately well-suited to manufacturing firms but can also be disastrous in organizations (such as human service agencies) where the goal is to meet unique needs of individuals. Indeed, many theorists subsequent to Weber have explored ways in which characteristics of the bureaucracy actually undermine its presumed strengths.

One example of these problems is offered by Merton (1952) in his study of the experiences of individuals working within bureaucracies. He found that over time, workers' concern for completing the key instrumental activities of their jobs was gradually replaced with a concern for meeting the procedural and paperwork requirements of the bureaucracy, regardless of whether the basic job was done. Merton called this the *bureaucratic personality.* He also coined the term *trained incapacity* to describe the ways in which bureaucratic personalities become incapable of meeting the real needs of the people they were intended to serve. These behaviors are often considered an inevitable consequence of tightly structured chains of command and expectations for unthinking compliance with rules. Most important, he believed these behaviors develop from individuals' realization that their own interests were best served not by doing the job well but by doing it "by the book."

A great deal of contemporary organizational thought has addressed ways such as these in which bureaucracies fall short of their goal of maximal organizational functioning. In particular, various schools of thought have addressed aspects of complex organizations that extend beyond the bureaucracy's emphasis on structural characteristics. As will be seen, many of these aspects were examined specifically from the perspective of how the bureaucratic model fails to account for their importance. Among these are organizational goals, decision-making process, technology, and the role of the individual within the organization.

In many ways, ethnic minorities and women have been disadvantaged in bureaucratically structured organizations. "It should be no surprise that feminists have asserted that bureaucracies have a male orientation and a male bias" (Kelly 1991, 97). As employees are promoted through lower and middle levels to upper-level administrative positions, there has been a tendency for white males to dominate the highest levels. This phenomenon has been referred to as the *glass ceiling.* Women and minorities can reach a level where they have a close-up view of functioning at the top, but they often cannot reach the top because those who select for top positions seemingly value sameness and fear diversity.

MANAGEMENT THEORIES

Scientific and Universalistic Management

One of the earliest and most important schools of thought on the management of tasks and functions in the workplace was the work of Frederick Taylor, an American industrialist and educator whose main works appeared in the first two decades of this century. Taylor had experience as both a worker and a mechanical engineer, and he was primarily concerned with management techniques that would lead to increased productivity. He believed that many organizational problems were tied to misunderstandings between managers and workers. Managers thought that workers were lazy and unmotivated, and they also mistakenly believed they understood workers' jobs. Workers thought that managers cared only about exploiting workers, not about productivity.

To solve these problems, Taylor developed what came to be known as *scientific management,* which derives its name from his emphasis on the need for managers to conduct scientific analyses of the workplace (1947). One of the first steps is to complete a careful study of the work itself, commonly by identifying the best worker and studying that person. The goal is to find the optimal way of doing a job—in Taylor's words the "one best way"—to develop the best possible tools for completing it, fit workers' abilities and interests to particular job assignments, and find the level of production the average worker could sustain.

Following this, a critical step is then to provide incentives to workers to increase productivity. Taylor's favorite tool for this was the piece-rate wage, in which workers are paid for each unit they produce. In this manner, more units are produced, unit cost is reduced, organizational productivity and profitability are enhanced, and workers earn more.

Taylor's focus on productivity enhancement was adapted and broadened by a group of writers often referred to as the *universalistic management* theorists. The best-known of these was French industrialist Henri Fayol, whose writings focused on specifying the structural attributes of organizations that managers should develop and promote. Scott (1981) condenses this work into the following six principles:

1. *Scalar principle* calls for a hierarchical structure with a pyramid-shaped chain of command;
2. *Unity of command principle* specifies that each person should have only one immediate supervisor;
3. *Span of control principle* limits a supervisor's number of subordinates to a manageable number, usually no more than six to eight;
4. *Exception principle* specifies that subordinates are responsible for routine matters covered by standard rules, leaving the supervisor responsible for exceptional circumstances not covered by these rules;
5. *Departmentalization principle* incorporates a strong emphasis on division of labor within the organization, and specifies that similar functions should be grouped together (e.g., functions that are similar in terms of purpose, process, clientele or location);
6. *Line-staff principle* distinguishes between line functions, which are those most central to completion of basic organizational activities, and staff functions, which are primarily supportive or advisory.

Though somewhat broader in scope, the outcomes intended from the application of these principles were similar to the goals of scientific management. These included stability, predictability (especially with respect to the manufacturing process) and maximum individual productivity.

Strengths and Weaknesses.   The works of both Taylor and Fayol were subsequently criticized for what Mouzelis (1967) termed a *technicist* bias; that is, that both tended to treat workers as little more than cogs in a wheel. No two people, and no two workers, are exactly alike, thus the "one best way" of doing a job may also be unique to the person doing it. In fact, forcing a similar approach on a different worker may decrease both productivity and worker satisfaction. Also, because these approaches addressed means for increasing the output of workers, they were subjected to considerable criticism (especially by writers in the labor movement) for allegedly assisting in the exploitation of workers by management.

Because both Taylor and Fayol were interested primarily in industrial organizations, their work was generally deemed to have little applicability to human service organizations during the first few decades that social work began drawing on management theories. For example, the predominant approach to allocating work responsibility followed that of physicians, assigning "cases" or clients to social workers who acted on a very loosely structured mandate to employ their professional skill to meet client needs. As a result, the focus of scientific and universalistic management on precision, measurement, and specialization of function fit poorly with this type of job design.

However, during the last decade, social work has begun to adopt a more "scientific" approach to practice. In many areas of specialization, procedures and protocols specify parameters for professional activity in certain types of cases.

Also, in the interest of improving practice, a great deal of emphasis has been placed on conducting formal research on clients in one's own caseload, often through the use of single-subject designs. Similarly, requirements for outcome evaluation have placed more rigorous demands on the design of interventions and the measurement of success. Though these trends do not necessarily embrace the more mechanistic aspects of Taylor's notions, they do echo his concern for organizational operations that are based on the most careful possible analysis of the work itself.

Human Relations

As the field of organizational management and analysis grew, the works of Taylor, Weber, and others were criticized for their focus on rational, structural approaches to understanding organizations. The earliest of these criticisms addressed Taylor's assumptions concerning factors that motivate organizational actors. In particular, they took issue with the notion that workers are oriented to the instrumental goals of the organization and respond most readily to material rewards (e.g., piece-rate wages) that are designed to further those goals. One such group began with the intention of testing Taylor's principles concerning productivity enhancement. Eventually, however, they concluded that organizations must be viewed as social institutions, and it is social factors—friendship, belongingness, and group solidarity—that are most important in both understanding and affecting the behavior of organizational actors.

Often referred to as the human relations school, this view had its origins in the well-known Hawthorne studies conducted in the 1920s. Experimenters placed a group of workers in a special room and then varied the intensity of the lighting and other environmental factors to observe its effect on productivity. The greater the intensity of lighting, the more productivity increased. When the researchers had clearly established the positive correlation between increased lighting and productivity, they attempted to confirm their findings by reducing the lighting, expecting to find reduced productivity. Instead, productivity continued to increase even in very dim lighting. The researchers concluded that the cause of the increase in productivity was *social factors.* Workers appeared not to respond to the lighting but instead to the fact that they were members of a group to which they wanted to contribute their best effort, and it was this sense of social responsibility that prompted improved performance.

Subsequent experiments on the effect of social factors in organizations (including many from the burgeoning field of industrial psychology), as well as on other research, examined more general questions concerning the behavior of groups. Etzioni (1964) summarizes the basic tenets of the human relations approach that developed from these findings:

1. *"The level of production is set by social norms, not by physiological capacities"* (p. 34).
2. *"Non-economic rewards and sanctions significantly affect the behavior of the workers and largely limit the effect of economic incentive plans"*

(p. 34). A number of studies found that workers who were capable of producing more often would not do so. The reason seemed to be that they were unwilling to exceed what the group as a whole was able to do, even if this meant a reduction in their earnings.

3. *"[W]orkers do not act or react as individuals but as members of groups"* (p. 35). For example, attempts by management to influence workers' behavior can sometimes be more successful if targeted toward the group as a whole rather than at individuals (who would be unwilling to change unless accompanied by group members).

4. *The role of leadership is important in understanding social forces in organizations, and this leadership may be either formal or informal.* The importance of informal leadership is that it influences behavior in ways that can either amplify or negate formal leadership acting through established organizational structures. In addition, democratic leadership is more effective in eliciting cooperation and willingness to change than more authoritarian forms.

The prescriptive lessons to be drawn from these tenets include the idea that organizational actors are more likely to draw satisfaction from social relationships within the organization than from its instrumental activities. Also important is the notion that workers' willingness to follow management comes from willingness to follow members of the work group. As a result, the key to making effective changes in organizational operations lies not in rules and formal structure but in the quality of personal affiliations and the coherence of informal structures. Managers who succeed in increasing productivity are most likely to be those who are responsive to the social needs of workers.

Strengths and Weaknesses.   No viewpoint fails to generate dissent, and in this case criticisms of the human relations school tend to fall into two major categories. First, a number of writers have raised concerns about the methodological soundness of some of the research on which these views are based. For example, the original Hawthorne experiments have gained a somewhat infamous place in the history of research methodology. The so-called *Hawthorne effect* refers to the fact that experimental subjects may perform in certain ways simply because of the knowledge that they are being studied. In other words, the workers in the Hawthorne plant may have raised production not because of lighting levels or a sense of group solidarity but because of self-consciousness about being in an experiment. Other critics have argued that the design of these studies was such that expectations about economic incentives might still have influenced the subjects, further undermining the supposed importance of social factors (Sykes 1965).

A second line of criticism argues that it is possible not only to underestimate but also to overestimate the importance of social factors in organizations. For example, various research has indicated that informal organizational structures may not be as prevalent or powerful as the human relations writers suggest, that democratic leadership is not always associated with greater productivity or worker satisfaction, and that economic benefits *are* of primary importance to many organizational actors. Moreover, Landsberger (1958) argued that this school's emphasis on worker contentedness at the expense of economic rewards could foster an administrative model that is even more manipulative and paternalistic than might be the case with scientific management.

Still, these theorists have had an important impact on organizational thinking. With respect to management practice, their views have provided a humanizing counterbalance to the very formalized approach of other management theories. They have also had an impact on descriptive approaches, serving as a reminder of how the needs and interests of individual actors can be critical determinants of organizational behavior.

The title *human relations* has been somewhat misleading to students of organizational theory. For example, ask any group of social work students to choose their favorite organizational or management theory and the vast majority will most likely select the human relations school. It has a nice ring to it—human relations—that suggests a real concern for human beings. However, it is interesting to note that some critics of management theories place human relations theory, along with scientific and universalistic management, among those that tend to dehumanize, oppress, and exploit workers. Indeed, human relations theory, like all other management theories to that point, concentrated power and decision making at the top. It was never intended to empower employees or assist them in gaining genuine participation in the running of the organization. If people were treated more humanely under human relations management, it was because managers believed that this would lead to greater productivity. It was not necessarily because of any sincere concern for the employee or effort to create a more democratic workplace.

The practice of dealing with people on the basis of their perceived personal/social relationships within the workplace is another phenomenon that may well have disadvantaged women and minority employees over the years. Networking in organizations has been credited with identifying and securing jobs for people, with including certain people in important decision-making groups, with opportunities for promotion, and with many other benefits of employment. Women and minorities have often been excluded from important networks that control these rewards.

Later theories would develop around genuine empowerment for employees, but human relations management eventually died out as an approach to running an organization when it was recognized that a happy workforce was not necessarily a productive workforce, and other variables began to enter the equation. Nevertheless, the lessons of the Hawthorne studies—the importance of teamwork, cooperation, leadership and positive attention from management—should not be lost on executives and staff of human service organizations today.

Theory X and Theory Y

Later writers drew on the work of human relations theorists but altered many of their tenets and incorporated them into more general theoretical frameworks of human motivation. One example is Douglas McGregor (1960), who adopted

Maslow's hierarchy of needs as a basis of understanding workers' actions. For McGregor, organizational actors were not simply social beings but *self-actualizing beings* whose ultimate goal in organizations is to meet these higher-order needs. To illustrate this point, he identified two contrasting approaches to management which he labeled *Theory X* and *Theory Y*. Theory X is a categorization of traditional approaches to management such as that of Taylor, Weber, and even Mayo, which, McGregor argued, make certain assumptions about why workers participate in organizational activities. These assumptions are that (*a*) people have an inherent dislike for work; (*b*) they must be coerced in order to work; (*c*) the average worker prefers to be told what to do; and (*d*) monetary reward is the worker's primary motivator. These assumptions (whether implicit or explicit) lead to what McGregor sees as the coercive, directive aspects of Theory X management.

In contrast, Theory Y assumes that the task of management is to recognize workers' higher-order needs and design organizations that allow them to achieve these needs. Its assumptions are that:

1. Work is as natural an activity as rest or play, thus people do not necessarily have to be forced to do it.
2. Workers will commit to organizational goals if they are able to meet their own needs in so doing.
3. Workers will accept responsibility for meeting goals that are congruent with their needs.
4. Organizational tasks should be structured to allow workers to exercise creativity and imagination in fulfilling these responsibilities.

The critical feature of this model was its break from the management-dominated approach of previous theories in favor of a genuine transfer of decision-making power to lower-level actors.

Strengths and Weaknesses. McGregor's analysis was supported by the research of Frederick Herzberg (1966). Herzberg studied motivation among employees, and divided motivational elements into two categories: extrinsic factors and intrinsic factors. Factors extrinsic to the job included considerations such as wages, hours, working conditions and benefits. Intrinsic factors were those that had to do with the actual conduct of the work at hand. Herzberg discovered that, in the long run, extrinsic factors tend to keep down the levels of dissatisfaction with the job, but they do not motivate workers to work harder. Only intrinsic factors, such as ability to use one's own creativity and problem-solving capabilities actually motivated employees to work harder and become more productive.

On the other hand, results of other studies indicated that there were limits to how loosely structured an organization's operations could become and still function effectively. For example, Morse and Lorsch (1970) found that organizations in which tasks were loosely defined and variable appeared to fit well with the tenets of Theory Y. However, those in which tasks were predictable, repetitive, and required great precision functioned better when organized according to principles that McGregor categorized as Theory X management.

The importance for social work is that its tasks are often loosely defined and apparently better suited to Theory Y management, yet many human service organizations are still managed with a Theory X mentality. These views will be discussed in greater length later, but one of their key points was that no single management model applies equally well across all types of organizations.

Management by Objectives

Fundamental to the conceptualization and functioning of an organization is *purpose,* a commonly shared understanding of the reason for existence of the organization. In most cases, purpose has to do with productivity and profit. Taylor, Weber, and Mayo each stressed a different approach to achievement of purpose, but all agreed that an understanding of purpose was basic to the construction of a theory of organizational management.

One management theorist, Peter Drucker (1954), proposed a somewhat different approach to organizational management. Drucker suggested that organizational goals and objectives be used in a rational way by making them the central construct around which organizational life would function. In other words, instead of focusing on structure or precision or efficiency and hoping for an increase in productivity and profit, Drucker proposed beginning with the desired outcome and working backward. A goal might, for example, be "to increase productivity by 10 percent" or "to improve customer satisfaction by 20 percent over the previous year." Organizational structure, job design, and resources would then be adapted to meet each objective so that efforts during the year would constantly be focused on their achievement. Success, then, would be measured in terms of the achievement of stated objectives. This approach was known as management by objectives (MBO) and its goal-oriented approach to organizational operation became widely used in the 1960s and 1970s. Some of the techniques have survived in organizations into the 1990s.

Strengths and Weaknesses.   One major advantage of MBO comes in its emphasis on producing clear statements, made available to all employees, about expectations for the coming year. Techniques are also developed for breaking goals and objectives into tasks, and for monitoring progress throughout the year. This type of activity tends to improve collaboration and cooperative activity.

On the other hand, MBO adopts a very particularistic approach to management, which some critics have argued tends to concentrate attention on the trees rather than on the forest. In other words, management requires large-scale strategic thinking in addition to small-scale tactical thinking, yet MBO may tend to focus more attention on the latter. Another criticism is that, while there is something admirable about being so clear and direct about organizational expectations, the concept of building organizational life around goals and objectives has its drawbacks. As we will see in the next section, organizational goals often change, and the stated goals of an organization can be subverted in the interest of promoting unstated goals.

Still, many human service agencies, both public and private, have adopted some aspects of MBO in their planning systems over the past three decades. Most state agencies still require the development of an annual plan in which goals and objectives in each programmatic area are made explicit. While many other theoretical concepts and perspectives permeate the management perspectives of the 1990s, MBO has clearly made its contributions. Among the most significant has been the focus on *outcomes* for programs and organizations. Social work as a profession has been very concerned with *process* in the development of its practice approaches over the years. MBO, together with the emphasis on accountability, emphasizes the importance of program outcomes for clients as a major focus in determining funding and program continuation.

MBO has also served to make program planning more proactive. Prior to the use of goals and objectives, results were something that organizations hoped for but that did not drive their structure and procedures. Now many human service organizations consciously pursue achievements that clearly benefit clients. In some instances this has served to guide allocation of resources, and has provided a focus for monitoring and evaluation efforts. So, while the full thrust of MBO as a theory of management has diminished over the years, many of the techniques still serve human service organizations very well.

One contribution that can be credited to the use of goals and objectives is the increasing diversity being found in the workplace. For many years, those responsible for hiring failed to employ women and minorities in significant numbers. The lack of qualified applicants was most often used as the rationale for this pattern. However, as affirmative action programs were developed within organizations, goals and objectives for hiring were established. This had the effect of changing recruitment approaches, the focus of job advertising, screening tools, and many of the activities that had previously kept women and minorities from securing employment.

ORGANIZATIONAL GOALS AND THE NATURAL-SYSTEM PERSPECTIVE

One theme made explicit in Drucker's MBO model is the assumption that organizations should be directed by rational actions designed to achieve certain goals. This assumption began to be questioned by writers concerned about whether rational, goal-directed, formalized structures are the best way of serving organizational goals, and indeed whether these goals provide a clear direction in which to go. In fact, the idea that the goals of an organization and its members could gradually change had been present in organizational literature for some time.

For example, in the early 1900s Robert Michels examined political parties as examples of large modern organizations (1949, originally published in 1915). He documented the rise of oligarchies, or small groups of key decision makers, within these parties. The results suggested that these and other organizations had identifiable life cycles that go through the following steps:

1. The organization develops a formal structure.
2. The original leaders move into positions at the upper levels of the hierarchy;

3. These individuals discover the personal advantages of having such positions;
4. They begin to make more conservative decisions that might not advance their original cause as forcefully as before but that are less likely to jeopardize their own security or that of the organization;
5. Eventually, the party organization puts aside its political goals and instead becomes a tool for achieving the personal goals of upper-level administrators.

Michels called this the "Iron Rule of Oligarchy" based on his conclusion that it is an unavoidable fate of large organizations that adopt bureaucratic approaches to structuring themselves.

Philip Selznick (1949) found yet another such mechanism in his classic study of the early years of the Tennessee Valley Authority (TVA). The TVA was a creation of the New Deal era, and its goal was to promote economic development in the poverty-stricken Tennessee river valley through an ambitious mix of public works projects and grassroots organizing. With its enormous scope and rather vague goals, it became essential for the organization to delegate decision making to subunits responsible for particular projects in local areas. In this way, its aims became vulnerable to *cooptation* by existing local authorities whose involvement brought needed power and influence but whose own goals began to turn the TVA's subunits in new and unintended directions. Eventually, the TVA became, in many ways, merely a structure for serving the specific goals defined by the interests of local units. Selznick (1957) refers to this as the process of *institutionalization* of the organization. By this he means that organizations can take on a life of their own that has as much or more to do with the interests of their own participants as with the instrumental goals the organization is supposedly serving.

Other writers refer to this more generally as the process of *goal displacement,* and mechanisms such as cooptation, the growth of oligarchies, and the development of the bureaucratic personality are all means by which organizational goals can be displaced. In Selznick's view, the consistency with which these processes appeared in formal organizations argued against theories (such as Weber's) that seek to describe them as rational systems. Instead, he believed the better analogy was the organization as a *natural system,* one that is similar in key aspects to a biological organism. The most important of these aspects is the system's awareness of its own self-interest. Just as the prime motivation of an organism is to protect itself, an organization's principal goal often is to maintain its own functioning, thus predicting organizational behavior on the basis of what it will do to survive may often be more accurate than predictions based on rational approaches to meeting task goals. Etzioni (1964) identifies this in terms of the distinction between organizations' *real* goals and *stated* goals. In situations in which both cannot be served simultaneously, it is real goals (e.g., self-preservation) that almost always determine eventual actions.

Strengths and Weaknesses.   Recognition of the importance of organizational goals, particularly survival goals, has proved to be an important contribution to the development of organizational and management theory. Moreover, these views have had considerable influence on the study of human service organizations, such as David Sills' well-known 1957 study of the March of Dimes. Organized originally to unify the efforts of volunteers attempting to raise money for polio research, the March of Dimes became one of the vanguard organizations in the fight against polio nationwide. These efforts were eventually successful, in that funding from the March of Dimes provided part of the support for Jonas Salk's development of the first polio vaccine. This vaccine proved to be so effective that polio eventually became a relatively rare medical problem, meaning that the activities of the March of Dimes were no longer needed. Since it had been successful in achieving its goal, the organization could have simply disbanded, but it did not. Instead, it adopted a whole new cause—birth defects—and its efforts shifted to this new direction.

Sills points out that this is exactly the behavior that would be predicted by the natural system model. That is, the survival imperative prevails even if it means the system must alter its original reason for existence. The result is not necessarily bad, as can be argued in this case where an experienced organization took up the cause of a new social need. However, as we will review at greater length in the next chapter, survival goals can also lead to the abandonment of client services, thus the recognition of the role of these goals remains an important component in organizational analyses.

DECISION MAKING

Other writers continued efforts to explain organizations as rational systems, but their work began to focus on assessing the limits of organizational rationality. One of the most prominent of these writers is Herbert Simon, whose wide-ranging work eventually earned him a Nobel Prize in economics, and who undertook the study of organizational behavior via the process of organizational decision making (1957).

Simon began by changing the primary unit of analysis from the organization as a whole to individuals within the organizations. More specifically, he was interested in individual *decisions* about organizational matters. He had been influenced by the growing body of psychological research and was particularly interested in behaviorist views about the importance of stimulus-response connections as explanations for human behavior. He believed organizations can be conceptualized as aggregations of individuals' decisions within the organization, and organizational decision making can be viewed as a behavior that occurs in response to certain stimuli.

Rather than searching for methods to achieve perfect rationality, March and Simon (1958) argued that the key to understanding organizational decisions is understanding the constraints that limit decision making. They termed this *bounded rationality,* and identified three major categories of limitations:

1. habits, abilities, and other personal characteristics that individuals bring with them into the decision-making process and that influence their

actions in certain ways irrespective of the circumstances surrounding a specific decision;

2. "motivations, values, and loyalties . . . [whereby] an individual's strong identification with a certain group whose values diverge from organisational values might limit the individual's rational behavior" (Mouzelis 1967, 124); and

3. the inability of the decision maker to know either all the variables that might influence the decision or all possible consequences of the decision.

Because all decisions carry some measure of risk, the process of decision making in organizations may therefore be thought of as a sort of risk-management process. The goal of the decision maker is not necessarily to achieve a "perfect" outcome, because this may never be possible. Instead, the decision maker seeks to reduce uncertainty as much as possible in order to make a decision that provides a reasonable likelihood of achieving an acceptable outcome. March and Simon called this *satisficing,* and argued that understanding how satisfactory outcomes are sought through decisions made in a context of bounded rationality is the key to understanding organizations.

Subsequent works expanded on these ideas in several directions. For example, Cyert and March (1963) suggested that decision making in aggregate is a process of bargaining between individuals and units having different views and goals. The eventual actions of the organization can be understood as the outcome of these on-going negotiations among organizational members. Later, March and Olsen (1976) proposed a "garbage can" analogy to describe the rather chaotic process in which decisions emerge from a mixture of people, problems, ideas, and "choice opportunities" that is unique to every organization and situation. This approach assumes that rationality plays a relatively minor role in these situations; instead, the process of interaction among these various elements is the key to the eventual decisions.

Strengths and Weaknesses.   One aspect of decision-making theory that has had considerable impact on organizational analysis is its concern with the nature and quality of information available to decision makers. This concern largely coincided with the advent of computers, and it has played a part in the rapid growth of interest in information management in organizations. The basic idea is that information systems, augmented by the unique data processing capabilities of computers, can be used to reduce the uncertainty that decision makers must confront and increase the likelihood that they will make effective decisions.

On the other hand, as a means of understanding organizations, the decision-making approach has a number of limitations. For example, in a critique of March and Simon's work, Blau and Scott (1962) argue that the model focuses too narrowly on formal decision making, ignoring the interpersonal aspects of organizations and the influence that informal structures can have on decisions that are made. Champion (1975) also notes that little attention is paid to situations in which a particular individual may not seek overall rationality but personal or local-unit gain. Most important, the decision-making model has been criticized for its focus on internal factors that lead to particular decisions. This emphasis ignores the fact that it is often influences internal to the organization that are most important to both eliciting and determining a decision. In fact, growing attention toward the importance of external factors provided the impetus for the next important developments in organizational theory.

ORGANIZATIONS AS OPEN SYSTEMS

Understanding Open Systems

In learning about practice with individual clients, most social workers are introduced to systems theory. This approach is based on the work of biologist Ludwig von Bertalanffy, who believed that lessons from fields such as ecology concerning organisms' interdependence with their surroundings provides a basis for conceptualizing other phenomena as systems engaged in environmental interactions (1950). Via this model, individual clients are viewed not merely as isolated entities that are driven primarily by internal psychological processes but rather as social beings whose personalities and behaviors can be analyzed in terms of their constant interaction with the world around them. As *open systems,* clients both give to and draw from elements external to themselves. The key to understanding clients lies in this ongoing process of exchange with the key elements (e.g., culture, community, family, etc.) that comprise their personal environment. Beginning in the 1960s, a group of writers argued that organizations can be understood in similar ways.

One influential example was the work of Katz and Kahn (1966), who used von Bertalanffy's ideas to lay the groundwork for an open-systems view of organizations. They began by arguing that previous writers had analyzed organizations as though they were closed systems whose functioning could be understood entirely through study of their internal structure and processes. Katz and Kahn considered this a naive view, arguing that organizations must be understood as open systems that "maintain themselves through constant commerce with the environment, i.e., a continuous inflow and outflow of energy through permeable boundaries" (p. 17). Simply examining internal aspects of an organization— whether its structure, management style, goals, etc.—was in their view insufficient to understanding it. Instead, organizations must be understood as systems existing within a particular environment, in large part defined by the process of exchange in which they act on and respond to their environments.

As illustrated in Figure 6.1, systems are comprised of collections of constituent parts (whether cells comprising an organism or people comprising an organization) that receive *inputs,* operate on them through some sort of process (called the *throughput*) and produce *outputs.* In human service agencies, inputs include resources vital to the agency, such as funding, staff, facilities, and services provided by other agencies in their organizational environment. Clients are important inputs, as are the types and severity of the problems for which they are seeking help. More subtle but also critical are inputs such as values, expectations,

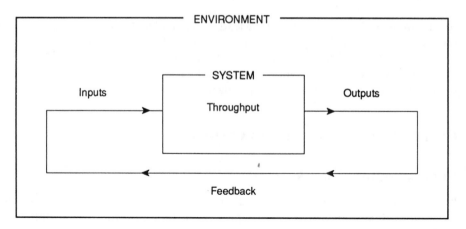

FIGURE 6.1   Diagram of Open Systems

and ideas that are held by community members, funding agencies, regulatory bodies, and other segments of the environment.

Throughput involves the services provided by the agency—often referred to as its *technology*—and the way it is structured to apply this technology to the inputs it receives. Outputs refer to the organization's products. In industrial firms this is usually some sort of material object; in social work agencies it is the completion of a service to a client. As we will discuss, the important aspect of service output is often defined as an *outcome,* which is a measure of a quality-of-life change (improvement, no change, or deterioration) on the part of a client.

Another key element of many open systems is a *feedback* mechanism, which is a defining characteristic of what are called cybernetic systems. Cybernetic systems are self-correcting systems that are able to act on information from their surroundings, interpret the data, and adjust their functioning accordingly. Biological systems are examples of cybernetic systems, in that they adapt themselves to changing conditions in their environments. Organizations are also cybernetic systems, and it is virtually impossible to envision one that could survive without gathering information from and taking steps to adjust to conditions in its environment. For example, manufacturers must constantly adjust to changing markets for their goods, and their survival often depends on the ability to adjust quickly to increase output of fast-selling items and decrease or change products that are not selling well. Likewise, human service agencies must be providing needed and relevant services or they will go out of business. This process of receiving feedback from the environment and making adaptations to fit external conditions is at the heart of the open-systems approach to understanding organizations.

Contingency Theory

Partly in response to these, the apparent soundness of open-systems thinking and partly because of doubts about management theories that promoted a single model of management for all organizations, a new outlook began to take shape in the

1960s. The underlying premise was that different organizational styles may be entirely appropriate due to the particular circumstances each organization faces. Known generally as *contingency theory,* this approach is summed up in three basic tenets. The first two, proposed by Galbraith (1973), summarize criticisms of both earlier management theorists and the decision-making model:

1. There is no one best way to organize.
2. Any way of organizing is not equally effective. (p. 2)

To these, Scott (1981), adds a third principle that incorporates the open-systems perspective:

3. The best way to organize depends on the nature of the environment to which the organization must relate. (p. 114)

The unifying theme across all these principles is that the nature of the organization and its management scheme are contingent upon a variety of factors that are unique to that organization. For example, a human service agency need not be managed like an auto-assembly plant in order to achieve maximum productivity.

Morse and Lorsch (1970) took issue with McGregor's notion that a decentralized, humanistic management model is the preferred approach across virtually all organizations. Their research findings showed that, to the contrary, high organizational effectiveness and a strong sense of personal competence could be found in organizations with relatively rigid rules and structure. Similarly, these measures were low in some organizations having a loose structure and a great deal of individual autonomy. The key contingency to which their results pointed was the nature of organizational tasks. Manufacturing organizations with very predictable tasks fared best with a tightly controlled structure. Those with less predictable tasks (in this case a research and development role) appeared to be much better suited to a loose structure and management style.

A typology of these differences was proposed by Burns and Stalker (1961), who described distinctions between two primary forms of management systems— mechanistic and organic. Mechanistic management systems, which reflect both the characteristics of bureaucracies as described by Weber and the managerial techniques laid out by Taylor, are associated with organizations existing in relatively stable environments. Organic forms occur in unstable environments in which the inputs are unpredictable and thus the organization's viability depends on its capacity to respond in ways that are not rigidly restrained by formal rules and structures.

Lawrence and Lorsch (1967) argued that the tenets of earlier schools of thought apply more or less well to a particular organization according to the characteristics of its environment at the time. In particular, they called attention to the importance of stable versus changing environments as the critical contingency on which an analysis of organizational structure and management should rest. For example, they noted that "in simplified terms, the classical [e.g., Weberian] theory tends to hold in more stable environments, while the human relations theory is more appropriate to dynamic situations" (p. 183).

Also, incorporating some of the notions of the decision-making approach, Lawrence and Lorsch focused on the importance of certainty versus uncertainty in determining organizational actions, but in this case the unit of analysis was organizational units rather than individual decision makers, and uncertainty was considered as a characteristic applying to the organizational environment rather than to individual decisions. Stable environments allow for greater certainty in structuring operations, thus a human service agency that deals mainly with particular clients having a particular problem (such as a food bank) may be expected to be characterized by fairly routinized operations and formal structure. Conversely, organizations that deal with a wide variety of clients and unpredictable client problems can be expected to be structured loosely and have a much less ''by-the-book'' approach to operational rules.

In his classic 1967 book *Organizations in Action,* James Thompson echoed the argument that the key issue in organization/environment interactions is the degree of *uncertainty* in the environment. Thompson stated that organizations seek predictability in the environment because this allows the ongoing operation of rational structures. However, as Simon and others point out, the environment is never perfectly predictable. Accordingly, the organization that structures itself too rigidly won't last long. The goal is to be able to respond to changes in the environment to ensure organizational survival.

Thompson focused considerable attention on the nature of the organization's technology. As illustrated in Figure 6.2, he described three levels of organizational functioning: (1) technical core, (2) managerial system, and (3) institutional system. The *technical core* includes the structures and processes within the organization's boundaries that allow it to carry out the principal functions for which the organization was created (i.e., the structure and processes that go into the assembly or the delivery of a service). Theoretically, the technical core works best when allowed to do the same thing in the same way; that is, when environmental inputs never vary. However, since the environment is constantly changing, the rational organization seeks to accommodate to environmental variations while still protecting its most vital elements, thus assuring survival. The *managerial system* includes those structures and processes that manage the work of the technical core. The *institutional system* deals with interactions between the organization and the environment.

FIGURE 6.2 Thompson's Organizational Model

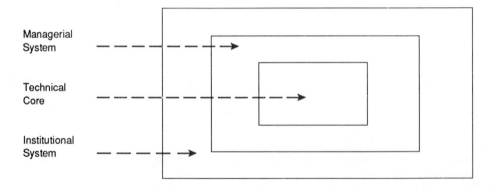

Managerial System

Technical Core

Institutional System

The means by which an organization structures itself to achieve this balance is at the heart of Thompson's analytical model. He argues that this is a rational process designed to assure organizational survival. Specifically, he hypothesizes that adaptive responses fall into a three-part sequence: (1) actions to protect the technical core of the organization; (2) actions to acquire power over the task environment; and (3) actions to absorb important elements of the environment by changing organizational domains. Actions to protect the technical core primarily involve responses that allow the organization to absorb necessary changes within itself, such as by increasing or decreasing output, hiring or laying off staff, or shifting resources among different internal units.

The *task environment* is the term Thompson uses to describe external organizations on which an organization depends, either as providers of needed input (money, raw materials, client referrals) or as consumers of its output. If internal responses are unsuccessful in accommodating to change, Thompson says the next step is for the organization to attempt to alter its relationships with members of the task environment in such a way that it has more control over the change. Examples of this might include negotiating long-term funding agreements or arranging for regular referral of clients from another organization (e.g., a residential treatment center may become the exclusive provider of treatment for a particular school district).

Finally, if the organization cannot accommodate to change by any of these methods, Thompson predicts that it will seek to incorporate into itself parts of the environment that relate to the change. For example, a human service organization dependent on providing services to substance-abusing clients that are paid for by contracts with a public agency may suddenly find itself jeopardized when governmental funding priorities shift toward prevention rather than treatment services. If a relatively small and new agency in the area appears to be in line for much of this funding, the older, larger agency may seek to merge with the smaller one in an effort to maintain its funding base by providing these new services. Because such a move involves changing at least part of the original agency's technical core, however, this type of response is likely to take place only after other adaptive strategies have been tried and proved inadequate.

Strengths and Weaknesses.   Open-systems models continue to have considerable influence on organizational analysis. The environment has come to be recognized as a critical variable in the life of every organization. This perspective has been particularly valuable in understanding human service organizations. Environmental considerations (such as development of funding and other resources) have always been prominent in agency concerns, and Thompson's theory has given them proper recognition. Identification of survival as the primary reason for existence of all organizations helps bring into a clearer focus the driving forces behind a good deal of organizational behavior. Thompson's postulates about techniques to protect the technical core add to our understanding of how it is that organizations survive.

In some ways, Thompson's work can help in understanding the increasing responsiveness within organizations to cultural diversity. No organization serving the public can afford to ignore the dramatically changing demographics in the communities in which they are located. For example, the Workforce 2000 report (Jamieson & O'Mara, 1991) estimates that, of every 10 new employees coming into an organization in the year 2000, 1.5 will be white males and the rest will be women and ethnic minorities. Many organizations are responding by providing training in developing collaborative relationships within diverse, multicultural work environments.

One of the major shortcomings of Thompson's conceptual framework was that he had a tendency to treat all organizations as though they were alike and behaved in essentially the same manner. Other work in the field of contingency theory makes it clear that it is important to understand the nature, purpose, and function of an organization in order to evaluate the appropriateness of organizational behavior and the relative influence of the environment.

CONTEMPORARY PERSPECTIVES

The history of organizational and management theory has been, in many ways, the history of a search for insights into the best ways to organize and manage—a search for the theory that will unlock the secrets of productivity. As we have attempted to illustrate in this chapter, the theme was different for each new theory. For Weber it was structure, for Taylor it was precision, for Mayo it was attentiveness to the human element, for Drucker it was a commonly shared sense of direction, for Simon it was the process of decision making, and for Thompson it was coping with environmental changes.

A major contribution of contingency theory was the introduction of the idea that no one theme or set of variables was right for every situation. For contingency theorists, when asked the question, "What is the best way to manage an organization?" the only correct answer was, "It depends . . ." The development of contingency theory over the last few decades has focused on the question, "On what does it depend?" In short, every organization is made up of a somewhat unique mix of variables, and the position of contingency theorists is that there can be no single formula for optimum structure and management style. The direction the organization takes will depend on the nature of the organization and its expectations for productivity.

Whether or not its tenets are always accepted, it is probably fair to state that the contingency approach has been a springboard for contemporary thinking about organizational and management theories. The 1980s saw a number of alternative perspectives introduced and, while none has dominated the field, each has contributed an interesting new dimension to how organizations are understood, analyzed, managed and led. Numerous terms are highly visible in the contemporary literature on organizations. These terms include vision, excellence, quality, culture, empowerment, diversity, and values. Leadership has become the word of choice over management, even though both are acknowledged as having their place. The following discussion will briefly introduce the reader to a sampling of the themes in recent organizational literature.

Power and Politics

Pfeffer (1981) argued that organizational actions are best understood in terms of power and politics. He defined power as the ability to influence actions, and politics as the process whereby this influence is used. Asked where power originates, Pfeffer would explain that power is derived from an individual's position within the organization. Therefore, power and organizational structure are closely tied to one another.

To illustrate the relationship of power and organizational structure, Pfeffer compared three models of organizational analysis: (1) the *bureaucratic model,* (2) the *rational choice model,* and (3) the *political model.* The bureaucratic model is based in the classic Weberian approach that assumes an organization is both structured and acts in a manner that maximizes its efficiency in achieving its goals. Pfeffer's criticisms of this model are essentially the same as those detailed earlier in this chapter. The rational choice model derives from the work of decision-making theorists such as Simon and March. Pfeffer agreed with their points concerning the constraints that limit rational decision making. However, he noted that these models still assume that decision making is oriented toward a clear organizational goal, thus the greatest drawback to rational choice models is that "they fail to take into account the diversity of interests and goals within organizations" (p. 27). It is for this reason that Pfeffer urged the use of a political model of structural analysis. Its benefit is in calling attention to the manner in which organizational actions may be either instrumental (that is, serving the presumed goals of the organization as a whole) or parochial, serving the perceived self-interest of a particular individual or organizational unit. Learning how power is acquired and then used to influence decision making was for him the key to the fullest understanding of how organizations operate.

Power has been discussed extensively in the feminist literature, both in relationship to politics within organizations and within the larger society in general. Gottlieb (1992) calls for a reconceptualization of empowerment and politics in organizations that serve women. She explains that "Women in both corners of the service relationship are affected by the societal definitions and oppression of women, although many members of both groups avoid seeing those effects" (p. 301). Because social work is a profession that has large numbers of women both as practitioners and as clients, Gottlieb encourages an increasing awareness of the political dimensions in the larger society that affect human service organizations.

Wamsley and Zald (1976) argue that structure and process in organizations is best understood in terms of the interplay of political and economic interests both internal *and* external to the organization. Political means the processes by which the organization obtains power and legitimacy. Economic means the processes by which the organization gets resources such as clients, staff, and funding.

The goal of this *political economy* perspective is to incorporate much of the work of previous schools into a more general conceptual model. Within this model elements such as individual interests and goals, the power wielded by the holders of these interests, and environmental resources and the relative influence of those who control them are all seen to interact in a way that creates the unique character of an organization. This character is not static but changes as the political economy of the organization changes.

Organizational Culture

The concept of *organizational culture* has had a profound influence on the development of contemporary theories. Schein (1985) defines culture as:

> a pattern of basic assumptions—invented, discovered, or developed by a given group as it learns to cope with its problems of external adaptation and internal integration—that has worked well enough to be considered valid and therefore, to be taught to new members as the correct way to perceive, think, and feel in relation to those problems. (p. 9)

Schein explains that an organizational culture develops through shared experiences. Newly formed organizations are heavily influenced by leaders who bring their perspectives to the organization and around which assumptions and beliefs emerge. "Culture, in this sense, is a learned product of group experience and is, therefore, to be found only where there is a definable group with a significant history" (p. 7). Schein argues that leadership and culture are intimately related, and understanding what assumptions leaders bring to organizations is central to analyzing how change occurs within an agency.

The connection of leadership to organizational culture has been explored in numerous ways. Of particular interest is the rapidly expanding literature on leadership and gender:

> By 1990 an ongoing debate had developed over whether women want the same type of success as men, whether they are able to demonstrate the behavior and leadership required for modern organizations to compete at high levels, and whether successful female managers need to adopt male behaviorial styles in order to lead or compete. (Kelly 1991, 96)

Feminist scholars have begun to analyze the processes of empowerment and collective action within organizations and the impact these processes have on changing cultural assumptions within organizations (Astin & Leland 1991). Language and communication, values, orientations toward power, perceptions of relationships, and leadership styles are fertile ground for exploration of gender and the development of organizational culture.

Organizational culture is important in understanding any organization; it is highly "visible" and "feelable" (Schein 1985, 24). When entering an organization, one quickly perceives that established patterns occur within that system even if they are not explicitly stated. The social worker who assumes a new place in an organization must be aware that these patterns may be so central to organizational functioning that they are taken for granted by members of that organization. When violated, members may respond emotionally because they are so invested in the "way things have always been done." It is difficult to understand how employees feel about an organization without considering the culture. Organizational culture, therefore, is much broader than looking at climate, ideology, or philosophy. It is a sense of group identity that permeates decision making and communication within the organization.

Theory Z

In the late 1970s and early 1980s attention in the United States began to be directed toward growing competition from Japan. Markets long dominated by American firms were being taken over by Japanese industries, and there was considerable curiosity about how Japanese industrial organizations had overcome their earlier reputation for poor quality work to such an extent that Japanese manufacturing was setting worldwide standards for quality and durability.

William Ouchi attempted to capture Japanese-style management in his 1981 best-seller *Theory Z*. The message of the title was that the philosophical and theoretical principles underlying Japanese management went beyond McGregor's (1960) conceptualization of Theory Y that we discussed earlier in this chapter.

An organization in Japan, said Ouchi, is more than just a structural or goal-oriented entity as it is in America. It is a way of life. It provides lifetime employment, it is enmeshed in the social, political, and economic network of the country, and its influence spills over into other organizations such as universities and public schools, all the way down to the nursery-school level.

The basic philosophy of Japanese-style management is that involved workers are the key to increased productivity. While this may sound a bit like the human relations school, it is dramatically different. The Japanese are concerned not simply about having workers feel that their social needs are met in the workplace, but rather that workers become a demonstrable part of the process through which the organization is run. Ideas and suggestions about how to improve the organization are regularly solicited and, where feasible, implemented. One example is the *quality circle,* where employees set aside time to brainstorm about ways to improve quality and productivity.

In contrast to American organizations, Japanese organizations tend to have neither organizational charts nor written objectives. Most work is done in teams, and consensus is achieved without a designated leader. Cooperation rather than competition is sought between units. Loyalty to the organization is extremely important, and it is rewarded by loyalty to the employee.

While Japanese productivity has remained high and its products continue to set the standard for quality in many areas, experiments designed to transplant Japanese-style management to this country have met with limited success. In most cases it has been concluded that the entire philosophy is compatible with a homogenous culture like Japan's, but does not fit well with the more heterogenous and individualistic character of the American workplace. Nevertheless, some of the concepts from *Theory Z* have been incorporated into contemporary management thought, and they have had an important influence on organizational and management theory.

"In Search of Excellence"

Another important management theme in the 1980s was the "excellence" theme, developed by Thomas Peters and Robert Waterman (1982). Peters and Waterman were employees at McKinsey and Company, a management consulting firm. Concern began to grow in the firm about problems with management, and the pair became the leaders of a project on organizational effectiveness.

They established a definition of what they considered to be excellent companies, and selected sixty-two of them for their study. They immersed themselves in the current thinking about the theory and practices of excellent companies and discovered that the dominant themes were such topics as organizational culture, a family feeling among employees, a preference for smallness, a preference for simplicity rather than complexity, and attention to individuals. In effect, they found that the prevailing management practices in these organizations focused more on the human elements emphasized by Mayo and McGregor than on the structure of the workplace as emphasized by Weber and Fayol.

While they discovered that a rational base built on collection and analysis of data is indispensable, they also concluded that analysis of data must be flexible and take into account a wide range of considerations, including the human element. Rational approaches, they determined, need to stop considering the human implementer a "necessary nuisance" and instead build on the strengths brought into the system by its employees.

Ultimately they translated their findings into eight basic principles which have become the focal point of the "excellence approach" to organizational management:

1. *A bias for action:* a preference for doing something—anything—rather than sending a question through cycles and cycles of analyses and committee reports.
2. *Staying close to the customer:* learning preferences and catering to them.
3. *Autonomy and entrepreneurship:* breaking the corporation into small companies and encouraging them to think independently and competitively.
4. *Productivity through people:* creating in all employees the awareness that their best efforts are essential and that they will share in the rewards of the company's success.
5. *Hands-on, value driven:* insisting that executives keep in touch with the firm's essential mission.
6. *Stick to the knitting:* remaining with the business the company knows best.
7. *Simple form, lean staff:* few administrative layers, few people at the upper levels.

8. *Simultaneous loose/tight properties:* fostering a climate where there is dedication to the central values of the company combined with tolerance for all employees who accept those values.

As the provision of human services has, over the years, moved closer and closer to a provider-consumer relationship, these principles and the findings of the Peters and Waterman study have taken on increased importance.

In 1989 Rosabeth Moss Kanter ushered in the 1990s with her book entitled *When Giants Learn to Dance.* Viewing the changes in management as a "post-entrepreneurial" revolution, Kanter concluded that "modest change everywhere in the corporation [was] becoming orthodoxy" (p. 10). Reaching beyond concepts such as "total quality" and "continuous improvement", she began to investigate not only what strategies organizations were using to solve their problems but what consequences these changes were having for those persons who were a part of these organizations. Breaking tradition with metaphors of war and sports, her book focused on whether "elephantlike" organizations heavily characterized by bureaucracy could actually learn to dance collaboratively with one another.

Emerging concerns in the 1980s carried over into the 1990s as change became a way of organizational life. Public as well as private agencies began quality improvement, quality assurance, and total quality programs. Strategies to cope with uncertain environments were joined with encouragement for organizations to engage in flexible and collaborative relationship building in order to survive.

Managing Diversity

Roosevelt Thomas Jr. (1991) takes a somewhat different approach to managing the workforce of the 1990s. He identifies diversity as the key variable affecting productivity, and sees effective management of diverse populations as a critical skill. He identifies three trends which, he believes, will dictate the need for dealing with a more diverse workforce:

1. American corporations must now do business in a global market which has become intensely competitive.
2. The makeup of the U.S. workforce is changing dramatically as it becomes more diverse.
3. The "melting pot" concept is becoming less applicable. Instead, individuals have begun to emphasize and take pride in differences.

In order to remain competitive, Thomas believes that American organizations will have to learn how to draw on the creative resources represented in a workforce made up of Asian Americans, African Americans, Latinos, Anglos, and other races, as well as a more even mix of males and females. To accomplish this objective, he proposes an analytical framework for understanding organizational culture that breaks diversity down into three phases: (1) *affirmative action,* (2) *valuing differences,* and (3) *managing diversity.*

Affirmative action refers to programs and efforts designed to bring ethnic minorities and women into the organization. The focus is on recruitment efforts, and success is measured by the numbers and percentages of minorities recruited and retained in the organization. Thomas sees affirmative action as a temporary step in moving the organization toward managing diversity.

Valuing differences focuses on enhancing interpersonal relationships among individuals. Much of the responsibility for these efforts falls on staff training and personnel development, with the objective of fostering acceptance and mutual respect across racial and gender lines, enhancing understanding of differences, assisting participants with understanding their own feelings and attitudes toward differences, and enhancing working relationships among people who are different.

Managing diversity, which is Thomas's vision, refers to a complete evaluation of the organization as a system to determine if it is as effective and productive as it can be and needs to be in an increasingly competitive environment. If the system is not effective, and if it is not prepared to deal with a diverse work force, Thomas suggests it may need to undertake a long-term strategy to modify the core culture. This requires a full understanding of the existing culture and a planned transition to a new culture where an environment is created that supports full utilization of a diverse work force. This requires a mind set that recognizes and values differences among all employees, including white males, and searches for opportunities to tap the reservoir of talent and strength represented in a diverse staff.

Thomas cites a number of major American corporations that have undertaken the challenge to change the organizational culture and increase productivity and competitiveness by effectively managing diversity. While most human service organizations have had a diverse work force for several decades, a thorough understanding of Thomas's conceptual framework would very likely lead many to the conclusion that they have not moved much beyond the phase of affirmative action, and that they have much to learn about valuing differences and eventually managing diversity well.

Summary and Analysis of Contemporary Theories

The perspectives discussed above come together in some interesting ways. Clearly the trend of the 1980s and 1990s is toward a better, more thorough understanding of organizational culture. Often this begins with an identification of the locus or centers of power and an understanding of the effectiveness of various individuals or groups in exercising political and leadership skills. These factors, together with others identified by Schein, make up what has come to be understood as organizational culture, a powerful and sometimes seemingly intractable force for continuation of "business as usual."

Most contemporary authors, however, are convinced that future organizational success and effectiveness will, to a great extent, be determined by an organization's ability to understand and even to change its culture. In contingency theory terms, this may mean that some some human service organizations must move away from a mechanistic structure and design toward a more organic approach. For others, however, it may mean moving away from an extreme entrepreneurial, laissez-faire style of management toward a more circumscribed, even mechanistic approach. As contingency theorists are fond of saying, "It depends . . .". The most useful organizational and management theories and approaches for human service agencies in the 1990s and beyond will depend on such factors as mission, objectives, target population served, personal, family and social problems addressed, the types of people employed, the state of the art of treatment or intervention, the clarity of outcome expectations, and other such variables. All things considered, it presents a rather exciting scenario for application of new knowledge and discovery of new approaches to understanding and managing human service organizations.

SUMMARY

The goal of this chapter has been to introduce theoretical notions about organizations and to begin tying these notions to the task of understanding organizations in which most social workers practice. These theories and perspectives can be understood partly in terms of the way they differ among themselves (Table 6.1). Some theories (such as scientific management and the human relations school) are prescriptive models, meaning that they provide guidelines on how to organize. In contrast, descriptive theories (such as the bureaucracy and the decision-making model) offer conceptual strategies for analyzing organizations and their operations.

These theories can be distinguished according to their approach to explaining organizational behavior. Some theories assume a rational model in which behavior is seen as the result of logical decision making oriented toward the instrumental goals of the organization. Other theories employ a natural systems approach, in which the organization is seen as being analogous to a biological organism and its behavior as responding to basic concerns for survival and self-maintenance.

Organizational theories differ on whether they adopt a closed- or open-systems perspective on the role of the organizations' environments. Closed-systems approaches implicitly focus on internal structure and process in organizations and tend to direct little or no attention to the role of the environment. By comparison, open-systems models emphasize organizations' dependence on their environment and adopt analytical strategies that view internal structure and process as the product of interactions with the environment.

Each theory we have reviewed can also be understood in terms of one or a small group of organization variables toward which it tends to direct attention. These variables include structure (the bureaucracy), productivity and the role of management (scientific and universalistic management), social interactions and self-actualization (human relations and Theory Y), organizational goals (the institutional school and management by objectives), strategic choice (the decision-making model), environmental interactions (contingency theory), the exercise of power and political influence (the political economy model), and organizational culture. As is often the case with theory-building in many different arenas, many of the models have developed out of criticisms of earlier works that have directed attention in new and fruitful directions. Nonetheless, even the earliest of these theories still has some validity, and the critical task in an organizational analysis is to glean from these various models the ideas that best explain the particular organization being addressed.

As we will see, organizational analysis in human service organizations has already produced a substantial body of literature that can be very helpful to macro practice. Chapter 7 will review this literature and discuss means for applying it to specific problems that may arise in human service organizations.

REFERENCES

Astin, H. S., and C. Leland. (1991) Women of influence, women of vision: A cross-generational study of leaders and social change. San Francisco, CA: Jossey-Bass Publishers.

Barker, R. L. (1987) *The social work dictionary.* Silver Spring, MD: National Association of Social Workers.

Blau, P. M., and W. R. Scott. (1962) *Formal organizations.* San Francisco: Chandler.

Burns, T., and G. M. Stalker. (1961) *The management of innovation.* London: Tavistock.

Champion, D. J. (1975) *The sociology of organizations.* New York: McGraw-Hill.

Cyert, R. M., and J. G. March. (1963) *A behavioral theory of the firm.* Englewood Cliffs, NJ: Prentice-Hall.

Drucker, P. F. (1954) *The practice of management.* New York: Harper.

Etzioni, A. (1964) *Modern organizations.* Englewood Cliffs, NJ: Prentice-Hall.

Galbraith, J. R. (1973) *Designing complex organizations.* Reading, MA: Addison-Wesley.

Gottlieb, N. (1992) *Empowerment, political analyses, and services for women.* In Y. Hasenfeld, ed., Human services as complex organizations, 301–19. Newbury Park, CA: Sage.

Herzberg, F. (1966) *Work and the nature of man.* Cleveland: World.

Jamieson, D., and J. O'Mara. (1991) *Managing workforce 2000: Gaining the diversity advantage.* San Francisco: Jossey-Bass.

Kanter, R. M. (1989) *When giants learn to dance.* New York: Simon & Schuster.

Katz, D., and R. L. Kahn. (1966) *The social psychology of organizations.* New York: John Wiley & Sons.

Kelly, R. M. (1991) *The gendered economy: Work, careers, and success.* Newbury Park, CA: Sage.

Landsberger, H. A. (1958) *Hawthorne revisited.* Ithaca, NY: Cornell University Press.

Lawrence, P. R., and J. W. Lorsch. (1967) *Organization and environment: Managing differentiation and integration.* Boston: Graduate School of Business Administration, Harvard University.

March, J. G., and H. A. Simon. (1958) *Organizations.* New York: John Wiley & Sons.

March, J. G., and J. P. Olsen. (1976) *Ambiguity and choice in organizations.* Bergen, Norway: Universitetsforlaget.

McGregor, D. (1960) *The human side of enterprise.* New York: McGraw-Hill.

Merton, R. K. (1952) Bureaucratic structure and personality. In R. K. Merton, A. P. Gray, B. Hockey and H. C. Selvin, eds., *Reader in bureaucracy,* 261–372. Glencoe, IL: Free Press.

Michels, R. (1949) *Political parties* (Paul, E. and C. Paul, trans.) Glencoe, IL: Free Press. (First published in 1915)

Morse, J. J., and J. W. Lorsch. (1970) Beyond Theory Y. *Harvard Business Review, 45*: 61–8.

Mouzelis, N. P. (1967) *Organization and bureaucracy.* London: Routledge & Kegan Paul.

Ouchi, W. (1981) *Theory Z: How American business can meet the Japanese challenge.* Reading, MA: Addison-Wesley.

Parsons, T. (1960) *Structure and process in modern societies.* Glencoe, IL: Free Press.

Peters, T. J., and R. H. Waterman. (1982) *In search of excellence: Lessons from America's best-run companies.* New York: Harper & Row.

Pfeffer, J. (1981) *Power in organizations.* Marshfield, MA: Pitman.

Rogers, R. E. (1975) *Organizational theory.* Boston: Allyn & Bacon.

Schein, E. H. (1985) *Organizational culture and leadership.* San Francisco: Jossey-Bass.

Scott, W. R. (1981) *Organizations: Rational, natural, and open systems.* Englewood Cliffs, NJ: Prentice-Hall.

Selznick, P. (1949) *TVA and the grass roots.* Berkeley: University of California Press.

Selznick, P. (1957) *Leadership in administration.* New York: Harper & Row.

Sills, D. L. (1957) *The volunteers.* New York: Free Press.

Simon, H. A. (1957) *Administrative behavior.* (2nd ed.). New York: Macmillan.

Sykes, A. J. M. (1965) Economic interests and the Hawthorne researchers: A comment. *Human Relations, 18*: 253–63.

Taylor, F. W. (1947) *Scientific management.* New York: Harper & Row.

Thomas, R. R., Jr. (1991) *Beyond race and gender: Unleashing the power of your total work force by managing diversity.* New York: AMACOM.

Thompson, J. D. (1967) *Organizations in action.* New York: McGraw-Hill.

von Bertalanffy, L. (1950) An outline of general system theory. *The British Journal for the Philosophy of Science, 1*(2): 493–512.

Wamsley, G. L., and M. N. Zald. (1976) *The political economy of public organizations.* Bloomington, IN: Indiana University Press.

Weber, M. (1946) *From Max Weber: Essays in sociology* (H. H. Gerth and C. W. Mills, trans.). New York: Oxford University Press.

Weber, M. (1947) *The Theory of social and economic organization* (A. M. Henderson and T. Parsons, trans.). New York: Macmillan. (First published in 1924)

CHAPTER 7

Practice in Human Service Organizations

Overview

INTRODUCTION

Having reviewed in the previous chapter a variety of approaches to understanding organizations in general, we now turn our attention specifically to human service organizations, in which most social workers are employed. These agencies have unique characteristics that distinguish them from other organizational types and that social workers must understand in order to employ their macro-practice skills effectively. However, the distinguishing features of these agencies are not always clear-cut, thus we begin with a discussion of how human service organizations are defined.

In Chapter 3, we quoted a definition of human service organizations as "the vast array of formal organizations that have as their stated purpose enhancement of the social, emotional, physical, and/or intellectual well-being of some component of the population" (Brager & Holloway 1978, 2). This definition provides a starting point, but it leaves some troubling questions. For example, manufacturing firms increase the well-being of the population by creating desirable products, but does this make them human service organizations? Also, any number of groups ranging from political lobbying firms to the Ku Klux Klan seek to promote what they perceive to be the well-being of some component of the population, but does this make them human service organizations? Hasenfeld (1983) addresses this question in part by noting that human service organizations "work directly with and on people whose attributes they attempt to shape. People are, in a sense, their 'raw material'" (p. 1). In other words, human service organizations operate in some way on people themselves, and though they may distribute or even produce certain goods (as in a food bank or housing cooperative) their focus is on improving the quality of life of their constituents, consumers, or clients.

However, many kinds of organizations work with or on people, and service providers from boutiques to barber shops to bistros are carefully designed to enhance at least the perceived well-being of their clients. Are these human service organizations? Hasenfeld addresses this point in the second part of his definition, which specifies that human service organizations "are mandated—and thus justify their existence—to protect and to promote the welfare of the people they serve" (p. 1). In other words, these organizations are expected to conform to societal expectations (both implicit and explicit) that services are provided to their constituents in a way that also promotes the overall welfare of the public. Agencies whose activities cannot be legitimized in the context of these expectations cannot be considered human service organizations.

A large variety of organizations may still be encompassed within this definition, and to make sense of this diversity the most important consideration is the auspice, or sectoral location, of the agency. As we discussed in Chapter 5, human service agencies may be classified as one of three types, corresponding to the three major sectors of the economy: public, nonprofit, or for-profit. These are important distinctions because the mission, service orientation, and nature of practice within an organization vary considerably across these types. Though for-profit agencies are growing in importance as employers of social workers, public bureaucracies, and nonprofit agencies remain the most common practice venues. The following vignettes illustrate the issues and problems encountered by social workers in public and nonprofit agencies.

TWO VIGNETTES OF HUMAN SERVICE ORGANIZATIONS

Vignette 1 focuses on a large public agency and its development. Issues concerning the growth of bureaucracy, hierarchical structure, the role of the elected officials, frustrations over slow change processes, limited creative application, and barriers to client services are illustrated in the vignette.

Our second vignette describes a medium-sized nonprofit agency established at the turn of the century. As times change, the organization grows through the receipt of government grants and contracts. Issues related to working with boards of directors and sponsoring groups, attempts to address the needs of multiple constituencies in an increasingly regulated environment, and the use of volunteers are presented.

We hope that these vignettes will set the stage for how a social worker can begin to analyze what is happening in diverse human service organizations. Immediately following the vignettes we will briefly discuss the issues raised, after which we will present a framework for analyzing human service organizations.

VIGNETTE 1: CANYON COUNTY DEPARTMENT OF CHILD WELFARE

Creating a Dynamic Organization

Canyon County Department of Child Welfare had, for a long time, considered itself a unique and innovative organization. Created in the early 1960s, its initial years of development came during a time when national attention was focused on the development of high-quality human service programs designed to address client needs and community problems. The director of child welfare was hired as a result of a national search. She had built a strong reputation in a northeastern state as a person who ran successful programs and was well liked by the community, her staff, and clients alike.

She took the job because she was excited by the challenge of building a department from scratch with more-than-adequate resources made available from federal, state, and county governments. She hired people who, like herself, were committed to teamwork, to collaboration, and to problem solving. Middle managers and supervisors were people with many years of experience, most of whom had MSW degrees; line workers tended to be recent graduates of MSW programs. The director stressed high energy, enthusiasm, collaboration, mutual support, morale, and competence in her hiring interviews.

During the 1960s and 1970s, Canyon County Department of Child Welfare built a reputation for providing high-quality services, for a high rate of success, and for an extremely positive work environment. It was an organization other counties looked to for leadership in dealing with emerging problems of the time—child abuse and neglect, family violence, drug and alcohol abuse, and other family-related problems.

Dismantling a Dynamic Organization

Toward the end of the 1970s, two things happened to change the direction of the department. First, as a county in a state with the fastest growing population in the country, the population of Canyon County doubled in size during the 1970s. Increasing fiscal and political conservatism influenced decisions of the county board of supervisors, and the child welfare budget became the focal point of a major budget reduction effort. Second, the director reached retirement age.

The board of supervisors used this opportunity to appoint a person who had spent his career in the insurance industry. They saw this as their opportunity to introduce some "hard-headed business practices" into the running of human service programs. Because of its strong national reputation, employment by the Canyon County Child Welfare Department served as a solid reference and made an individual highly marketable in other counties and states. Many managers and supervisors took advantage of other employment opportunities, and their positions were filled by people who had political connections to the board or to the director. The team approach which had dominated for two decades was replaced by a more rigid bureaucratic structure, and collegial practices were replaced by strictly enforced administrative policies.

By the end of the 1980s, the department bore little resemblance to the one that had built such a strong reputation during the 1970s. The most noticeable change was in the structure of the organization. The organizational chart reflected clearly defined work units, with reporting lines from entry level all the way through to the director. Standardized workloads were assigned regardless of the difficulty or complexity of cases. Specialization was eliminated. Likewise, employee-oriented efforts such as job rotation, job sharing, and flex-time were eliminated.

Involvement of the County Board

The members of the county board of supervisors began to experience mounting complaints about the child welfare department. Child abuse and neglect reports went uninvestigated. Annual reports revealed a steady decline in the successful resolution of problems for families served by the department. A consultant was hired to do an organizational analysis and to make recommendations to the board of supervisors.

The consultant found little personal involvement in organizational objectives. Line staff felt that their opinions did not matter, so they either kept comments to themselves or complained to colleagues. When problems were identified, little effort was expended to analyze them or propose solutions. Most staff members believed that success was defined in terms of adherence to policies and procedures. Ambitious staff members who hoped for successful careers in the department became experts on existing policy, not on understanding problem families or on professional practice with families as the previous staff had done.

For those who were hired into management positions, the emphasis was on control. Virtually all decisions about cases had to pass through and be signed by a supervisor and a program manager. Managers felt that staff ignored their efforts to enforce policies and procedures, especially when it came to keeping paperwork up to date. Conflict was mostly covert and managed by office politics. A personal relationship with the director or deputy director was perceived as being more important than a problem or issue faced by the organization.

VIGNETTE 2: LAKESIDE FAMILY SERVICES

Historical Development

Lakeside Family Services Agency was originally incorporated as the Methodist Home for Orphaned Children in 1902. Begun by the Methodist Church, this home served children with no living relatives. Situated on a large parcel of donated land on the outskirts of a metropolitan area, the home was the site of many church gatherings as well as fund-raising events over the years. Volunteers from the church and community were part of almost every activity at the home.

During the 1920s the home was the recipient of generous contributions from wealthy church and civic-minded leaders, and in the 1930s it became a Red Feather Agency. The Red Feather fund-raising campaign was the forerunner of what was now the local United Way. As campaign contributions increased, so did the scope of the home. By the mid-1940s, the home had expanded to include services for unwed mothers and family counseling, and had hired several professionally trained social workers.

Originally, the fifteen-member voluntary board of directors was elected by the Annual Conference of the Methodist Church. The bylaws specified that at least 75 percent of the members must be members of the church and that the executive director should also be a member. Although it was not required, the majority of staff were church members and there was an active volunteer auxiliary of over 100 persons.

Major Changes Occur

During the 1960s, the board engaged in a number of controversial meetings to determine the future of the home. Not only had service needs changed, but there were fewer and fewer orphans. The United Way was putting pressure on the home to merge with two other family service agencies in the same city. The percentage of the home's budget that came from the Methodist Church was getting smaller, even though actual dollar amounts increased each year. Several board members were encouraging the home to rethink its mission and to actively seek state and federal funding.

By 1970, after a decade of controversy, the home changed its name to Lakeside Family Services Agency, disaffiliated from the Methodist Church, and became a major nonprofit provider of government contract services to children, families, and the aged. The agency relocated and the church-owned property on which the home stood reverted back to the church. Lakeside remained a United Way agency, and dollar amounts increased yearly. By 1980, however, a majority of the agency's budget (70 percent) came from government contracts and grants.

The remnant of the board that had supported these changes in the agency's mission, funding, and structure were joined by persons carefully selected for their expertise in fund raising and politics. They selected an executive director with an MSW and hired a director of development.

The agency was structured into three program components: (1) children's services, (2) family services, and (3) aging services. Each program component received government contracts, as well as United Way funds and private contributions, and within each component there was service diversification. For example, aging services included homemaker/chore, home health, and adult day care.

Program directors began complaining that contract dollars never truly covered the full cost of services and that state and federal regulations were restricting their ability to provide adequate care to their respective clientele. The executive director searched for strategies to deal with these complaints and spent a great deal of time conferring with directors of other nonprofit organizations.

The Search for Strategies

The 1980s witnessed a period of government retrenchment. Lakeside Family Services experienced cutbacks in two of its program areas. When the executive director talked with other providers, she perceived a new sense of competitiveness that she had not sensed before.

When staff suggested the use of volunteers to help keep services going, the executive director realized that the previously active volunteer pool of earlier days had not been nurtured and maintained. In fact, only the aging program was using volunteers—in this case to do home visits to frail elderly. Even this use was limited, because the volunteers' activities were carefully structured and greatly limited by state service specifications.

At the executive director's request, the board approved a fee-for-service schedule and instructed the director of development to develop a plan for recruiting fee-paying clients. Staff were angered by the agency's new focus on private fee-payers when they could not serve those persons they considered in greatest need.

In 1990, the agency was in great financial difficulty. In desperation, the executive director began unsuccessful negotiations with United Methodist Church officials to see if they would be interested in taking the agency back under their wing.

It is not unusual for organizations, over time, to exhibit the symptoms of unhealthy behavior described in Vignettes 1 and 2. When this happens, it is often tempting to opt for a seemingly simple solution like changing the director in Vignette 1 or attracting more paying clients in Vignette 2. However, cultural change in organizations usually occurs over a long period of time. Attitudes and behaviors tend to permeate all levels of staff, so a simple change in the organization rarely solves all problems.

The two vignettes differ in that one agency is public and exists because of a government mandate, whereas the other evolved in the private nonprofit sector. However, there are a number of parallels. Both organizations developed in growth climates, only to face severe financial and political constraints in recent years. Whereas Canyon County became more bureaucratic, Lakeside became more professionalized. Just as rigid rules developed within Canyon, Lakeside experienced the constraints of state and federal regulations when they began receiving more and more government monies. Both organizations searched for answers to complex problems that could not be easily solved. In this chapter, we propose a method of conducting organizational analyses that will enable practitioners to understand more fully what is happening in organizations like Canyon and Lakeside.

A FRAMEWORK FOR ORGANIZATIONAL ANALYSIS

In Chapter 5, we presented a framework with which to analyze community human service systems. In this chapter, we offer a similar model for use in analyzing organizations. As before, the model is presented in the form of tasks to be completed in the analysis and questions to be asked within each task. Completion of these tasks is intended to lead to a more complete and accurate understanding of the organization that will in turn facilitate change efforts. Table 7.1 provides an overview of the framework.

Focus A: Identifying the Agency's Task Environment

The process of using the framework in Table 7.1 may be thought of as collecting information through a funnel, the broadest part of which incorporates considerations of an organization's environment, after which the focus narrows toward the internal workings of the organization. To understand considerations external to the organization, we will use the concept of *task environment* to describe the critical elements of an organization's environment. These critical elements are

TABLE 7.1 Framework for Analyzing Human Service Organizations

Focus	Tasks
A. Identifying the Agency's Task Evironment	1. Identify funding sources 2. Identify sources of noncash revenues 3. Identify clients and client sources 4. Identify other constituents
B. Recognizing the Dynamics of Agency/Environment Relations	5. Observe relationships with clients 6. Observe relationships with resource sources 7. Observe relationships with competitors
C. Analyzing the Organization	8. Identify corporate authority and mission 9. Understand organizational structure 10. Understand administration, management, and leadership 11. Recognize the organization's culture 12. Assess the organization's programs and services 13. Assess organizational technology 14. Evaluate personnel policies and procedures 15. Recognize how the organization deals with community relations 16. Recognize methods of financial management and accountability 17. Identify facilities, equipment, computer utilization, and records management

those which provide the organization with its raw materials and resources (e.g., revenues, clients, constraints).

As noted in our review of the work of James Thompson (1967) in Chapter 6, the task environment consists of elements outside an organization that enable it to operate and that set the basic context for these operations. Thompson notes that, as originally defined by Dill (1958), the task environment includes four key components:

> (1) customers (both distributors and users); (2) suppliers of materials, labor, capital, equipment, and work space; (3) competitors for both markets and resources; and (4) regulatory groups, including governmental agencies, unions, and interfirm associations. (pp. 27–8)

Dill's work focused on industrial firms and must be altered to fit the circumstances of human service organizations. For example, defining the customers of human service organizations is a bit more complex undertaking than with commercial firms. Sometimes clients are equivalent to customers, sometimes not. For example, a person who has sought counseling and is willing to pay for this service is very much a customer in the traditional sense. On the other hand, an adult son who has abused his elderly father is not exactly a customer who has sought out protective services. He receives these services involuntarily.

Martin (1980) designed a model that identifies the many environmental entities important to human service organizations (see Chapter 3). The most critical of these elements are:

1. Funding sources;
2. Sources of noncash revenues;
3. Clients and client sources;
4. Other constituents.

We will use these four elements as a guide for the questions to be asked in analyzing an organization's task environment.

Task 1: Identify Funding Sources.   Questions to be asked:

- What are the agency's funding sources?
- How much and what percentage of funds are received from each source?
- Which funds are earmarked to certain programs or services and which are flexible?

There is a twist on the "golden rule" that states, "the one who has the gold makes the rules." This revision of an old adage is perhaps cynical but undeniably accurate when applied to almost any complex organization. Indeed, understanding how a particular agency is financed is often the key to understanding the agency itself. However, this process can be a difficult one given that in modern human service organizations funds are obtained from a multitude of different sources that are combined in complex ways. Moreover, most organizations do not typically make funding information easily available, thus simply determining how an agency obtains necessary funds can be a demanding task. (Where public funds are used, however, budget documents are often, by law, considered public documents.)

The first step in analyzing organizational funding is to determine the sources from which funds come. The following lists major sources of revenue for human service organizations, including important types of funds available from each source.

Major Revenue Sources for Human Service Organizations
Government funds

Direct government appropriation

Government purchase-of-service contract funds

Government grants

Matching funds

Tax benefits

Donated funds

Direct charitable contributions (from individuals, groups, and associations such as religious groups)

Indirect contributions (e.g., through United Way)

Private grants (e.g., foundation monies)

Endowments

Fees for service

Direct payments from clients

Payments from third parties (e.g., private or public insurers)

Other Agency Income

Investments (e.g., interest, dividends, royalties)

Profit-making subsidiaries

Fund raisers and appeals

Though it is unlikely that any two organizations will have an identical distribution of revenue sources, certain patterns do exist. The most important of these relates to agency auspice. In general, public agencies rely more heavily than others on direct governmental appropriations; nonprofit agencies make more extensive use of donated funds; and for-profit agencies emphasize fee-for-service revenues. However, it is also important to note that this is only a *rough* trend, and it is in the process of change.

In the public sector, direct appropriations are virtually the exclusive source of revenues for organizations at the federal level. This source is primary for many state, county, and local agencies as well, but these organizations also make use of a mixture of funds from higher levels of government. In general, the lower the level of government, the larger the number of funding sources from which organizations at that level are likely to draw revenues. Among the most important mechanisms for dissemination are block grants (lump-sum appropriations in which specific allocations are left to local governments), matching funds (which, for example, provide a certain amount of federal funds for each dollar expended by state-level agencies), and grant programs in which funds are targeted toward a specific use and are restricted to that program. In the vignette regarding Canyon County discussed earlier in this chapter, the Child Welfare Department was funded solely by government funds.

Nonprofit agencies, like Lakeside Family Services in Vignette 2, tend to have an even greater range of funding sources. Moreover, though by definition these are the agencies toward which charitable contributions are targeted, such contributions make up only a small portion of the annual budget of most nonprofit agencies. In one national study conducted in 1987, nonprofit organizations as a whole drew an average of 27 percent of their funds from charitable contributions, as compared to 39 percent from dues, fees, and charges, 26 percent from government sources, and 16 percent from other sources (Hodgkinson & Weitzman 1989).

In a study that we conducted in 1989, focusing specifically on nonprofit human service organizations, the average distribution across funding sources was 34 percent from government contracts, 33 percent from charitable donations, 13 percent from client fees, 10 percent from public grants, 5 percent from private grants, and 5 percent from other sources (McMurtry et al. 1991). Government contract funds are those in which a nonprofit or for-profit agency contracts with a public agency to provide specific services to specific clients. Combining these funds with those received via public grants—the average agency in this study drew almost half (44 percent) of its funds from government sources—and some agencies reported receiving all their funds from these sources. This suggests that many human services agencies, though nominally part of the nonprofit sector, may be more accurately viewed as quasi-public agencies. The most important elements of the task environments of these organizations will thus be the public agencies that set contract policies and service reimbursement rates.

For-profit firms are a growing arena for social work practice, and among such organizations as hospitals and nursing homes they are major service providers. In fact, Stoesz (1988) notes that in 1985 two hospital corporations each had revenues exceeding all charitable contributions collected nationwide by the United Way that same year. Other areas in which large human service corporations are developing include child care, home-based nursing care, and corrections. Also, private counseling firms, though traditionally small in scale, are a part of this sector. All these organizations share a predominant reliance on fee-for-service revenues. However, individual consumers are a less important part of the task environment of these organizations than insurance companies and other third-party payors who establish policies and rates for reimbursement.

For example, a private social work firm may draw a majority of its clients from the employee assistance program of a nearby manufacturing plant, thus relationships with the manufacturer will likely be the paramount environmental consideration for this firm.

In general, a critical point in understanding funding sources is that most funds come with strings attached, and decisions on how to spend them may rest much more with the funding agency than with the recipient. This means, using governmental organizations as an example, that a county agency which appears to be subject to local decision-making processes may in fact be more accurately viewed as a local extension of the state agency that provides the bulk of its funds. A change episode that attempted to influence the use of these funds would thus be likely to succeed only if it recognized that decision-making power over the funds rested with organizations in the agency's task environment rather than inside its own boundaries.

The number of sources from which an agency's funds are drawn is also a key consideration. Somewhat paradoxically, an agency with many funding sources often has greater autonomy and flexibility than one with few because the loss of any single source might not jeopardize the overall viability of the organization. On the other hand, the greater the number of funding sources, the more complex the agency's operations become. With each new source comes another layer of regulatory constraints, program diversity, and accountability expectations. Whereas the agency with a single funding source may risk becoming rigid and highly specialized, the agency with many sources may have difficulty defining and focusing on its mission.

Task 2: Identify Sources of Noncash Revenues.   Questions to be asked:

- Does the organization use volunteers? If yes, how many and for what purposes?
- What material resources (e.g., food, clothing, physical facilities, etc.) does the organization receive?
- What tax benefits does the organization receive?
- How important are noncash revenues to the organization's operation?

In considering resources, it is also important to keep in mind that actual dollars coming into a human service organization are not the only form of resources. Many other assets on which agencies rely are not as obvious as cash revenues but may be equally important. Three such assets are volunteers, material resources, and tax benefits.

Volunteers have traditionally been a mainstay of human service organizations. As noted in Chapter 2, the entire nonprofit human service sector originated with the activities of individual volunteers who began to work together in order to better organize their efforts. In the Lakeside vignette presented earlier in this chapter, volunteers were critical to the organization's early development. Today, the contribution of these individuals to human service organizations is enormous. Hodgkinson and Weitzman (1989) summarize these contributions:

> Approximately 80 million adults 18 years of age or older or 45 percent of the adult population volunteered an average of 4.7 hours per week in 1987. They contributed 19.5 billion hours in [formal and informal volunteering] . . . The 14.9 billion hours in formal volunteer commitments is the equivalent of 8.8 million full-time employees valued at nearly $150 billion. (p. 60)

Study results indicate that 7 percent of volunteer time was devoted directly to human services and welfare organizations in 1987, with an additional 3 percent devoted to fund raising for multipurpose human welfare services, meaning that the monetary value of direct volunteer services to human service agencies that year totaled roughly $15 billion (Hodgkinson et al. 1988).

Volunteers perform many different roles in human service agencies. Nonprofit agencies may rely heavily upon professional staff to deliver services, but it is important to recognize that boards of directors are volunteers. Volunteers also contribute time to public and for-profit agencies. For example, a large for-profit corporation may allow their workers release time to volunteer for a human service project or a government department may recruit volunteers to work with their staff. In settings such as hospitals, hospices, and nursing homes volunteers perform numerous duties such as delivering patient mail, friendly visiting, telephone reassurance, and assisting at mealtime.

A second type of resource is contributions of material goods. Examples are food, clothing, physical facilities, real estate, vehicles, and a wide variety of household and office materials. In some cases these goods are provided for use directly by the agency, in other cases they are donated for the purpose of resale in order to generate cash revenues, and in still other cases they simply pass through the agency for distribution directly to clients. In each circumstance, though, the total value of these resources to organizations is again substantial. Though specific figures are difficult to obtain, one example of the magnitude of this source of income is deductions on individual and income taxes claimed for noncash charitable contributions. In 1988, over 10 million individual filers claimed noncash charitable contributions, the cash value of which totaled more than $6.7 billion dollars (Internal Revenue Service 1991).

Tax benefits are particularly important for private, nonprofit human service organizations. Indeed, one defining characteristic of nonprofit agencies is an official designation as a charitable organization under section 501(c)(3) of federal Internal Revenue Service regulations. Meeting the requirements of this section allows nonprofit agencies to avoid income taxes that for-profit firms must pay, and this can be a critical benefit in service arenas such as health care, where nonprofit and for-profit hospitals often engage in intense competition for patients and physicians. Tax laws are also important in terms of their effect on other revenue sources, particularly charitable contributions. For example, Karger and Stoesz (1990) note that the Tax Reform Act of 1986 may have reduced contributions to nonprofit agencies by limiting tax breaks for contributors to those who itemize deductions on their tax returns.

Noncash resources are important considerations in an organizational analysis because an agency's behaviors may be understood as efforts to acquire and protect these assets. For example, an organization that relies heavily on volunteers may seek to protect this resource even if in so doing it comes into conflict with the interests of professional staff. Similarly, the structure of an agency may be adapted to take advantage of one of these resources, as with the growing number of nonprofit agencies that are raising funds by collecting donated material goods and reselling them through thrift stores. On the other hand, attention to noncash resources may also be important in initiating change efforts. For example, some organizational problems are often left unaddressed due to pessimism about the ability to raise funds to add or augment services, and a change agent's awareness of the possibilities posed by the use of noncash resources may be a key to overcoming this barrier.

Task 3: Identify Clients and Client Sources.   Questions to be asked:

- What client groups does this organization serve?
- How many unduplicated clients are served by each program?
- How are client needs determined?
- Within each client group, how many (or what percentage) are able to pay? Contract eligible? Unable to pay (low-pay or no-pay)?
- What percentage of clients are ethnic/racial minorities, women, gays or lesbians, or members of other oppressed groups?
- How and by whom (i.e., self, family, provider) are clients referred to this organization?
- How and to which agencies does this organization refer clients?

In commercial firms, clients are primarily those who purchase goods or services, thus the organization carefully designs its outputs to meet the needs of this group. In human services agencies, those who pay for services often are not the same as those who receive them. This is an important distinction, and for our purposes we will define the clients of human service organizations as *those who are direct recipients of services.*

Within this definition, clients can be divided into two groups. In the first group are those who are able to pay the agency (either personally or through third-party reimbursement) at least as much as their services cost. Paying clients are important resources that agencies both seek to attract and are most likely to serve. In the Lakeside vignette, the board approved a plan to attract fee-paying clients to the agency. This angered staff who felt that indigent clients were being ignored.

The second group are those persons who are able to pay only part or none of the cost of their services (Netting et al. 1990). These clients are usually seen as liabilities, because serving them means the agency must expend resources that it has to offset by generating revenues elsewhere (e.g., through fund raising, profits earned from serving paying clients, or other means). Clients also differ in terms of their fit with the agency's technology. Clients whose problems or needs are among those the agency serves are more likely to be evaluated as assets, whereas those having different problems or needs may be evaluated as fiscal liabilities. These evaluations can strongly influence the likelihood that clients will receive services, sometimes regardless of their intrinsic level of need.

Because clients are evaluated in these terms, important elements in the task environments of human service organizations are other agencies that serve as *referral sources* and *referral targets*. Referral sources are agencies that refer clients who are likely to be evaluated as resources, and referral targets are those who accept referrals of clients evaluated as liabilities. Formal and informal referral arrangements among agencies for exchange of clients form the basis for interactions that are often viewed with equal importance as relationships with funding sources.

Task 4: Identify Other Constituents.   Questions to be asked:

- What state and federal regulatory bodies oversee programs provided by this organization?
- What agencies contract with this organization for service delivery?
- What professional associations, labor unions, or accrediting bodies influence agency operations?
- Is this organization affiliated with or sponsored by religious, ethnic, or fraternal bodies?
- How does this organization define its "public" and what groups are part of this definition?

Within an organization's task environment are groups that do not necessarily provide resources but that set the context in which the agency operates. One example is regulatory bodies that are responsible for setting the boundaries of acceptable service practices. Many of these are governmental licensing agencies that inspect and certify both the physical environment and services of certain organizations (e.g, nursing homes, child-caring institutions, residential treatment facilities, etc.). Others are contracting agencies that often require provider agencies to conform to detailed procedural guidelines in order to be reimbursed for the services they deliver. Still others are local, state, and federal revenue departments that levy taxes and monitor financial accounting procedures. Extensive accounting and funding-usage requirements are also imposed by nongovernmental funding sources such as the United Way.

Organizations such as professional associations, labor unions, and accrediting bodies also help to establish the regulatory boundaries of practice. However, their influence may be exerted through individuals within the organization rather than upon the organization as a whole. For example, standards established in the NASW Code of Ethics and for members of the Academy of Certified Social Workers (ACSW) govern the activities of staff who are members of these bodies. State licensing bodies impose similar constraints, and organizations with a high proportion of employees who meet these requirements may function differently than those with relatively few.

The "general public" is another part of this set of constituents. By their nature, human service organizations are dependent on some form of social sanction for their activities, and loss of the public support may jeopardize their existence. Unfortunately, views of members of the general public are not always apparent. Moreover, public opinion is seldom unanimous. Organizations must determine which of a typically wide variety of expressed views represents the predominate attitude.

Within the task environment, public opinion is often conveyed through a bewildering diversity of elements. These include elected representatives, interest and advocacy groups, civic organizations, and others. In addition, funding organizations are indirect but nonetheless important representatives of public views. Patterns in the ebb and flow of charitable donations, for example, suggest both general levels of public concern and particular problems toward which this concern is directed (as do the priorities of private foundations). Finally, mass media outlets are critical purveyors of public attitudes, though by their nature they often emphasize the most extreme rather than the most typical opinions.

Child protective services provides an example of the relationship between agencies, public opinion, and mass media (as both a carrier and shaper of public opinion). Deciding whether to remove an at-risk child from his or her home involves a delicate balancing act between concern for the child's well-being and concern for parental rights. In one well-publicized case in Washington state, for example, the fatal abuse of a child led to public outcry, which in turn resulted in legislative changes that instructed protective service workers to favor the safety of the child in such decisions. However, publicity on cases in other locations has featured allegations of "child-snatching" by protective service workers, which in turn led to legislative imposition of stricter guidelines for the removal of children. The point is that public opinion is dynamic rather than static, and similar agencies at different times or in different places may encounter very divergent public attitudes and expectations. Identifying the task environment is therefore an ongoing process as new groups develop and as public attitudes change.

Focus B: Recognizing the Dynamics of Agency/Environment Relations

Having identified important elements of the task environment of human service organizations, an equally important area to be addressed is the way in which organizations interact with these elements. Based on organizational theory and subsequent research growing out of open-systems models, two concepts appear to be critical in analyzing these dynamics: *resource dependence* and *domain setting.*

Resource dependence means that because organizations are open systems, they must rely on elements in their environment in order to obtain resources necessary for survival. Because of this dependence, organizations try to establish relationships that minimize uncertainty regarding the availability of these resources. Relationships with elements of the task environment are based on exchanges (e.g., of funds, clients, or services), and exchanges are always reciprocal to some degree (Thompson, 1967). An exchange may be a more or less equal one that benefits both organizations and in which each member holds roughly equal power. Other exchanges, however, may be dramatically unequal.

A related concept that also arises from open-systems models is the notion of organizational domains (Levine & White 1961). A domain refers to what the organization does and who it serves, and it is the means by which the organization establishes its role or niche within its environment.

Domain setting refers to this process by which organizations establish their domains among others within their task environment. One part of the process is domain legitimation, whereby the organization wins acknowledgment of claims it makes as to its sphere of activities. Legitimation is not always immediately forthcoming, and there is usually a disparity between what an organization says are its boundaries, the *claimed domain,* and what these boundaries actually are, the *de facto domain* (Greenley & Kirk 1973). Also, claims regarding domains evolve along with circumstances in the environment. Specifically, agencies seek to take advantage of available resources, and most are constantly adjusting their domains as a means of doing so.

These concepts provide the basis of a discussion of human service organizations' interactions with their environments. In addressing these dynamics, we will refer to the major elements of the task environment identified in the previous section. A key theme will be changes during the last decade that have substantially altered the environments of most human services organizations.

Task 5: Observe Relationships with Clients.   Questions to be asked:

- Has this organization targeted new or different clients within the last five years?
- What is the organization's domain (specifically, what types of clients does the organization serve)?
- Are these clients ones who bring resources to the agency or for whose services resources must be obtained elsewhere?
- Does the organization claim a larger domain than it serves, and are significant numbers of clients turned away?
- What types of clients does the organization refuse (e.g., are most of these the poorest or most troubled clients; are most of these minorities as opposed to nonminorities)? What happens to these clients?

As noted earlier, clients can be either resources or liabilities for an agency, depending on whether they fit within the organization's domain and whether they can pay for services. Recognizing this dynamic, a longstanding concern relative to agencies' relationships with clients is whether certain groups of clients, especially the most needy, are being excluded from access to services (Cloward & Epstein 1965). Results of a variety of studies over the past twenty years suggest this may indeed be the case.

In an early study, Kirk and Greenley (1974) examined clients' efforts to obtain services. Their results showed that only 47 of every 100 clients were served by the first two agencies they visited; the rest were either rejected or referred at least twice. In a companion piece (Greenley & Kirk 1973), they analyzed the dynamics of these outcomes and identified domain selection as a key factor. Because most agencies had larger claimed domains than de facto domains, they attracted clients that they were unable to serve. Nevertheless, this disparity was apparently seen as desirable by many agencies, since it afforded them the opportunity to "cream" the best-fitting clients who could pay and to refer or reject the remainder.

In addition, important distinctions appeared between agencies in terms of *boundary control,* meaning the ability of the agency to reject clients that it did not wish to serve. Agencies with high boundary control (usually for-profit and prestigious nonprofit organizations) were those most likely to engage in creaming, leaving clients who were rejected to seek out agencies with low boundary control. This resulted in the clients with the greatest difficulties and the least ability to pay being directed to agencies that were already the most overcrowded and had the fewest available resources (Greenley & Kirk 1973).

As a general rule, boundary control is highest in for-profit organizations, where the primary goal is making a profit, and lowest in governmental organizations, which are intended to provide the "safety net" for clients who cannot obtain services elsewhere. However, during the 1980s the policies of the Reagan administration concentrated on accelerating an existing trend toward shifting a greater burden of services to the private sector. The presumption was that private sector organizations could provide services more efficiently and effectively than large governmental bureaucracies, and that, in the case of nonprofit organizations, they could also draw on their traditional commitments to the poor to ensure that these clients were served.

Unfortunately, a number of studies suggest that this trend has often led to service reductions or restrictions, particularly on the part of nonprofit agencies. Among the reasons for these cutbacks have been changes in governmental rules (Berg & Wright 1981) and delays in reimbursement for contract services (Kramer & Grossman 1987). Gronbjerg (1990) studied the effects of changing governmental policies on nonprofit agencies in the Chicago area. She argues that services often diminished because these policies misunderstood the nature of the private sector, noting:

> . . . these [policies] were unrealistic because only a few nonprofit organizations focus on the poor and their problems, and relatively few made significant efforts to move in that direction during the early to mid-1980s. . . . Nonprofit organizations are not as responsive to the poor as public stereotypes might suggest, probably because they have enough to do without focusing on the poor and their difficult problems. . . . [The policies] falsely assumed that nonprofit organizations have a strong commitment to the poor that is independent of the incentives provided by government funding. (pp. 228–29)

The important point is that human service agencies adjust their boundaries according to a wide range of factors, and a misunderstanding of these may lead to critical service gaps. One key criterion in boundary setting is the nature of the clients themselves, and being poor or having numerous problems are characteristics that simultaneously increase the level of need yet, ironically, decrease the likelihood of being served.

Task 6: Observe Relationships with Resource Sources.   Questions to be asked:

- How are the relationships between funding sources and organizational leaders?
- How does the organization use and work with volunteers?
- How are the relationships between various constituencies and organizational members?
- What types of changes have recently affected the organization, particularly in the area of access to resources?

The dynamics of client selection can be better understood in terms of the resource dependence model described earlier. As we noted, the resource dependence model posits that external bodies upon which an organization depends for vital resources are often more powerful determinants of organizational actions than internal factors (Pfeffer & Salancik 1978). Within this model, clients can be seen as simply one of a variety of resources for which agencies contend. As a result, actions that may be detrimental to client services when viewed from the perspective of an agency's service mission become less puzzling (though not necessarily less problematic) when viewed from a resource dependence perspective.

Cash funding remains the most important of all resources, and the extent and consequences of external control are affected both by the source of funds and the circumstances of the agency acquiring them. For example, Hardina (1990) studied the funding base of fifty-three organizations to determine the impact on client involvement and access to service of the agencies' relative reliance on various sources. Her results showed that agencies restricted to grassroots funding (primarily local donations) were less able than those who drew funds from outside the community to establish and maintain reliable service availability. In general, the greater the variety of funding, the greater the fiscal health and service flexibility of the organization. The exception was government funds, which were found to limit service flexibility and client self-help, stiffen eligibility requirements, and reduce citizen participation.

Wardell (1988) developed a set of four propositions embodying the dynamics of both resource dependency and domain setting in his study of Youth Advocate Programs in Pennsylvania:

1. An organization's survival is a function of its ability to learn and adapt to changing environmental contingencies.
2. The degree of a focal organization's dependence on some element of its task environment is (1) directly related to the focal organization's need for

resources or legitimation which that element can provide, and (2) inversely related to the ability of other elements to provide the same resource or legitimation.

3. Organizations which are perceived as threatening to an existing organizational configuration and institutional thought structure in a local setting will evoke defensive reactions by established local organizations.

4. The persistence (or survival) of a focal organization over time is directly related to the degree of formalization it attains in exchange agreements with other organizations constituting its task environment. (pp. 92–3)

Task 7: Observe Relationships with Competitors.   Questions to be asked:

- What other agencies provide the same services to the same clientele as this organization?
- Are there mechanisms for interagency cooperation and are they used?
- With whom does the organization compete?
- With whom does the organization cooperate? Are there relationships formal or informal (e.g., is the organization part of a coalition or an alliance)?

One further element of the environment that also plays a role in these dynamics is other service providers. Relationships between agencies within each others' task environments can be competitive, cooperative, or a mixture of the two, depending on the circumstances.

In Chapter 5, Figure 5.3 delineated five levels of interaction leading to improved programming. These levels were communication, cooperation, coordination, collaboration, and confederation. These levels can be used to assess how a human service organization relates to other members of its task environment.

Competitive relationships characterize circumstances in which two or more agencies seek the same resources (clients, funds, volunteers, etc.) from the same sources. Increasingly, this competition takes place between nonprofit and for-profit agencies for fee-for-service and contract-eligible clients. More specific to nonprofit agencies is also competition for charitable donations and for government and private foundation grants. For example, McMurtry et al. (1991), found that nonprofit agencies reported competition for both funds and clients to have risen during the previous three years, with the greatest source of competition being other nonprofit organizations rather than for-profit agencies.

Competition is not the exclusive rule of thumb, however. Cooperative arrangements are also common, as in the case of referral agreements between agencies, which are used as a means of exchanging clients that do not fit the referring agency but are considered resources by the agency to whom they are referred. More generally, agencies have also developed more large-scale coalition-building efforts designed to improve their ability to advocate for particular client needs (Weisner 1983). Others have developed community-oriented cooperative arrangements to ensure more complete service coverage within particular areas (Merritt & Neugeboren 1990). Factors contributing to this behavior include community awareness of service needs, resource scarcity, and the capacity of local governments to coordinate these arrangements.

The dynamics of relationships between agencies and their funding sources, clients, and competitors follow closely the principals of resource dependence and domain legitimation summarized in Wardell's propositions outlined above. These, in turn, can be phrased in the form of questions that we have posed after each task.

Focus C: Analyzing the Organization

Analysis of organizations, like analysis of communities, requires a breakdown of a large, complex entity into elements. The objective is to be able to identify the points or locations within the organization that help to explain organizational strengths and to understand its weaknesses or problem areas. In examining each element, the objective is to determine its relative health or strength, to understand how it relates (or does not relate) to the current problem, and to understand how interactions between and among elements support (or fail to support) the continuation of the problem.

For an illustration of organizational analysis, let us return to the examples of the Canyon County Department of Child Welfare and Lakeside Family Services Agency used at the beginning of this chapter. When an organization such as Canyon is experiencing problems in productivity, in quality of client service—in morale, and in worker-management relationships—it is not unusual that the county board of supervisors would hire a management consultant to do an analysis of the department. Similarly, in a nonprofit organization that has become more professional, has become dependent upon government funds, whose mission has evolved, and which is now experiencing cutbacks in funding, a consultant is often hired to analyze the organization and the strategies needed to become economically self-sufficient.

It is possible that consultants, after interviewing representative staff, consumers, board members, and others would be able to document all the problems identified above, would pose some reasons for existence of the problems (working hypotheses), and would recommend some solutions. Using such an approach, consultants are often misled into recommending short-term solutions such as staff development and training, morale building activities such as social events, relationship building activities between management and staff, attempts to humanize the chief executive officer, and other such activities. These kinds of undertakings rarely solve the kinds of fundamental problems that necessitated the use of a management consultant in the first place.

An alternative approach to organizational analysis would be to conduct a systematic examination of a number of organizational elements. These elements might include: (1) organizational mission; (2) organizational structure, including location, management, staffing and workload of programs and services; (3) goals and objectives of programs; (4) adequacy of funding; (5) personnel policies and practices; (6) management style; (7) problem solving and communication patterns; and other such elements.

Within each element one could examine ideal models or optimal levels of functioning as illustrated in current theoretical or research literature. From the ideal, one would then move to an examination of data and documentation that depict the actual situation, and finally to an examination of the gaps between ideal and real. The attempt is to put one's finger on the underlying cause(s) as precisely as possible in the interest of solving long-term problems and avoiding dealing merely with symptoms.

In this section we propose a framework for analysis that identifies elements to be examined within the organization, that explores relevant theoretical frameworks, that identifies the questions to be answered, and that proposes data and documentation to be collected or examined.

The elements to be examined include:

1. Corporate Authority and Mission
2. Organizational Structure
3. Organizational Administration, Management, and Leadership
4. Organizational Culture
5. Planning, Delivery, and Evaluation of Programs and Services
6. Technology
7. Personnel Policies and Practices
8. Community Relations
9. Financial Management
10. Facilities, Equipment, and Resources

Task 8: Identify Corporate Authority and Mission. Questions to be asked:

- Is the organization operating in a manner that is consistent with its mission and authority?
- To what extent is the mission supported by staff who perform different roles within the organization?
- Are policies and procedures consistent with mission and authority?

Basic to understanding any organization is understanding its domain, as described earlier in this chapter. A statement of mission establishes the problems to be addressed and the populations to be served. Mission statements are relatively permanent expressions of the reason for existence of an organization, and they are not expected to change unless the fundamental reason for existence of the organization changes. Lack of clarity in a mission statement or differences between mission and organizational activity can be indicators of problem areas. For example, Lakeside Family Services is a prime candidate for reexamining its original mission established in the early 1900s when the agency was an orphanage. If this organization has not revised its mission, then it may find that its stated reason for existence does not accurately reflect what it actually does. Rethinking the mission and what the organization wants to be may begin the process of redirecting the agency.

Peters and Waterman (1984) are unequivocal in their commitment to the notion of shared vision as integral to the success of an organization. Without some common understanding of mission and direction there will inevitably be individuals and groups working at cross purposes. With a shared vision, there may still be differences about strategies, but there will be commitment to the same ends or outcomes.

Examining corporate authority involves an attempt to understand the legal basis on which the organization operates. If the organization is public (governmental), the legal basis is in statute or executive order. If it is not public, the legal basis is in articles of incorporation. In some situations it can be important to examine these documents firsthand rather than accept secondary interpretations. There have been instances where organizations are incorporated for one purpose, and perhaps even funded through a trust that specifies that purpose, such as the running of an orphanage. This was the case for Lakeside Family Services. Over the years new populations and services were added to the mission, such as services to pregnant teens. It is possible that such expansion can reach the point where an agency is operating outside of its legally authorized area.

Some of the more important documentation and data sources to be examined in understanding corporate authority and mission might include:

1. Articles of incorporation, statutes, or executive orders;
2. Mission statement;
3. Relevant policies and procedures;
4. Minutes of selected board meetings;
5. Interviews with selected administrators, managers, and staff.

Task 9: Understand Organizational Structure.   Questions to be asked:

- What is the organizing theme for the basic organizational structure (e.g., bureaucratic, organized around programs, organized around professional disciplines, alternative or nontraditional, etc.)?
- Is this the most logical structure? Is it consistent with and supportive of the mission?
- Are staff clear about reporting lines and accountability?
- Is supervision logical and capable of performing expected functions?
- Is there an informal organization (people who carry authority because they are respected by staff, and thus exert influence outside those in formally designated positions)?
- Are there clear distinctions between staff and line functions?

When we think of organizational structure we tend to think of an organizational chart with boxes and lines indicating a hierarchy from the highest level down through entry-level positions. The chart helps with understanding who reports to whom, who is responsible for what divisions of the organization, and how the chain of command proceeds from bottom to top.

This system, of course, is patterned after the bureaucratic model described by Weber (1946). This model of organizational structure is used widely because it is easy to understand and apply, it insures that everyone has one and only one supervisor, and it provides for lines of communication, exercise of authority, performance evaluation, discipline, and the many other functions which are necessary to the running of an organization.

However, there are many critics of bureaucracy, and many who believe that it is not the best structure for human service agencies for a number of reasons. Critics argue that bureaucratic structure causes problems in human service organizations because such standardized techniques work well only in predictable circumstances, whereas individual clients and their problems are quite unique. Rules that govern the production process in manufacturing enterprises, for example, may be helpful in ensuring consistent quality of the product, but in a human service organization these rules may serve only to constrain workers' ability to exercise professional judgment.

A number of terms have been used to describe the dysfunctions of bureaucracies. Merton (1952) uses the term "learned incompetence" to signify the performance of employees who rely so heavily on a policy manual to make their decisions that they are unable to think logically or creatively about the problems clients bring to the agency.

Lipsky (1984) uses the term *bureaucratic disentitlement* to describe situations in which clients fail to receive benefits or services to which they are entitled due to decisions that are based on internal organizational considerations rather than service needs. Hasenfeld (1983) calls attention to *goal displacement,* which describes the tendency of organizations to lose sight of organizational mission and goals, and to focus on the concerns of units and subunits within the organization. Still, Etzioni (1964) argues that bureaucratic structure both persists and expands because its highly rational approach to structuring complex systems leads to greater efficiency and predictability.

Contingency theorists, in addressing the question of what organizational structure is best, contend that it depends on what it is that the organization is expected to produce. Morse and Lorsch (1970) demonstrated that higher productivity in one type of organization (a container manufacturing plant) was achieved through a traditional structure with clearly defined roles, responsibilities, and lines of supervision. Another type of organization (a research lab) achieved higher productivity through a very loose structure which allowed researchers maximum flexibility to carry out their own work unfettered by rules, regulations, and supervision.

Alternative organizations that focus on the need for social change require a very different structure than do large public organizations. Although these non-traditional agencies do not always survive or eventually become more traditional as they grow and develop, they offer new and different ways of approaching organizational structure. Focusing heavily on process and charismatic leadership, many alternative agencies are formed in response to a service delivery system that is often perceived as dehumanizing for both clients and staff (Perlmutter 1988).

Miles (1975) proposes several alternatives to bureaucratic structure. One option, adapted from the work of Likert (1961), is called a *linking-pin structure.* In this type of organization, rigid lines of reporting and one-to-one relationships are abandoned in favor of placing an emphasis on work units. One or more persons within a work unit are then selected to play a linking role to other work units where collaboration is important. By serving as a fully functioning participant in both units, the person(s) in the linking role are able to facilitate better communication and working relationships than are possible through the traditional structure.

Another option is *matrix structure,* where supervision is assigned to a function rather than to a person. Under this type of structure, staff are likely to have more than one supervisor, and constant communication is a necessity. A matrix management structure might be used in a ward of a mental hospital, where supervision for the activities of the ward falls to one person, while supervision of professional functioning and performance evaluation falls to another person.

Still another structure is the *project team structure,* where teams working on the same effort take responsibility for different functions and work relatively independently. For example, in starting up a community project, one team might conduct a needs assessment, another explore funding, another handle incorporation responsibilities, and another secure a facility. Work is coordinated by a committee of team leaders to insure that the project teams are headed in the same direction and that their efforts are oriented toward a common end.

A final structural option proposed by Miles is the *collegial structure.* In this type of organization, individual professionals operate relatively independently and come together only in circumstances where their work overlaps. A medical clinic would be a good example. Five physicians may collaborate on the purchase of a building and equipment and the hiring of receptionists and nursing staff. No single individual has more authority than any other. Each generates her or his own income. Each operates as an entrepreneur, except in situations where the functioning of the organization requires overlap.

Probably no single organizational structure could be said to be superior to another as applied to the field of human services. For large public agencies, some type of bureaucratic structure will probably be required because of sheer size and accountability considerations. For a small, community-based agency, a collegial model may work very effectively. Much will depend on the mission, purpose, and goals of the organization, the services provided, and the expectations for accountability.

Documentation and data to be examined in order to understand organizational structure might include:

1. Organizational chart;
2. Policy manuals indicating job descriptions and responsibilities; and
3. Interviews with selected administrators, managers staff, and volunteers.

Task 10: Understand Administration, Management, and Leadership. Questions to be asked:

- How is the workplace organized and work allocated?
- Is appropriate authority passed on along with responsibility?

- How close is supervision and what, exactly, is supervised? Is it tasks, or is it functions, or is it the employee, depending on need?

- How are people treated in the workplace, including the very lowest level employees?

- Do employees feel valued at every level? Do they believe they are making a contribution to the success of the organization?

- How are decisions made? Is information solicited from those affected? Is it used? Are there individuals or units within the organization that are left out of decision making? If so, why?

- How is conflict handled?

A wealth of literature exists concerning the approaches to administration, management, and leadership. Miles (1975) classifies managerial theories or models into one of three categories: (1) the *traditional model,* (2) the *human relations model,* and (3) the *human resources model.*

The traditional model is characterized by very close supervision of work, control of subordinates, breaking work down into simple tasks that are easily learned, and establishing detailed work routines. Assumptions are that people inherently dislike work, that they are not self-motivated or self-directed, and that they only do it because they need the money. The traditional model would include such theorists as Weber, Taylor, and others committed to the basic tenets of bureaucracy or scientific management (as discussed in Chapter 6).

The human relations model is characterized by efforts on the part of management to make each worker feel useful and important. Management is open to feedback, and subordinates are allowed to exercise some self-direction on routine matters. Assumptions are that people want to feel useful and important, that they have a need to belong, and that these needs are more important than money in motivating people to work. Theories that support the human relations model would include Mayo's human relations theory, as well as many of the theorists who expanded on Mayo's work and focused on motivation.

The human resources model is characterized by a focus on the use of untapped resources that exist within employees. The manager is expected to create an environment in which all members may contribute to the limits of their abilities. Full participation is encouraged on all matters, and self-direction and self-control are supported and promoted. Assumptions are that work means a great deal more than merely earning a paycheck. It is an important part of people's lives, and they want to contribute to the success of the total work effort. Furthermore, people are assumed to be creative, resourceful, and capable of contributing a great deal more when they are unrestricted by the constraints of the traditional or the human relations models. The theories that support the human resources model are drawn essentially from the work on contingency theory (Burns & Stalker 1961) and well supported by a number of contemporary authors (Peters & Waterman 1984).

This philosophy of management is important to understand because it affects so many facets of organizational life. It can affect, for example, whether adult protective service workers are allowed merely to collect facts from a battered elderly person and then turn to a supervisor who will direct the next steps, or whether they are allowed to use professional judgment to intervene as they see fit.

Some of the more important documents and data sources to be examined to understand organizational administration, management, and leadership might include:

1. Job description of the chief executive officer (CEO) and other staff in positions of leadership;
2. Interviews with board members (if the agency is private) or the person to whom the CEO is accountable (if the agency is public) to determine their expectations of the CEO;
3. Criteria used for performance evaluation of the CEO and other staff in positions of leadership;
4. Interview with the CEO to determine expectations for other staff in positions of leadership;
5. Organizational chart;
6. Interviews with staff in various roles to determine perceptions about the job, the workplace, supervision, and administration.

Task 11: Recognize the Organization's Culture.   Questions to be asked:

- How would one begin to describe the organization's culture?
- What are the organization's artifacts and creations?
- What are the organization's stated values and what is actually valued within the organization?
- How do leaders within the organization influence organizational values and assumptions?
- What are the taken-for-granted patterns within this organization?
- Is behavior consistent with culture?
- Are there minorities or others who feel left out of the accepted organizational culture?

In Chapter 6, we touched upon the concept of organizational culture and its importance in contemporary thinking about how organizations behave and function. Most people have experienced the uncertainty of entering an unfamiliar organization and immediately sensed dynamics that are not easily interpreted. For example, a social work intern described her feelings about entering a particular nursing home for the first time. She stated that she did "not feel good about it" but when questioned about what that meant, she was at a loss of words to describe why she felt this way. Thinking that this student might not be familiar with nursing-home settings, her instructor asked about her previous experience. The student had been to many nursing homes, but this one was upsetting to her. Several weeks later she was able to identify reasons for her concern. The nursing home's odor, the observed interactions between staff and residents, the receptionist's lack of interest in greeting visitors, the arrangement of furniture in the lobby which was not conducive to interaction, the fact that residents were lined up in hallways, and the staff's discouragement of residents who wanted to bring personal possessions into the home were problematic for her. These elements began to paint a picture of an organization that did not fully value its residents, staff, or visitors.

Having completed tasks 8 through 10, one begins to gain a sense of the organizational culture. Fully understanding the culture requires intensive and long-term observation, but a beginning "sense" of the organization can still be gained at this point in the analytical process. Also, for the social worker who is just entering a new organization there is great opportunity. Using oneself as an instrument to experience what is happening means that the beginning practitioner may identify patterns that seasoned staff take for granted and perform without even considering the implications. Observing interactions will tell much about how clients, staff, and volunteers are valued. Seeing what artifacts are displayed (e.g., publications, documents, mission statements, pictures, political or religious symbols, etc.) will tell much about what is important to the organization and what clients first see when they enter this setting. Listening for comments that express values and feelings will add insight. We encourage the social worker to observe and study all these things as the analysis continues.

It is also important to recognize that professed culture may be different from actual day-to-day behavior. For example, an agency's statement of philosophy may say that creativity is valued in this organization, yet the social worker observes that staff who come up with new ideas are not heard. Similarly, a human service manager may be a member of NASW and say she is committed to the code of ethics in which primary responsibility is toward one's clients. However, in practice, this same manager may ask staff to recruit fee-paying clients rather than focus their efforts on the poorest of the poor. Just because mission and philosophy statements profess certain cultural attributes does not mean that they will be exemplified in what happens within the organization. The norms and beliefs that emerge in dealing with these types of value conflicts are important elements of organizational culture. Oftentimes, they are so much a pattern within the organization that they are difficult to uncover and to understand.

Some of the more important documents and data sources to be examined to understand organizational culture include:

1. Pictures, documents, plaques, and symbols on agency walls and in display cases;
2. Observations of interactions (both verbal and nonverbal) between staff members; between staff and clients; and between staff, clients, and volunteers;
3. Arrangement and location of office space, lobby areas, common areas, furniture, and provisions for privacy;
4. Discussions with staff regarding what is valued in the organization;
5. Observation of leadership style and what values are expressed (both verbally and through actions) by organizational leaders;

6. Board minutes and other documents in which value conflicts are discussed and decisions are made.
7. Grievance procedures, both formal and informal.

Task 12: Assess the Organization's Programs and Services.   Questions to be asked:

• What programs are offered? What services are offered within each program? Are the services consistent with the goals and objectives of the program?

• Is there a common understanding among management and line staff within each program about problems to be addressed, populations to be served, services to be provided, and outcomes to be achieved?

• Are staffing patterns appropriate to the services to be provided? Are any staff over or under qualified? Are workload expectations reasonable given expectations for achievement with each client and within each service and program? Is consideration given to cultural and racial understanding of workers and clients?

• What data is collected on clients and how is it used?

• What evaluative information is expected from the evaluation plan? Is there a plan to gather information about clients and the extent of improvement at the point of termination and in a follow-up survey or interview? Is there an effort to determine level of client satisfaction with services? What do the findings reveal to date?

Some of the central questions for all human service organizations in the 1990s and beyond include: (1) Are the programs and services offered effective in terms of resolving the problems they are funded to address? (2) Are clients any better off after coming to this organization than they were before they came? (3) If services are effective, are clients being served at the lowest possible cost without reducing the level of effectiveness?

These questions need to be dealt with in the context of understanding what goes into the planning, delivery, and evaluation of programs. A complete program should include a problem analysis, goals and objectives, program and service design, a data collection and management information system, and a plan for evaluation (Kettner et al. 1990).

Each program should be based on a clear understanding of the problems it is intended to address and the populations it is intended to serve. It is not unusual to find that in some longstanding programs there has been a shift in emphasis over the years. For example, a program that was designed to keep families together may, over time, shift emphasis to protecting the children, then to protecting the rights of the parents, and finally to insuring legal soundness of all actions. Each of these emphases requires a different analysis of the problem and population served, different resources, different patterns of staffing, and clearly different ways of evaluating effectiveness.

Some of the more important documents and data sources to be examined to understand the planning, delivery, and evaluation of programs and services might include:

1. Program plans;
2. Organizational charts;
3. Roster of staff and job descriptions;
4. Annual reports of programs and services;
5. Needs assessment surveys;
6. Evaluation findings, including client satisfaction surveys;
7. Case records.

Task 13: Assess Organizational Technology.   Questions to be asked:

• What are the job expectations for each level of staff within the organization? What background education and experience is required to perform these jobs? Do those who hold these jobs have the appropriate credentials?

• Are staff members performing competently in their positions? Are they meeting expectations? Are they effective (do they get good results) in working with clients?

• Is each discipline supervised and evaluated by someone with appropriate knowledge, values, skills, and professional identification?

• In what ways are various units representing different disciplines (e.g., social work, psychology, medical, data processing, etc.) linked with each other for the purposes of collaboration and communication?

The issue of technology is an important one for organizational and program analysis in the field of human services. The field encompasses a wide range of specializations including, but not limited to, such services as mental health, drugs and alcohol, developmental disabilities, child welfare, services to the aging, residential treatment for a variety of populations, adult and juvenile corrections, services to special populations, and many others.

Each organization providing service within these fields employs people from a wide variety of disciplines for direct services to clients. These may include social work, counseling, psychology, child care, nursing and other health professions, education, and others. Support services may be provided by people from such fields as accounting, management, public relations, fund raising.

The important issue in examining technology is the organization's standards governing the job expectations, hiring, performance, supervision, and evaluation of that technology. What, for example, are the educational requirements for each position? Does the organization adhere to these requirements? What experience is required? What licenses or certifications are necessary?

In the early work on technology, both Taylor (1947) and Weber (1946) emphasized the importance of clearly defined job expectations, workers who were well-prepared to perform expected functions, supervision, performance evaluation, and feedback to improve performance. Taylor, of course, focused his efforts on what would be considered essentially assembly-line technologies. Weber's work is more applicable to the definition, supervision, and evaluation of professional functions.

Miles (1975) refers to this issue as job design. He points out that in organizations where the prevailing management philosophy comes from the traditional model, jobs are designed in a manner that permits only the carrying out of routine physical and mental tasks. Sometimes this type of job design is appropriate when the work is something like forms completion or data processing. When complex professional responsibilities are assigned and the staff member has professional training, however, and is allowed to perform only routine tasks, conflicts will eventually emerge.

Operating under a human relations philosophy, while it sounds more employee-oriented, can be deceptive. Constraints are often the same as those under the traditional model. The only differences are that a concern is expressed for the human needs of the employee, such as the desire for self-esteem. Teamwork may be emphasized in order to support employee needs for belonging, but the fundamental approach to job design is still carrying out routine physical and mental tasks.

Job design under the human resources model is more complex. In this type of an organization, employees are involved with management in joint goal setting. Work is performed under conditions of self-direction and self-control. Data and information generated about individual performance and program performance are shared with the employee in the interest of promoting professional growth and development. This type of job design, while ideal for the experienced employee with professional education, may be inappropriate for positions where the job requires more task definition and supervision.

Some of the more important documentation and data sources to be examined might include:

1. Job descriptions;
2. Relevant policy and procedure manuals;
3. Evaluation reports;
4. Case records;
5. Interviews with representatives of each discipline.

Task 14: Evaluate Personnel Policies and Procedures. Questions to be asked:

- How diverse is the workforce? Are differences valued in this organization?
- How do managers and administrators view staff? As people who carry out tasks? As members of teams or units? As creative problem solvers who have an important stake in organizational success?
- What formal and informal criteria are used for evaluating performance?

- What kinds of behaviors does the organization reward?
- What is the organization's philosophy and policy about staff development and training? What resources are invested in it?
- How attractive are wages, hours, working conditions, and fringe benefits? How attractive is the facility and the work environment?
- What are the affirmative action policies and how are they implemented?
- To what extent does the organization groom people for higher level positions, and to what extent do they promote from within?

Most organizations go to great lengths to insure that their equipment will be in good working order. They purchase maintenance contracts for their photocopy machines, computers, printers, vehicles, and anything else that needs to be in good running order. Unfortunately, not all organizations invest the same level of concern or resources in their employees. And yet employees have a variety of needs to be met if they are to function at their optimal levels of productivity.

The pioneering work on understanding and nurturing employees' human needs was done by human relations theorists (as discussed in Chapter 6) and by other theorists such as Maslow (1943). The human relations school discovered that the way management treats employees and the sense of loyalty and identification employees feel with the organization can be important factors in determining levels of productivity. Maslow was helpful in pointing out that human needs are not all the same for all employees at all times; that needs change and become more complex, higher level needs as those at lower levels are met and satisfied.

Miles (1975) examines employee motivation and its relationship to reward systems in the context of the traditional model, the human relations model, and the human resources model. Under the traditional model, the prime purpose of rewards is to attract and hold a stable, predictable work force. Wages and working conditions are designed to attract job applicants and fringe benefits are designed to hold employees. This approach tends to produce very conservative, non-risk-taking behaviors, and leads to low productivity. Supervisors generally have very little discretion to allocate anything other than small rewards within their own units.

Under human relations management, symbolic recognition tends to flourish. Five-year pins, employee of the month, and other such symbols are used as awards, generally by managers and administrators in accordance with their own criteria. There may be some attention to staff development and training, but sending employees to workshops and conferences tends to be seen as a benefit bestowed by the organization, as a reward for loyalty and performance, rather than something that is fundamental to capable and competent functioning on the job.

Under a human resources approach to management, the manager's key task is to facilitate employee performance by removing barriers and allowing the employee to achieve the highest possible levels of excellence. Barriers may include lack of adequate job-related knowledge. In these cases, staff development and training would be considered as necessary to the achievement of optimal performance. Motivation is believed to emanate from job satisfaction, and rewards are tied to creativity, initiative, and high levels of performance.

As mentioned in Chapter 6, managing diversity is an important theme of the 1990s. Thomas (1991) explains that "managing diversity is a comprehensive managerial process for developing an environment that works for all employees" (p. 10). In analyzing any human service organization, the practitioner will want to examine how diversity is handled. Is there a clear effort to value gender, racial, ethnic, sexual preference, lifestyle, and other types of diversity within the organization? Is there a focus on empowerment of staff and volunteers that work toward removing the barriers referred to in the human resources approach to management?

Some of the more important documentation and data sources to be examined in order to understand personnel policies and practices might include:

1. Manual of personnel policies and procedures;
2. Personnel records;
3. Job descriptions and recruitment brochures;
4. Statistics on absenteeism, turnover, usage of sick leave;
5. Grievances and complaints filed with the personnel officer;
6. Affirmative Action/Equal Employment Opportunity plans and documents;
7. Performance evaluation forms;
8. Interviews with representative staff who perform different roles.

Task 15: Recognize How the Organization Deals with Community Relations. Questions to be asked:

- Is there a clearly defined public image, and is there a strategy for communicating this image to the public? What kinds of resources, including funding, does the organization invest in promoting its public image?
- What is the reputation of the agency, its programs and services, its board, executive, management, and line staff with the general public, other agencies, funding sources, clients, and other relevant constituencies such as minority communities?
- Do the agency's facilities and published materials contribute to its desired public image?
- Does the agency respond when needed by other community agencies for political activities, fund raising, dealing with community social problems, or other issues?

In the field of human services, the issue of community relations is approached a bit differently than in other fields. In for-profit, commercial enterprises, for example, overriding considerations have to do with attracting and keeping customers in a highly competitive environment. Human service systems, in communities all over the country, are becoming highly complex networks of public, private not-for-profit, and private for-profit organizations that are interdependent in many ways. When federal or state funding is reduced, it is not a matter of concern only to public agencies. Private agencies are also affected through their contracting relationships. When insurance companies refuse to cover family counseling or individual therapy, it is not a matter of concern only to private agencies. Budget shortfalls and the continued viability of private agencies is of great concern to state and county human service agencies as well.

Community relations, then, for human service organizations, often requires a multifaceted approach. For agencies and programs that need to attract clients, it is important that there be a public relations and publicity strategy. The public should be informed of organizational purpose and mission, the services they provide should be made clear, and staff competence and credentials need to be publicized.

A human service organization cannot forget, however, that they are a part of a communitywide system. As such, credibility with colleagues, with referral sources, and with government contracting agencies is critical. In many communities there is an expectation that agency personnel will participate in community-planning efforts to achieve interagency cooperation. When funding is threatened and lobbying efforts are needed, it is expected that the agency director, board members, and staff will become involved. When fund-raising efforts such as United Way and other campaigns are undertaken, agency participation is again expected.

In all cases, it is prudent for agencies to establish policies and procedures for communicating to the news media and other agency publics about the work of the agency. Accurate and timely information distributed to the news media will often protect the agency from undue loss of public esteem and ultimately from loss of valuable financial resources.

For an understanding of the importance of good community relations from a theoretical perspective, we turn again to the work of James Thompson (1967). Probably his most valuable contribution to the understanding of organizational community relations is his emphasis on the importance of organizational environment. While most theories focus on internal functioning, Thompson makes it clear that organizations are parts of systems and, as such, are interdependent with other organizations and with consumers. In human services, where funding is so heavily interdependent on community, state and federal sources, this is especially true.

This is why the first six tasks in this chapter dealt with the organization's environment. At this point, it is important to analyze how the organization seeks to enrich and nurture its relationships with community constituents and what mechanisms are in place to do so.

Some of the more important documentation and data sources for understanding agency/community relations might include:

1. Publicity materials;
2. Newspaper articles;
3. Client satisfaction surveys;

4. Relevant policies and procedures;
5. Interviews or surveys of clients and other community agency personnel.

The final two categories of (1) financial management and accountability and (2) facilities, equipment, computer utilization and records management really have very little support from the major organizational and management theories cited above. Yet, they are important enough to organizational health and strength that they should not be ignored as elements to be examined in any good organizational analysis. Consequently, we will discuss these two elements, but will not attempt to relate them to the theoretical frameworks discussed in Chapter 6.

Task 16: Recognize Methods of Financial Management and Accountability.   Questions to be asked:

- Is the budget prepared in accordance with accepted standards of accounting and financial reporting? Are annual audits conducted?

- Are program staff involved in a meaningful way in preparing the budget, and do they get useful feedback about expenditures and unit costs during the year? Do program staff use budget data as a measure by which they attempt to improve efficiency?

- Do resources appear to be adequate to achieve stated program goals and objectives?

- What are the major sources of revenue for the organization? What demands and restrictions does each funding source place on the organization and its programs?

Budgeting and budget management is often an activity left to upper administration and treated as though line staff, first-line supervisors, and other people involved in service delivery need not be involved. Good financial management practices, quite to the contrary, involve all levels of staff. Fiscal soundness and budgeting practices affect programs and services in a very profound way. To put it simply, organizations cannot run without money. Yet, good financial management practices would dictate that programs and services drive the budget, not the other way around.

For many years human service agencies were limited to a very simplified type of budgeting called *line-item budgeting.* This involved identification of expenditure categories and estimating the number of dollars that would be needed to cover all expenses in each category for one year. Categories typically included personnel, operating expenses such as rent, utilities, supplies, travel, and other such items.

In the more recent literature, more sophisticated budgeting techniques have been developed for application to human service agencies (Lohmann 1980; Kettner et al. 1990). These techniques, referred to as functional budgeting and program budgeting, are based on program planning and budgeting systems (PPBS) (Lee & Johnson 1973). Both approaches to budgeting operate within the conceptual framework of programs. Both produce cost and expenditure data in relation to programs rather than in relation to the entire agency. Functional and program budgeting techniques produce such data as total program costs, cost per unit of service, cost per output (client completion of program or service), and cost per outcome (the cost of producing measurable change in a client's quality of life).

This data become increasingly important in an environment of increasing competition for scarce and diminishing resources. In the same manner that individuals shop for the best buy with their own personal purchases, government contracting agencies—in competitive environments—shop for the lowest unit cost. Organizations that do not have the type of budgeting system or data base that permits calculation of unit costs increasingly find themselves at a distinct disadvantage in a competitive market.

Some of the more important documentation and data sources to be examined in order to understand the approach to financial management and accountability might include:

1. Annual reports;
2. Audit reports;
3. A cost allocation plan;
4. Program goals and objectives;
5. Communitywide comparative studies of unit costs;
6. Interviews with all levels of program staff.

Task 17: Assess Facilities, Equipment, Computer Utilization, and Records Management. Questions to be asked:

- Do employees feel that they have enough space? Is the physical work environment attractive and conducive to high productivity?

- Have problems been identified with current facilities and equipment? Is there a plan to address the problems and to fund solutions?

- Are there conditions related to facilities or equipment that appear to act as barriers to productivity or work flow?

- Is the agency able to produce data that will answer important questions about clients, programs, and services? Does the agency have a computerized record-keeping and management information system that includes client data?

Considerations in the areas of facilities include adequacy of space, physical condition and maintenance of facilities, and geographical location of agency and branches. The important points are that offices and work space allotted to personnel are suited to the needs and resources of the agency and provide as pleasant a work environment as possible for staff. Plans for renovation and expansion should be in place and appropriate to reasonable expectations for growth.

Equipment analysis should include an assessment of all mechanical, electrical, and other fixed building equipment to insure compliance with health and safety codes, and adequacy to serve the needs of staff for proper work flow without disruption. Agencies that use computers only for word processing and billing, with no plans to build and maintain a client data system, are in jeopardy of becoming obsolete very quickly as demands for data outstrip their ability to compile data and information by hand.

The type of client records kept is often determined by the reporting requirements of funding sources. However, agencies that collect only the data necessary to satisfy the demands of funding sources are limiting their ability to make good use of client, program, and funding data to improve the quality of services and the efficiency of agency operations. A management information system that incorporates data about clients, services provided, evaluation of services, cost of services, and other such relevant data is invaluable in this era of data-based decision making. Software is available that will permit aggregation of data by caseworker, by unit, by program, or by agency. The organization that builds such an information system is clearly in a position to compete successfully in the 1990s and beyond.

SUMMARY

The seventeen tasks in this chapter provide a beginning framework for analyzing a human service organization. We began with the agency's environment as a reminder that each organization exists within a larger community. In chapters 4 and 5 we explored the complex nature of community systems, and tasks 1 through 4 require the analyst to look explicitly at the unique combination of units that comprise a specific organization's defined community.

Tasks 5 through 7 require one to examine how the organization actually interacts with community elements. Patterns of interaction are explored with clients, sources from which resources are garnered, and competitors who provide the same or similar services. These dynamics are essential to understanding the politics of what happens between organizational and community actors.

The remaining tasks focus on the internal aspects of organizational functioning. It is our hope that the reader is aware of how multifaceted organizational analysis can be, given the number of tasks required to gain a beginning understanding of what occurs within one agency.

Once an organization is analyzed, the stage is set for identifying opportunities for change within that organization. Chapters 8 through 10 provide a model for approaching change in organizations and communities.

REFERENCES

Berg, W. E., and R. Wright. (1981) Goal displacement in social work programs. *Administration in Social Work, 20*: 25–39.

Brager, G., and S. Holloway. (1978) *Changing human service organizations: Politics and practice.* New York: Free Press.

Burns, T., and G. M. Stalker. (1961) *The management of innovation.* London: Tavistock.

Cloward, R. A., and I. Epstein. (1965) Private social welfare's disengagement from the poor. In M. N. Zald, ed., *Social welfare institutions* (pp. 623–44). New York: John Wiley & Sons.

Dill, W. R. (1958) Environment as an influence on managerial autonomy. *Administrative Science Quarterly, 2*(1): 409–43.

Etzioni, A. (1964) *Modern organizations.* Englewood Cliffs, NJ: Prentice-Hall.

Greenley, J. R., and S. A. Kirk. (1973) Organizational characteristics of agencies and the distribution of services to applicants. *Journal of Health and Social Behavior, 14*: 70–79.

Gronbjerg, K. A. (1990) Poverty and nonprofit organizations. *Social Service Review, 64*(2): 208–243.

Hardina, D. (1990) The effect of funding sources on client access to services. *Administration in Social Work, 14*(3): 33–46.

Hasenfeld, Y. (1983) *Human service organizations.* Englewood Cliffs, NJ: Prentice-Hall.

Hodgkinson, V. A., and M. S. Weitzman. (1989) *Dimensions of the independent sector: A statistical profile* (3rd ed.). Washington, DC: The Independent Sector.

Hodgkinson, V. A., M. S. Weitzman, and The Gallup Organization (1988) *Giving and volunteering in the United States.* Washington, DC: The Independent Sector.

Internal Revenue Service. (1991) *Statistics of Income—1988, Individual Income Tax Returns (Pub. 1304).* Washington, DC: Author.

Karger, H. J., and D. Stoesz. (1990) *American social welfare policy: A structural approach.* New York: Longman.

Kettner, P. M., R. M. Moroney, and L. L. Martin. (1990) *Designing and managing program: An effectiveness-based approach.* Newbury Park, CA: Sage.

Kirk, S. A., and J. R. Greenley. (1974) Denying or delivering services? *Social Work, 19*(4): 439–47.

Kramer, R., and B. Grossman. (1987) Contracting for social services. *Social Service Review, 61*(1): 32–55.

Lee, R. D., and R. W. Johnson. (1973) *Public budgeting systems.* Baltimore: University Park Press.

Levine, S., and P. E. White. (1961) Exchange as a conceptual framework for the study of interorganizational relationships. *Administrative Science Quarterly, 5* :583–601.

Likert, R. (1961) *New patterns of management.* New York: McGraw-Hill.

Lipsky, M. (1984) Bureaucratic disentitlement in social welfare programs. *Social Service Review, 58*(1): 3–27.

Lohmann, R. (1980) Financial management and social administration. In F. D. Perlmutter and S. Slavin, eds., *Leadership in social administration.* Philadelphia: Temple University Press.

Martin, P. Y. (1980) Multiple constituencies, dominant societal values, and the human service administrator. *Administration in Social Work, 4*(2): 15–27.

Maslow, A. (1943) A theory of motivation. *Psychological Review, 50*: 370–96.

McMurtry, S. L., F. E. Netting, and P. M. Kettner. (1991) How nonprofits adapt to a stringent environment. *Nonprofit Management and Leadership, 1*(3): 235–52.

Merritt, J., and B. Neugeboren. (1990) Factors affecting agency capacity for interorganizational coordination. *Administration in Social Work, 14*(4): 73–85.

Merton, R. K. (1952) Bureaucratic structure and personality. In R. K. Merton, A. P. Gray, B. Hockey, and H. C. Selvin, eds., *Reader in bureaucracy* (pp. 261–372). Glencoe, IL: Free Press.

Miles, R. E. (1975) *Theories of management: Implications for organizational behavior and development.* New York: McGraw-Hill.

Morse, J. J., and J. W. Lorsch. (1970) Beyond theory Y. *Harvard Business Review, 48*: 61–8.

Netting, F. E., S. L. McMurtry, P. M. Kettner, and S. Jones-McClintic. (1990) Privatization and its impact on nonprofit service providers. *Nonprofit and Voluntary Sector Quarterly, 19*(1): 33–46.

Perlmutter, F. D. (1988) *Alternative social agencies: Administrative strategies.* New York: Haworth Press.

Peters, T. J., and R. H. Waterman. (1984) *In search of excellence: Lessons from America's best-run companies.* New York: Harper & Row.

Pfeffer, J., and G. R. Salancik. (1978) *The external control of organizations: A resource dependent perspective.* New York: Harper & Row.

Stoesz, D. (1988) Human service corporations and the welfare state. *Society, 25*(5): 53–8.

Taylor, F. W. (1947) *Scientific management.* New York: Harper & Row.

Thomas, R. R. (1991) *Beyond race and gender.* New York: AMACOM.

Thompson, J. D. (1967) *Organizations in action.* New York: McGraw-Hill.

Wardell, P. J. (1988) The implications of changing interorganizational relationships and resource constraints for human services survival: A case study. *Administration in Social Work, 12*(1): 89–105.

Weber, M. (1946) *From Max Weber: Essays in sociology.* (H. H. Gerth and C. W. Mills, trans.) Oxford, England: Oxford University Press.

Weisner, S. (1983) Fighting back: A critical analysis of coalition building in the human services. *Social Service Review, 57*(2): 291–306.

Framework for Analyzing a Human Service Organization

FOCUS A: IDENTIFYING THE AGENCY'S TASK ENVIRONMENT

Task 1: Identify Funding Sources

- What are the agency's funding sources?
- How much and what percentage of funds are received from each source?
- Which funds are earmarked for certain programs or services and which are flexible?

Task 2: Identify Sources of Noncash Revenues

- Does the organization use volunteers? If yes, how many and for what purposes?
- What material resources (e.g., food, clothing, physical facilities, etc.) does the organization receive?
- What tax benefits does the organization receive?
- How important are noncash revenues to the organization's operation?

Task 3: Identify Clients and Client Sources

- What client groups does this organization serve?
- How many unduplicated clients are served by each program?
- How are client needs determined?
- Within each client group, how many (or what percentage) are able to pay? Contract eligible? Unable to pay (low-pay or no-pay)?
- What percentage of clients are ethnic/racial minorities, women, gays or lesbians, or members of other oppressed groups?
- How and by whom (i.e., self, family, provider) are clients referred to this organization?
- How and to which agencies does this organization refer clients?

Task 4: Identify Other Constituents

- What state and federal regulatory bodies oversee programs provided by this organization?
- What agencies contract with this organization for service delivery?

- What professional associations, labor unions, or accrediting bodies influence agency operations?
- Is this organization affiliated with or sponsored by religious, ethnic, or fraternal bodies?
- How does this organization define its "public," and what groups are part of this definition?

FOCUS B: RECOGNIZING THE DYNAMICS OF AGENCY/ENVIRONMENT RELATIONS

Task 5: Observe Relationships with Clients

- Has this organization targeted new or different clients within the last five years?
- What is the organization's domain (specifically, what types of clients does the organization serve)?
- Are these clients ones who bring resources to the agency or for whose services resources must be obtained elsewhere?
- Does the organization claim a larger domain than it serves, and are significant numbers of clients turned away?
- What types of clients does the organization refuse (e.g., are most of these the poorest or most troubled clients; are most of these minorities as opposed to nonminorities)? What happens to these clients?

Task 6: Observe Relationships with Resource Sources

- How good are the relationships between funding sources and organizational leaders?
- How does the organization use and work with volunteers?
- How good are the relationships between important external various constituencies and organizational members?
- What types of changes have recently affected the organization, particularly in the area of access to resources?

Task 7: Observe Relationships with Competitors

- What other agencies provide the same services to the same clientele as this organization?
- Are there mechanisms for interagency cooperation and are they used?
- With whom does the organization compete?
- With whom does the organization cooperate? Are these relationships formal or informal (e.g., is the organization part of a coalition or an alliance)?

FOCUS C: ANALYZING THE ORGANIZATION

Task 8: Identify Corporate Authority and Mission

- Is the organization operating in a manner that is consistent with its mission and authority?
- To what extent is the mission supported by staff who perform different roles within the organization?
- Are policies and procedures consistent with mission and authority?

Task 9: Understand Organizational Structure

- What is the organizing theme for the basic organizational structure (e.g., bureaucratic, organized around programs, organized around professional disciplines, alternative or nontraditional, etc.)?
- Is this the most logical structure? Is it consistent with and supportive of the mission?
- Are staff clear about reporting lines and accountability?
- Is supervision logical and capable of performing expected functions?
- Is there an informal organization (people who carry authority because they are respected by staff, and thus exert influence outside those in formally designated positions)?
- Are there clear distinctions between staff and line functions?

Task 10: Understand Administration, Management, and Leadership

- How is the workplace organized and work allocated?
- Is appropriate authority assigned along with responsibility?
- How close is supervision and what, exactly, is supervised? Is it tasks, or is it functions, or is it the employee, depending on need?
- How are people treated in the workplace, including the very lowest level employees?
- Do employees feel valued at every level? Do they believe they are making a contribution to the success of the organization?
- How are decisions made? Is information solicited from those affected? Is it used? Are there individuals or units within the organization that are left out of decision making? If so, why?
- How is conflict handled?

Task 11: Recognize the Organization's Culture

- How would one begin to describe the organization's culture?
- What are the organization's artifacts and creations?
- What are the organization's stated values and what is actually valued within the organization?

- How do leaders within the organization influence organizational values and assumptions?
- What are the taken-for-granted patterns within this organization?
- Is behavior consistent with culture?
- Are there minorities or others who feel left out of the accepted organizational culture?

Task 12: Assess the Organization's Programs and Services

- What programs are offered? What services are offered within each program? Are the services consistent with the goals and objectives of the program?
- Is there a common understanding among management and line staff within each program about problems to be addressed, populations to be served, services to be provided, and outcomes to be achieved?
- Are staffing patterns appropriate to the services to be provided? Are any staff over or under qualified? Are workload expectations reasonable given expectations for achievement with each client and within each service and program? Is consideration given to cultural and racial understanding of workers and clients?
- What data is collected on clients and how is it used?
- What evaluative information is expected from the evaluation plan? Is there a plan to gather information about clients and the extent of improvement at the point of termination and in a follow-up survey or interview? Is there an effort to determine level of client satisfaction with services? What do the findings reveal to date?

Task 13: Assess Organizational Technology

- What are the job expectations for each level of staff within the organization? What background education and experience is required to perform these jobs? Do those who hold these jobs have the appropriate credentials?
- Are staff members performing competently in their positions? Are they meeting expectations? Are they effective (do they get good results) in working with clients?
- Is each discipline supervised and evaluated by someone with appropriate knowledge, values, skills, and professional identification?
- In what ways are various units representing different disciplines (e.g., social work, psychology, medical, data processing, etc.) linked with each other for the purposes of collaboration and communication?

Task 14: Locate Personnel Policies and Procedures

- How diverse is the workforce? Are differences valued in this organization?
- How do managers and administrators view staff? As people who carry out tasks? As members of teams or units? As creative problem solvers who have an important stake in organizational success?
- What formal and informal criteria are used for evaluating performance?
- What kinds of behaviors does the organization reward?

- What is the organization's philosophy and policy about staff development and training? What resources are invested in it?
- How attractive are wages, hours, working conditions, and fringe benefits? How attractive is the facility and the work environment?
- What are the affirmative action policies and how are they implemented?
- To what extent does the organization groom people for higher level positions, and to what extent do they promote from within?

Task 15: Recognize How the Organization Deals with Community Relations

- Is there a clearly defined public image, and is there a strategy for communicating this image to the public? What kinds of resources, including funding, does the organization invest in promoting its public image?
- What is the reputation of the agency, its programs and services, its board, executive, management, and line staff with the general public, other agencies, funding sources, clients, and other relevant constituencies such as minority communities?
- Do the agency's facilities and published materials contribute to its desired public image?
- Does the agency respond when needed by other community agencies for political activities, fund raising, dealing with community social problems, or other issues?

Task 16: Recognize Methods of Financial Management and Accountability

- Is the budget prepared in accordance with accepted standards of accounting and financial reporting? Are annual audits conducted?
- Are program staff involved in a meaningful way in preparing the budget, and do they get useful feedback about expenditures and unit costs during the year? Do program staff use budget data as a measure by which they attempt to improve efficiency?
- Do resources appear to be adequate to achieve stated program goals and objectives?
- What are the major sources of revenue for the organization? What demands and restrictions does each funding source place on the organization and its programs?

Task 17: Assess Facilities, Equipment, Computer Utilization, and Records Management

- Do employees feel that they have enough space? Is the physical work environment attractive and conducive to high productivity?
- Have problems been identified with current facilities and equipment? Is there a plan to address the problems and to fund solutions?

- Are there conditions related to facilities or equipment that appear to act as barriers to productivity or work flow?
- Is the agency able to produce data that will answer important questions about clients, programs, and services? Does the agency have a computerized record-keeping and management information system that includes client data?

PART **IV**

Macro Change

In the previous three parts of the book we have attempted to provide the basic knowledge necessary to understand the context of macro practice and to analyze two major macro systems—communities and organizations. In Part IV, the final part of the book, we will present a model for acting within and upon these systems. Specifically, we will detail means for bringing about change in communities and organizations that will lead to improvements in these systems' abilities to provide appropriate and effective services.

The three chapters in Part IV address the planned change process in sequential order. Chapter 8 looks at the tasks involved in planning the change episode, including identifying the problem and target population, analyzing the problem, and developing an intervention hypothesis. Chapter 9 outlines a variety of tasks such as identifying relevant groups, assessing political, interpersonal, and resource considerations, and setting goals and objectives. Chapter 10 completes the process by discussing change tactics and the means by which all the preceding tasks are organized into a comprehensive plan.

CHAPTER **8**

Preparing for Macro-Level Interventions

INTRODUCTION

Social work is a profession oriented toward action and change. People who practice social work commit themselves to serve as a resource for those who have problems, who have limited or no control over the changes that need to be made in order to resolve their problems, and who request or are willing to accept help.

The majority of social workers deal with change directly with clients, usually working with individuals one to one or with families or small groups. Some practitioners focus on communitywide problems. Others practice in the areas of planning, management, and administration of organizations. Regardless of the professional social worker's practice orientation, it is crucial that practitioners of all types understand that, while some problems can be resolved at an individual or family level, others will require intervention at higher levels, including the need to effect changes in organizations and communities.

Managing macro-level change requires a good deal of professional knowledge and skill. Poor management and flawed decision making in the change process can result in serious setbacks, sometimes making things worse for those already in need. On the other hand, many very positive changes in organizations and communities have been orchestrated by social workers and others who have carefully planned, designed, and carried out the change process.

It is not unusual for direct practitioners to have clients ask for help with problems that appear to be individual or interpersonal but, upon further probing are clearly macro-level problems. A family that loses its primary source of income, is evicted, and finds that there is a three-month waiting list to get into a homeless shelter represents a symptom of a community problem. Clearly their immediate shelter problem must be resolved, but just as obviously the communitywide lack of emergency housing must be addressed. A mother may describe the pressures put on her son to join a gang and become involved in the drug trade. While the immediate need for this family can perhaps be met by building a support system for the boy designed to keep him in school, in a part-time job, and in constructive activities, this casework approach would not solve the problem for the many other families who must live daily with the same threats.

Identifying and dealing with organizational and community conditions, problems and needs presents a complex set of challenges to a social worker. Over the years, the image of the change agent has developed around some of the early social change pioneers—people like Dorothea Dix or Florence Kelley. Others view change agents as superorganizers like the late Saul Alinsky, or as high profile individuals like Ralph Nader who has had great success in bringing about social change through nationwide organization and exceptional political skill. In reality, most social workers have neither the resources, the media exposure, the charisma, the experience, the following, or the power that these leaders have had available to them. Yet, in spite of seemingly overwhelming challenges, social workers have been effective in bringing about changes in organizations and communities.

Effectiveness, however, does not necessarily come from the power of personality or the ability to mobilize thousands to a cause. It comes from careful, thoughtful, and creative planning undertaken by a group committed to change.

The change effort may be led or coordinated by a professional social worker, but those involved will represent a broad range of interest groups.

GUIDELINES FOR PLANNING CHANGE

The three tasks and their accompanying steps outlined in Table 8.1 represent guidelines for planning an organizational or a community change. The tasks described in this chapter will require input from knowledgeable and experienced people. They are also tasks that fall within the capacity of a professional social worker who can skillfully draw on various talents present among a group of committed professionals, volunteers, and consumers.

Focus A: Identifying the Population and the Problem

Although many macro-level interventions seem to begin at the point of proposing solutions, they should begin with a focus on developing a clear understanding of the problem. While this may sound simple and straightforward, in practice it can become quite complex. Take, for example, a community in which highway deaths due to alcohol are up 37 percent in the last two years. How might the problem in this case be defined? One group will be convinced that the problem is the lack of strict enforcement of existing laws prohibiting driving under the influence of alcohol. Another group will describe it as a problem of easy availability of alcohol to teenagers. Another will see alcohol abuse as a symptom of increasing stress. Still another will see it as a symptom of family breakdown. These represent just a few of the perspectives that might be introduced in an attempt to understand some of the reasons behind drunk driving, even when there is agreement that the increase in alcohol-related highway deaths is the problem.

TABLE 8.1 Framework for Planning Change

Focus	Tasks
A. Identifying the Population and the Problem	1. Identify organizational or community conditions
	2. Collect supporting data
	3. Identify barriers to condition resolution
	4. Determine whether a condition is a problem
B. Analyzing the Problem	5. Identify relevant historical incidents
	6. Identify and apply relevant theoretical perspectives
	7. Apply findings from research, program evaluation, and practice
	8. Examine ethnic, gender, and target-population perspectives
	9. Speculate about the etiology of the problem
	10. Refine the problem statement
C. Developing the Intervention Hypothesis	11. State a hypothesis
	12. Propose relationships between changes and results

The important point is that identifying and defining the problem in different ways leads to very different interventions. The way the problem is conceptualized and defined, therefore, can be critical in achieving the desired result—reducing the number of alcohol-related highway deaths. For this reason, quick responses should be resisted while the necessary discipline is employed to conduct a careful study and documentation effort.

We propose that change agents proceed through a series of steps designed to gather as much useful information about the problem as can be made available. The steps involved in compiling this information include: (1) identifying an organizational or community condition; (2) collecting supporting data; (3) identifying barriers to condition resolution; and (4) determining whether the condition is seen as (or can be made to be seen as) a problem.

Task 1: Identify Organizational or Community Conditions.   A condition is a phenomenon that is present in an organization or a community that may be troublesome to a number of people, but that has not been formally identified or publicly labeled as a problem. Every organization and community is full of both conditions and problems. Social consequences of urban living such as traffic, air pollution, crime, drug abuse, broken families, and suicide can all be considered social or community conditions. Similarly in rural communities isolation, inaccessible health care, or a declining economic base can all be considered social conditions.

The same concept applies to organizations. Troublesome phenomena are also present in organizations, but they have not always been formally identified or labeled as a problem. For example, staff in a long-term care facility for the elderly may be concerned about what they consider to be overmedication of some of the residents. Similarly, program managers may recognize a troublesome trend to extend services to those who can pay and to put those who cannot pay on a waiting list.

To be recognized as a problem, a condition must in some way be incorporated into a community's or an organization's agenda for action. This may mean that elected officials propose formal programs or policy solutions. It may mean that a task force within an organization is officially sanctioned to address the condition. Whatever the proposed action, formal recognition is important for legitimization.

The distinction between a condition and a problem is significant to a social worker planning a macro-level intervention. If a condition has not been formally recognized in some way, the first task must be to obtain that formal recognition. For example, for many years homelessness was dealt with as a personal employment problem and AIDS was dealt with as a personal health problem. Most communities simply viewed these as existing conditions, not as social or community problems. When these conditions began to affect greater segments of society, and reached the point where they could no longer be ignored, national, state, and local community leaders began to perceive them as problems. Once formally recognized and acknowledged as problems (usually as a result of persistent media attention), these conditions become candidates for organized intervention efforts. The creation of task forces for the homeless in cities across the country and federal funding for AIDS research are results of recognizing conditions and defining them as problems.

The first step in problem identification, then, is to develop a condition statement. A condition statement must include a target population, a geographical boundary, and the difficulty facing that population. Statements should be descriptive and free of qualifying or judgmental words or phrases, such as *poor* or *disadvantaged,* as possible.

Statements will be adapted depending on whether the condition exists within a community or in an organization. For example, a condition statement might be, "Suicide among teenagers in Preston County is increasing." Generally speaking, the more precise the statement, the greater the likelihood of a successful intervention. The above statement, for example, could vary from extremely general to very precise, as depicted below.

Sample Condition Statements
General   Teen suicide is increasing.

Teen suicide in Preston County is increasing.

Teens from lower socioeconomic families in Preston County have shown increasing suicide rates.

Teens from lower socioeconomic families in Preston County, primarily in the Washington and Lincoln High School attendance areas have shown increasing suicide rates.

Specific   Etc.

A similar process within an organization would begin with a general statement. For example, an organizational condition might involve an increasing dropout rate among low-income families in a family counseling program. Data and information would need to be compiled to help pinpoint the condition as precisely as possible.

Condition statements are made more precise through a process of research and documentation of the nature, size, and scope of the problem. As one proceeds with the steps in Task 1, the condition statement may be refined many times as new facts arise.

Task 2: Collect Supporting Data.
There was a time when a community could become sensitized to a condition and recognize it as a problem based on a few incidents. Churches started orphanages and counties started poor houses with little or no data beyond personal knowledge of a few people in need and the expectation that there would be more.

Today, however, with so many social and community problems competing for limited resources, data must be compiled to justify the existence of a problem or need. Collecting data on a community social problem can be a challenge.

Ideally, in dealing with teen pregnancy, for example, one would hope to find those powerful statistics that clearly demonstrate something like the following:

There are 3,279 pregnant teens in Clifton County.

Lack of early intervention can be expected to result in 1,200 premature births, including high-risk stillbirth or mental retardation.

Lack of help with child care and parenting can be expected to result in an abuse and neglect rate of 22 percent or 721 abused and neglected children.

The retarded, abused, and neglected children born this year can be expected to cost the state $4.5 million per year for various forms of care and treatment.

An early intervention program for 3,279 pregnant teens will cost $1.5 million and can be expected to reduce the incidence of premature delivery to 300 and the incidence of abuse and neglect to 8 percent.

These kinds of figures make it clear that it is a case of paying something now for prevention or paying many times more that amount later for care, maintenance, or perhaps rehabilitation. However, though these kinds of statistics are much desired and preferred, they are rarely produced. Instead, individuals initiating change must rely on what is available—census data, community needs assessments, levels of demand for service as reported by agencies, rates of service, data generated by hospitals, schools and police departments, and any other source available. These are often the same data sources used in the community and organizational assessment processes outlined in earlier chapters.

A few techniques can be helpful in cases where data and information are needed. One resource is national, regional, or state studies where an incidence rate per thousand (or hundred thousand) has been established. If, for example, it has been found that one out of every two marriages performed in a community will end in divorce, one can track down the average number of marriages performed in that community in a given year and calculate the number of divorces that can be expected to follow over time.

Basic to all statistical support is a knowledge of the number of people in various categories (e.g., men, women, age groupings, ethnic minorities, etc.). Valuable information like this is available in the *County and City Data Book* published by the Bureau of the Census available in the government documents section of a library. Taken from census data, this resource book includes such data categories as household composition, occupation, age, gender, etc.

In addition, state and/or county departments of social services, health, mental health, and corrections often collect data which can be useful in documenting the existence of social problems. Other sources include local social service agencies, United Ways, community councils, centralized data collection resource centers, centralized information and referral agencies, law enforcement agencies, hospitals, and school district offices. The process of tracking down information is often similar to a scavenger hunt where one clue leads to another until finally the persons initiating change feel that a credible amount of support data has been compiled.

Comparative data are generally more useful than a single statistic, and several techniques can be used to collect this type of information. These include cross-sectional analysis, time-series comparisons, comparisons with other data units, standards comparisons, and epidemiological analysis (Kettner et al. 1985).

Cross-Sectional Analysis. This approach focuses on a single population but provides a number of different perspectives on that population at a particular point in time. For example, a survey might focus on areas of need experienced by a particular target population and display the percentage of the population who report a problem in this area, as shown in Table 8.2.

As problems are identified, subpopulations can usually be assessed by demographic characteristics such as age, gender, ethnic minority status, census tract, and others. The most serious limitation is that a cross-sectional analysis does not reveal changes over time.

Time-Series Comparisons. When available, data from repeated observations over time are preferred over cross-sectional analysis because they display longitudinal changes. Assuming data were collected on an annual basis, a time-series comparison would look at trends in the variable(s) of interest. For example, the number of requests for overnight stays in a homeless shelter might be displayed, as shown in Table 8.3.

Statistics like these can help project need and cost into the future, based on assumptions about trends identified through a series of observations. Comparisons between these observations can provide the change agent with valuable information. For example, they can be used to document how client need is

TABLE 8.2 An Illustration of Cross-Sectional Analysis, Examining the Percentage of Each Population Experiencing a Problem

	% of Population	Housing	Employment	Nutrition	Transportation
Age					
0–18	19%	6%	N/A	5%	N/A
19–30	29%	14%	7%	9%	16%
31–64	39%	17%	11%	8%	19%
65 +	13%	19%	33%	15%	33%
Sex					
Female	52%	5%	7%	6%	18%
Male	48%	16%	24%	11%	17%
Ethnicity					
Anglo	75%	10%	5%	4%	7%
African American	10%	17%	11%	12%	15%
Hispanic	8%	7%	10%	9%	11%
Native American	4%	11%	23%	8%	14%
Asian American	3%	3%	4%	5%	9%

TABLE 8.3 Illustration of a Time-Series Analysis Examining the Number of Requests for Overnight Shelter by Homeless Persons

1989	1990	1991	1992
18,250	20,474	25,689	30,410

increasing, why additional resources are needed, and the projected dollars necessary to fill anticipated need.

Comparison with Other Data Units. A great wealth of both regularly and specially assembled information is available for use as supporting data. For example, over the past twenty years, many federal programs have contributed to the generation of data on rates per 1,000, 10,000, or 100,000 for social and health problems. These statistics allow for comparison regardless of the size of the city in question. Studies have also identified state and local per capita expenditures for various social and health problems. Based on these findings, states and cities can be ranked as to the incidence and prevalence of a problem as well as their efforts to address the problem.

Comparisons are particularly useful in making a case that a disproportionate share of resources should go to a particularly needy community. By comparing census tracts within a county on selected variables, it readily becomes evident that problems and needs are not always equally distributed across communities and neighborhoods within the county.

Standards Comparisons. This technique is helpful when comparative data are not available. A standard is defined as "a specification accepted by recognized authorities that is regularly and widely used and has a recognized and permanent status" (Buck et al. 1973, cited in Kettner & Martin 1987, 66). Standards are developed by accrediting bodies, governmental entities or professional associations. The Child Welfare League of America publishes comprehensive sets of standards related to community and agency programs for child abuse and neglect, adoption, and other child welfare services. Similarly, the National Council on the Aging has developed case management standards.

Standards also provide a useful basis against which an existing condition can be compared to determine its qualitative status. For example, a standard could be established specifying the minimally acceptable ratio of child protection workers to cases. Conditions considered to be below health, educational, housing, and other standards often become more readily accessible as targets for change.

Epidemiological Analysis. This is a technique adapted from the health care field. Analysis of factors contributing to a disease helps to establish relationships even when a clear cause/effect relationship cannot be demonstrated. For example, Piven and Cloward (1971) established relationships among the variables of poverty, poor education, poor housing, and welfare dependency. While it cannot be said that any of these conditions cause welfare dependency, its relationship to the combination of factors is well established. Also, as with standards comparisons, epidemiological analysis can be useful when comparative data are not available.

This type of original study is beyond the scope of most macro practitioners, and it is mentioned here not to suggest that a social worker should attempt to conduct an original study, but so that existing studies will be recognized as viable resources. The American Public Health Association, the National Center on Child Abuse and Neglect, the American Public Welfare Association, the Urban Institute, and other such organizations have provided many sound epidemiological studies that can be used as resources by social workers.

Task 3: Identify Barriers to Condition Resolution.   What is it about the condition that seems to prevent or interfere with change? Why has it persisted over time? What barriers must be dealt with in order to change the condition? Preliminary identification of these barriers is important in clarifying the change effort.

Before exploring barriers, however, it is important to understand the types of barriers to be identified. When examining conditions and problems in the human services, there seems to be a strong temptation to identify lack of resources as a barrier to condition or problem resolution. If the study is focused on an organizational problem, barriers tend to be defined in terms of a need for more staff, more equipment, expanded facilities, and so on. In defining a community problem, barriers tend to be seen in terms of lack of resources for a program— more day care slots, more training, and so on. We caution against this type of superficial assessment for several reasons.

First, resources have to do with the intervention, and they should be considered only after a specific approach has been proposed and resource issues can be addressed in detailed, not general, terms. Second, lack of resources is so universal that it is relatively meaningless as a part of problem analysis. Third, "lack of adequate resources" does not tell us what must be done in order to achieve condition or problem resolution. The statement simply assumes more of whatever is already being done. The need for additional resources in macro-level change can usually be assumed, but it should be addressed later in the change process.

The types of barriers to be addressed are those that stand directly in the path of condition or problem resolution. They are substantive factors or conditions that prevent progress toward solutions. They are not necessarily causes of the problem but they are factors which have been demonstrated to have a relationship to the problem. The purpose in identifying them is to help clarify the complex nature of the condition. One method useful for identifying barriers is to diagram the condition as in Table 8.4.

In the left-hand column, a condition statement is written. Below the statement, some of the significant supporting data can be listed. In the right-hand column, a condition resolution statement is written. It is usually stated as the converse of the condition statement. The center column is then used to identify barriers. In this column all factors are listed that are known to the planning group that may have some bearing on the problem. As new ideas emerge, they are added to the list. This becomes a centralized collection point for identification of all those factors that must be addressed if the problem is to be resolved.

Identification of barriers to condition resolution is intended not so much as a systematic pursuit of knowledge as a beginning attempt to examine some

TABLE 8.4   Identification of Barriers to Condition Resolution

Condition Statement	Barriers	Resolution Statement
The incidence of teen suicide is increasing in Preston County	An increasing number of teens suffer from low self-esteem in Preston County	Teen suicide should be declining or non-existent in Preston County
	Many parents are only minimally involved with their teenage children	
Examples of supporting data:		
The number of suicides increased from two in 1984 to seven in 1990	Teens are experiencing increased stress	
	Teen depression is increasing	
Stress related illness in high-school students increased 48 percent in five years	Many teens feel increasingly isolated and alienated from their peers	
	Use and abuse of drugs and alcohol is increasing among teens	

of the factors that appear to be associated with the condition. A more thorough study will be undertaken in the problem analysis phase. Examination of data supporting the existence of the condition together with identification of barriers helps to build an understanding of the scope and complexity of the condition. This is useful in bringing sufficient attention to the condition that it becomes recognized as a problem by those whose support is needed to bring about change.

Task 4: Determine Whether a Condition Is a Problem.   There is no precise definition of when a condition becomes a problem in terms of time of appearance, size, or severity. Except in crisis situations, problems are identified and labeled gradually due to shifting perspectives, changing political positions, or increasing awareness. Is homelessness a problem in any given community? Drug abuse? Crime? Air pollution? The answer to all these questions is, "It depends."

A condition becomes a problem when it receives enough public attention that it can no longer be ignored by community leaders, or when one or more leaders declare a condition unacceptable and decide that something must be done. For example, when a city councilperson's son is arrested for possession of crack, a community leader may suddenly become very interested in what others have long perceived as the "drug problem." Note that people may suffer from a condition long before it is recognized as a problem. However, for the macro practitioner, recognition of the problem is important because it is only with such recognition that efforts to solve the problem can be mounted on a meaningful scale.

For the change agent, it is then important to consider the question of who will support and who will oppose the proposed change. If it is already recognized as a problem by many community or organizational leaders, or by community citizens or agency staff members, then a proposed change may be readily accepted. If not, it must first receive enough attention that decision makers cannot ignore it. This raises a pivotal question for the change agent. Has the problem been acknowledged and does a commitment exist to address the need, or must efforts first be directed toward having the organization or community in some way formally acknowledge its existence and agree that intervention is appropriate? The answer will affect the immediate and long-range focus of the change effort. Ultimately significant decision makers must be persuaded that the condition is a problem. If this cannot be done, the chances of successfully bringing about change are slim. For this reason, the focus of a change effort is sometimes shifted from the substantive change to an effort to bring attention to the problem.

Summary of Steps Involved in Problem Identification.   In summary, the following important points have been made so far about identifying a condition and creating an awareness that it is a problem.

1. Initiating, macro-level interventions in organizations and communities begins with the identification of a condition or problem.
2. For a condition to be considered a problem, some type of formal recognition is necessary. Securing this recognition may become a subsequent step in the intervention process.
3. When a condition statement has been framed, relevant data should be collected to support the contention that a problem exists and to aid in understanding its nature, size, and scope.
4. Data displays should be carefully designed to illustrate the perspective on the problem that the change agent wishes to convey. Displays can illustrate comparisons to other conditions, changes in conditions over time, relationship of conditions to standards, or relationship to contributing factors.
5. Identification of barriers to condition resolution help to make clear the complexity of the condition and the sources of support needed for change.
6. The purpose of the presentation of data is to convince the appropriate individuals or systems that the condition is a problem in need of attention and intervention.

Focus B: Analyzing the Problem

Human problems are complex phenomena and, as such, often require a good deal of study and thoughtful consideration. While the lay public may have simple answers to many social problems, the professional can afford no such luxury.

Analyzing social or community problems is undertaken in an attempt to understand *why* the problem exists. Why are some people chronically unemployed? Why do some parents neglect their children? Why do some teens attempt suicide? This is no time for simplistic answers! It is a time for the most thorough study and analysis that time and resources will allow.

To conduct the analysis in as efficient a manner as possible, we propose that the change agent proceed through a series of steps: (1) identifying relevant historical incidents; (2) identifying and applying relevant theoretical perspectives on the problem; (3) using research, program evaluations, and practice findings; (4) identifying and incorporating ethnic, gender, and target population perspectives on the problem and the need; (5) speculating about the etiology of the problem; and (6) refining the problem statement.

Task 5: Identify Relevant Historical Incidents.   A social problem in any community or organization has its own history. This history can affect the ways in which people currently perceive the problem. It is, therefore, important to understand what has happened in the past, how the community or organization perceived and reacted to it, how the problem was addressed, how effective the attempts were to alleviate the problem, and who the major participants were in any previous change efforts.

If one looks merely at the problem as it is defined at the current time, much will be missed. Instead, it is crucial to determine the history of the problem, particularly in terms of critical incidents that have shaped this history. A task force might, for example, be concerned about a high dropout rate from the local high school. The following chronology of critical incidents helps them to better understand factors that may have influenced the development of issues in the high school over the years:

1982   Riverview High School was a predominantly lower-middle class high school with an 87 percent graduation rate.

1984   School district boundaries changed, and the new group of students included 30 percent for whom English was their second language.

1985   Enrollment dropped 20 percent, and the graduation rate fell to 67 percent.

1986   Riverview High School initiated a strong vocational training program designed to prepare high-school graduates for post-high-school employment; the college preparatory curriculum was de-emphasized.

1987   Enrollment increased, attendance patterns improved.

1988   Local employers hired only 32 percent of the graduates; unemployment rates among Riverview graduates one year later was as high as 37 percent.

1990   Enrollment dropped back to 1985 levels; the dropout rate hit 23 percent, its highest mark yet.

1991   Riverview High School was written up in the local newspaper as one of the ten worst schools in the state in terms of quality of education, retention rates of students, and post-high-school employment. A blue ribbon panel was formed to make recommendations to improve the quality of education.

Tracing these historical events lends insight into some of the incidents the faculty, staff, administration, students, and families associated with Riverview High School have experienced. In this case, the task force should expect to encounter a discouraged and cynical response to any sort of a "Stay in School" campaign. The critical incidents list indicates that many of the arguments for staying in school simply did not prove true for those who graduated. When the employment, career, and financial incentives for remaining in high school are removed, the challenge to keep students in school is greatly increased and the approach needs to be adapted in a way that seems relevant to those who are intended to be the primary beneficiaries.

Task 6: Identify and Apply Relevant Theoretical Perspectives.   Theories are intended to explain phenomena and to provide a framework for research and testing of hypotheses. As opposed to the random listing of facts and observations, theories allow for categorizing one's findings, making sense out of them, and turning seemingly unrelated bits of data into explanatory propositions that lead to logical, testable hypotheses.

Continuing with the example of high-school dropouts, one might draw on the work of B. F. Skinner (1971), Erik Erickson (1968), Carol Gilligan (1982), or Abraham Maslow (1943) to understand the behavior of the target population. Using some of Skinner's most basic concepts such as reinforcement, extinction, or desensitization, one might examine the high-school experience for selected students. Negative reinforcements in the form of poor grades and criticism (it might be hypothesized) may lead to discouragement on the part of poor students. These negative responses may also extinguish certain behaviors and limit the effort a student is willing to invest in academic success. Or perhaps school disciplinary experiences such as detention, suspension, and others systematically desensitize some students to organizationally imposed sanctions. In this case, efforts would have to be expended to discover what this group of students would consider positive reinforcement, and how the academic experience could be designed so that they could achieve success.

Erickson's concept of identity might cause one to focus on the need of high-school age youth for a positive self-image. The high-school experience might then be examined to determine the degree to which it supports the development of a positive identity for some and destroys it for others. Activities would be designed to build self-esteem on the assumption that increased self-esteem will act as a motivator to academic success.

Gilligan's work raises consciousness in understanding the psychological development of women and the importance of gender on how one views the world. If dropout rates for women are related to teen pregnancy, one may want to consider the importance of gender identity. Gilligan theorizes that women seek connection and affiliation as they develop, not having to separate from the mother in the same way that boys do. Becoming pregnant, which contributes to dropping out of school, may be a young girl's way of establishing intimacy and of feeling needed.

Maslow, on the other hand, would examine the phenomenon of high-school dropout in terms of the congruence between the high-school experience and students' needs. The pertinent question would be whether the educational programs were appropriately tailored to meet the social, esteem, and fulfillment needs of students. Each level of need, once met, is no longer a motivator, so new challenges would have to be designed toward the goal of self-fulfillment.

These examples simply provide a cursory application of the theories. A thorough explication of a theoretical perspective on dropout behavior would be required in an actual change effort.

Selecting an explanatory theoretical framework is an important decision in the problem analysis process. Theoretical understandings give the problem analysis internal consistency and ultimately provide a rationale for the intervention. Explanatory theories should be selected carefully based on what fits best with the problem and population. Theories should be critically evaluated for their biases and given credibility based on how thoroughly they have been tested.

Task 7: Apply Findings from Research, Program Evaluation, and Practice.   Over the past decade, literature reporting empirical testing of theoretical and practice-related questions has increased dramatically. A number of journals are now devoted almost exclusively to reporting research in social work and related fields (e.g., Social Work Research and Abstracts, Journal of Social Service Research). Others examine practice issues (e.g., Practice Digest, Social Work with Groups, Journal of Marriage and the Family, Journal of Gerontological Social Work).

Research, evaluation, and practice findings can be useful in problem analysis. Formally structured, rigorously designed research projects hold the greatest promise for generalizability, assuming that populations, problems, and conditions are comparable. Evaluations of existing social service programs can be informative, but they often lack the methodological rigor of organized research. Reports of practice findings tend to be the least formal in terms of their data collection, analysis, and reporting of findings, yet, they can be helpful and informative as long as the user is cautious in interpreting findings and deriving applications.

One feature of research and evaluation projects that can be helpful in problem analysis is the manner in which populations and problems are categorized for data collection and analysis. For example, continuing with the population of high-school dropouts, one source lists the following categories (Data Network for Human Services 1987):

- Student withdrawn due to ten or more consecutive days of unexcused absence. Student not known to have entered another public or non-public school district and/or the student's whereabouts are unknown.
- Student discontinuing studies due to academic difficulties.
- Student discontinuing studies due to behavioral difficulties.
- Student discontinuing studies due to economic or personal reasons. (p. 16)

Subcategories such as these may be more helpful than listing all high-school dropouts under a single statistic. In addition, using definitions and categories commonly used by other researchers and evaluators can be helpful in building a knowledge base about the population and problem and in comparing subpopulations in one community to those in another.

Task 8: Examine Ethnic, Gender, and Target-Population Perspectives.
A full understanding of a social problem requires increasing attention to varying
perspectives. Problems can be understood in a number of ways including working
closely with people who have experienced them or through systematic study and
research. It is important to distinguish, however, between these types of secondhand experiences and the firsthand experiences of one who has actually lived
with the problem.

When it comes to representing the perspectives of a population of people
who have experienced a problem, it should be understood that those who have
only secondhand experiences usually are not accepted as spokespersons by those
who have experienced the problem. For example, people who have experienced
day-to-day life on welfare may not be willing to accept a social worker as a spokes-
person to articulate their feelings and needs. They may be more likely to turn
to a fellow welfare recipient. Describing the experiences that led to a posttraumatic
stress disorder for a Vietnam veteran can be done with credibility only by someone
who was there. People of an ethnic group usually can speak for the experiences
of their own group, but not for another group. One gender may not be credibly
able to represent the other. For these reasons, it is important to find spokespersons
and literature that aid in understanding these important perspectives.

Culture can be defined in many ways. One definition is "those elements of
a people's history, tradition, values, and social organization that become implicitly
or explicitly meaningful to the participants during an encounter" (Green 1982, 7).
One might, for example, look at Asian culture, Mid-Eastern culture, Eastern
European culture, or Western culture to aid in understanding the behaviors of
a group of people who shared a common experience. Specifically, a social worker
who speaks English to a Hispanic client may discover that the client finds meaning
in the fact that a dominant language is used to express the professional's thoughts.
Language may be perceived as a cultural expression of oppression within a society
that is not sensitive to Hispanic people.

A term frequently used in connection with culture is *ethnicity*. As with
culture, there are numerous definitions of ethnicity. Green suggests that there
are three elements common to most definitions. First, ethnic group members share
a past and related backgrounds. Second, persons who identify with ethnic groups
believe that they are distinctively different from others in some important manner.
Third, ethnicity becomes significant when members of a group come in contact
with persons who are from different ethnic groups. Comparison is necessary
because it highlights the uniqueness of one group in relation to another (Green
1982). Major ethnic groups in this country include African Americans, Hispanic
Americans, Native Americans, Asian Americans, and others.

Members of ethnic groups in this country today often draw on customs
and traditions of their culture of origin. Their perceptions and experiences
can make a difference in the way a problem is perceived and understood. A
framework helpful in understanding and dealing with the complexities of ethnicity
and gender is the dual perspective. Initially conceptualized by Norton (1978),
the dual perspective views an individual as being at the center of two surrounding
systems which Norton calls the nurturing system and the sustaining system, shown
in Figure 8.1.

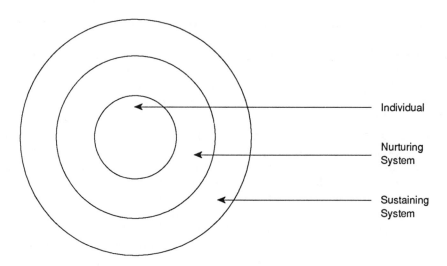

FIGURE 8.1 The Dual Perspective

SOURCE: Norton, D. G. (1978) *The dual perspective: Inclusion of ethnic minority content in the social work curriculum.* New York: Council on Social Work Education.

Immediately surrounding the individual is a *nurturing system,* represented by the parenting and extended family or substitute family practices, community experiences, beliefs, values, customs, and traditions with which the person was raised. Surrounding the nurturing system is a *sustaining system* represented by the dominant society. The sustaining system also reflects beliefs, values, customs, and traditions.

The focus of analysis for the change agent is the degree of fit between an individual's, family's, or group's nurturing system and the sustaining system within which they function. The nurturing system may, for example, support the importance of family over individual, while the sustaining system emphasizes and rewards individual competition and merit. Sustaining systems are made up of influential and powerful people—teachers, employers, elected officials and others. Some segments of sustaining systems may reflect racist and sexist attitudes, and therefore can be perceived by ethnic minorities and women to represent some-what alien and hostile environments. Yet they usually have little choice but to interact with these environments.

A good deal of problem analysis and service provision comes from a sustaining or dominant perspective. Even the theories used to explain the problem and the research on which the practitioner builds hypotheses may reflect sustaining system biases. Members of diverse ethnic groups, on the other hand, may have very different perspectives of the problem and how to resolve it. For example, if a community's elderly are experiencing a decreasing quality of life, some may attribute this to an inability to maintain elderly parents in the home as a part of the extended family. Others may attribute it to escalating costs of nursing care. Still others may see it as a change in values. And one's perception of this problem is likely to be linked to culture and ethnicity. It is therefore essential that the social worker understand those perspectives derived from the nurturing system.

As discussed in Chapter 5, informal and mediating units such as self-help groups and voluntary associations may guide the practitioner into a more sensitive realization of how nurturing and sustaining systems conflict. Whenever ethnic minorities, women, or other special population groups make up a part of the target population and are expected to benefit from the change effort, expertise reflecting these diverse perspectives must be sought and incorporated into the problem analysis and intervention design.

The target population represents a third perspective to be understood as part of the problem analysis. People who have experienced the problem should be sought out for their opinions and interpretations. Literature published by researchers and writers who represent a target population can be helpful, but they should not substitute for dialogue with those who are a part of the immediate community or organization under study, and who have firsthand experience with the problem.

A further complicating factor in understanding perspectives is the issue of representativeness. Who speaks for an ethnic group? For women? For any target population? In many cases, opinions and perspectives may fall along a continuum, and it is helpful if the outsider (in many cases the professional social worker) can understand the nature of the continuum in terms of its extreme positions as well as its moderate or central position. For example, the social worker may want to develop skills in ethnic-sensitive interviewing (Fetterman 1989).

Task 9: Speculate about the Etiology of the Problem.   Etiology is defined as "the science that deals with origins or causes . . . the act or process of assigning a cause" (Barnhart & Barnhart 1979). Speculating about the etiology of a problem is an attempt to arrive at an understanding of cause/effect relationships.

Examination of history, theory, research, and other literature on the population and problem come together at the point where cause/effect relationships are postulated. The change agent looks for patterns of events or factors that seem to be associated so that a case can be made for hypothesizing selected causal factors.

In many cases, alternative explanations of cause/effect are all logical and, in a sense "correct," but they may apply to different subgroups of the target population. For example, all of the following statements are probably true about a subgroup of dropouts:

Some students drop out of school because of inability to handle the academic demands.

Some students drop out of school because income is needed by their families and they are the only resource at the time.

Some students drop out of school because they suffer discrimination and rejection from their peers and leaving the situation is a way of avoiding emotional pain.

Some students drop out of school because there is such intense discord in their home and family life that they are incapable of dealing with the added stress of academic demands.

The decision that must then be made is not one of choosing the "correct" perspective on etiology, but rather on selecting the subgroup to be served. As with many (probably all) target populations and problems, one understanding of etiology and one intervention does not fit all.

Task 10: Refine the Problem Statement. When the above activities have been accomplished, the *working draft* of the condition statement can be refined into a problem statement. A simple, clear statement that includes a target population, boundary, and problem is most appropriate. Explanatory statements or supportive documentation may follow, but the statement should provide a consensus position for all those who are expected to support the change effort. The following might be used in the high school dropout example: Dropouts from the Washington, Lincoln, and Jefferson attendance areas of the Preston City school district have been increasing steadily over the last five years and have reached a level that is unacceptable to the citizens of this community.

Additional statements might be added highlighting whatever is considered necessary to build consensus and support, such as specific dropout rates for the five-year period and a listing of what are considered to be the major causes. This statement will serve as a focal point around which a support system will be built.

Summary of Steps in Problem Analysis. The following is a summary checklist reviewing all the important points made so far about developing a thorough understanding of the problem and gaining consensus from the participants about a common or shared understanding.

1. Analysis is undertaken in the interest of gaining a better understanding of the problem. The professional practitioner never jumps directly from problem identification to intervention.
2. Thorough problem analysis requires an understanding of problem history, theory, research, ethnicity, gender, target population perspectives, and problem etiology.
3. The focus of a study of problem history is on understanding how it has been framed in the past, what are the critical incidents in the history of the problem, how it has been addressed, and how the community has responded to various attempts to deal with it.
4. The use of theory brings to the problem contexts or frameworks within which various explanations can be explored. In the selection of theoretical frameworks one should be aware of the potential for bias in whatever explanation is drawn from the theory.
5. Journal articles on research and program evaluation from a variety of interdisciplinary journals are useful in developing an understanding of what has worked and not worked in other attempts to address the same or similar problems.

6. Ethnic and gender perspectives are sought in the interest of learning how various ethnic groups may perceive a problem differently from each other or women differently from men.

7. Target population perspectives are solicited as directly as possible from people considered to be in a position to represent this group. Perspectives developed through data analysis or through the use of theory and research should be put to the test in direct contact with target population representatives.

8. All knowledge, information, and value perspectives gathered are weighed, and cause/effect relationships are postulated. A shared understanding of causes is pursued in the interest of bringing focus to a proposed intervention.

9. Finally, the working draft of the condition statement is rewritten into a clear, concise problem statement which, together with supporting documentation, is used to provide direction, build consensus, and lead to proposing a change or recommending a specific intervention.

Focus C: Developing the Intervention Hypothesis

During the early phases of problem identification, many people involved in change efforts, both professionals and volunteers, are eager to propose a specific intervention. Many have experienced the frustration of working in what they perceive to be flawed programs or under what they perceive to be oppressive organizational policies, and they are eager to propose immediate change.

A disciplined, scholarly approach to macro-level change requires that the foregoing tasks associated with problem identification and analysis be addressed. However, it is the unusual change agent who is not constantly mindful of a preferred intervention and who is not continually molding and shaping it as the analysis unfolds.

Decisions about the nature, shape, and design of the intervention should wait until the problem analysis has been completed. When an acceptable degree of consensus has been achieved about the nature of the problem and its etiology, an intervention hypothesis is proposed.

Task 11: State a Hypothesis. Based on all the information gathered in the problem identification and analysis phases, an intervention hypothesis is developed. The hypothesis is a declarative statement (or series of statements) that proposes a relationship between a specific intervention and a result or outcome. The statement identifies the following: (1) a target population (or specific subgroup) and problem, (2) the change or intervention proposed, and (3) the results expected from the intervention. These elements combine to form a complete sentence that makes clear the expected relationship between problem, intervention and result. For example, a hypothesis for a program to prevent teens from dropping out of high school might read: If teens with economic problems are placed in a work study program which allows them to earn at least minimum wage for at least 30 hours a week and take evening classes, then the dropout rate among this group will decline at least 10% per year for the next five years.

This would be considered a testable hypothesis, and the expectation would be that the intervention would be designed to provide the features specified in the hypothesis. One method of developing this statement is discussion and brainstorming among a representative group of participants who are knowledgeable about the information produced in the process of problem analysis. Representatives should also be included from groups that can be crucial to the success of the change effort, such as ethnic groups, women, and target population members.

Task 12: Propose Relationships Between Changes and Results.   A proposed policy change might be hypothesized to affect the target population in the following way: If family counseling by a licensed clinical social worker is required as a condition for readmission of all students expelled for behavioral problems, then the readjustment rate of these students will improve and the dropout rate will decline.

It is not necessary at this point to flesh out the intervention in detail. However, for the change effort to proceed, it is necessary to make at least a preliminary decision about the nature and form of the intervention so that planning a strategy to introduce the change may proceed.

Summary of Steps in Developing the Intervention Hypothesis.   The following is a summary checklist reviewing all the important points made so far about developing an intervention hypothesis:

1. The macro practitioner should reexamine data, history, theory, research, ethnicity, gender, target population perspectives, and shared understanding of etiology.
2. Drawing on the knowledge base built on the above content areas, ideas about interventions that appear to be relevant to the need as it is currently understood should be discussed.
3. Using these proposed interventions, a set of intervention hypotheses (and possibly subhypotheses) should be developed. These statements should lay out a clear set of understandings about the population and problem, the nature of the intervention, and the expected outcomes.
4. These hypotheses and subhypotheses should be spelled out in a series of if/then statements; for example: If (*population*) with (*problem*) can be identified and recruited into this program and if they receive (*services*), then we expect that they will achieve (*outcomes*).

SUMMARY

This chapter has proposed a methodology for planning macro-level change in organizations and communities. The methodology begins with a thorough examination of the current condition in the organization or community that has led to the perception that there is a problem. Condition is seen as a more neutral and objective term; its use recognizes that not everyone agrees on the existence of a problem (or negatively defined condition). Someone must first identify the negatives that make this condition a cause for concern. This is accomplished by developing a clear statement of the condition, by collecting data about the incidence and prevalence of the condition, by assisting individuals whose support is needed to see the condition as a problem, and by identifying barriers to problem resolution.

As a clear picture of the problem begins to emerge, problem analysis is undertaken. This requires drawing on knowledgeable individuals for their insights and on the existing literature in order to understand history, theory, research, and the perspectives of various special populations on the subject. Gathering information from these sources leads to a shared understanding of etiology—cause(s) and effect(s)—which, in turn, leads to a refinement of the problem statement.

The final task is to propose, based on information gathered during problem identification and analysis, an intervention hypothesis which identifies a population, a problem, a proposed change, and an outcome, and speculates on their relationship in a series of if/then statements. This methodology is intended to maximize the professional social worker's understanding of a problem and the relationship between problem, change, and result, thereby increasing the possibility that the proposed changes, if implemented, will be successful in achieving the desired results.

REFERENCES

Barnhart, C. L., and R. K. Barnhart, eds. (1979) *The world book dictionary.* London: World Book International.

Data Network for Human Services. (1987) *Socio-economic indicators for Maricopa county.* Phoenix, AZ: Author.

Erickson, E. (1968) *Identity: Youth and crisis.* New York: Norton.

Fetterman, D. M. (1989) *Ethnography: Step by step.* Newbury Park, CA: Sage.

Gilligan, C. (1982) *In a different voice.* Cambridge, MS: Harvard University Press.

Green, J. W. (1982) *Cultural awareness in the human services.* Englewood Cliffs, NJ: Prentice-Hall.

Kettner, P. M., J. M. Daley, and A. W. Nichols. (1985) *Initiating change in organizations and communities.* Monterey, CA: Brooks/Cole.

Kettner, P. M., and L. L. Martin. (1987) *Purchase of service contracting.* Newbury Park, CA: Sage.

Maslow, A. H. (1943) A theory of motivation. *Psychological Review, 50*: 370–96.

Norton, D. G. (1978) *The dual perspective: Inclusion of ethnic minority content in the social work curriculum.* New York: Council on Social Work Education.

Piven, F. F., and R. Cloward. (1971) *Regulating the poor: The functions of public welfare.* New York: Pantheon.

Skinner, B. F. (1971) *Beyond freedom and dignity.* New York: Knopf.

CHAPTER 9

Developing an Intervention Strategy

INTRODUCTION

Macro practice in social work can be viewed as having three major parts: (1) conceptualizing and developing the substantive parts of a change effort, (2) preparing a strategy designed to get the change accepted, and (3) implementation of the strategy. Chapter 8 dealt with part one. This chapter and the next focus on the preparation of a strategy. Implementation issues are incorporated into these chapters as well, but they are not discussed as a separate topic. Implementation issues are highly individualized to the change effort, and sound professional practice involves constant interaction between the plan, the strategies and tactics proposed, and the realities of the actual intervention experience.

Strategy is a critical element of macro practice. Tropman and Erlich (1987) regard strategy as "an orchestrated attempt to influence a person or a system in relation to some goal which an actor desires" (p. 258). Brager, et al. (1987), link strategy to long-range goals and tactics to the short-range and specific behaviors of groups: "Groups having widely different long range goals (strategies) may engage in the same kinds of behaviors (tactics). . . . And a specific group may utilize a wide range of tactics in pursuit of their goals" (p. 177).

The terms strategy and tactics as used here are intended to be consistent with the definitions of Brager, et al. Strategy refers to the overall efforts designed to insure that the proposed change is accepted. Tactics, to be discussed at length in Chapter 10, refer to the specific techniques and behaviors employed in relation to the target system designed to maximize the possibility that the strategy will be successful and the proposed change adopted. The development of strategies and tactics involves some critical decisions. The approach taken can have far-reaching effects on the success of the change effort and its impact on the problem and the target population.

GUIDELINES FOR DEVELOPING
AN INTERVENTION STRATEGY

As in previous chapters, we will present the process of developing a strategy in terms of a number of areas toward which the macro practitioner must focus his or her attention. These foci include: (A) defining participants, (B) examining system readiness for change, (C) selecting a change approach, (D) assessing political and interpersonal considerations, (E) assessing economic considerations, (F) weighing the likelihood of success, (G) setting goals and objectives, (H) selecting appropriate tactics, and (I) preparing a written plan. This chapter is organized around the first seven foci, whereas Focus H and Focus I will be discussed in Chapter 10. Table 9.1 summarizes the major foci and relevant tasks involved in developing an intervention strategy.

Focus A: Defining Participants

Up to this point in the change process it is not unusual for the people involved to be a small core of committed individuals, possibly even close friends or fellow employees, who recognize a condition or problem and are concerned enough

TABLE 9.1   Framework for Developing an Intervention Strategy

Focus	Tasks
A. Defining Participants	1. Identify the initiator system 2. Identify the change agent system 3. Identify the client system 4. Identify the support system 5. Identify the controlling system 6. Identify the host and implementing systems 7. Identify the target system 8. Identify the action system
B. Examining System Readiness for Change	9. Assess general openness to change 10. Identify anticipated or actual response 11. Determine availability of resources 12. Examine outside opposition to change
C. Selecting a Change Approach	13. Select a policy, program, project, personnel, or practice approach
D. Assessing Political and Interpersonal Considerations	14. Address public image and successful change 15. Identify alternative perspectives 16. Assess duration and urgency
E. Assessing Resource Considerations	17. Determine the cost of change 18. Determine the cost of doing nothing
F. Weighing the Likelihood of Success	19. Assess support from individuals, groups, and organizations 20. Assess support from facts and perspectives
G. Setting Goals and Objectives	21. Identify goals 22. Formulate outcome and process objectives 23. Plan activities

to take action. It is perfectly appropriate for this small group to undertake some of the early activities of problem identification and analysis, as long as they do not become totally committed to a particular perspective on the problem.

In order for effective macro change to occur it is necessary to have allies. A good deal of strategy development involves the building of coalitions. People willing to commit themselves to change rarely accept someone else's definitions and perspectives without some revision. (If full participation of all critical actors was accomplished in the problem identification and analysis phases, then achievement of consensus on the problem and proposed solution should not be a barrier to progress at this point.)

One method of identifying, in an orderly, systematic manner, the participants critical to the success of a change effort is to identify people who are affiliated in some way with certain groups or organizations that make up the many systems and subsystems of the change effort.

We will use the term *system* to describe these critical participants. This term is used in the context of systems theory, implying that participants should be viewed as more than simply a collection of individuals who happen to have some common interests and characteristics. As a system or subsystem critical to the success of the change effort, they represent a complex set of interrelationships having system-like attributes that must be recognized and attended to by the core planning group. One of these attributes, for example, is called entropy and refers to the natural tendency of systems to expire without input and regeneration from outside the system. The concept is directly applicable to the types of systems involved in planned change. (For further discussion of systems theory, see von Bertalanffy 1956, or Katz & Kahn 1987.)

The systems to be considered include (1) an initiator system, (2) a change agent system, (3) a client system, (4) a support system, (5) a controlling system, (6) a host system, (7) an implementing system, (8) a target system, and (9) an action system (see also Kettner et al. 1985). It is worth noting here that these terms are used strictly for conceptual purposes to assist in understanding who should be involved and why. They are not terms commonly used among people involved in change efforts. It is more likely that terms like *committee* or *task force* will be used to designate groups, but the professional person who coordinates the effort should be aware, conceptually, of what systems are represented by the significant participants.

Task 1: Identify the Initiator System. The initiator system is made up of those individuals who first recognize the existence of a problem and bring attention to it. This could be a group of parents raising concerns with a school board about increasing violence in their schools or a group of staff members concerned about a lengthening waiting list for service in the counseling program. Individuals who first raise the issue may or may not also become a part of the initial planning process.

It is sometimes necessary and worthwhile to work with a group of individuals who fill appropriate roles and have a thorough knowledge of the problem, but see themselves as powerless to affect the system. Empowerment strategies such as teaching, training, group counseling, or consciousness-raising efforts at this point can pay rich dividends in the long run, and can place appropriate spokespersons into leadership positions rather than substituting less appropriate leaders.

Task 2: Identify the Change Agent System.   From the initiator system, the issue moves to identification of the change agent system. In a professionally assisted change effort this involves an individual designated as the leader of the change effort. We will refer to this person as the change agent. The change agent, together with an initial core planning committee or task force, comprises the change agent system. If the change activity will require drawing on the resources of an organization, it is essential that the organization sanction the change and also be identified as part of the change agent system. This may involve getting formal approval from executive or board, and may require released time from other duties, secretarial support, and other allocation of resources.

The makeup of this system is critical to the change effort because much of what is accomplished will be framed in the perspectives of these individuals. Ideally this system will include representation from the initiator system, people who have experienced the identified problem, people who have had experience in trying to solve the problem, and people who can be influential in getting the change accepted.

The function of the change agent system is to act as a central coordinating point. Many participants in the change effort will be taking on different activities at the same time. It is the job of the change agent system to insure that the change effort is properly organized and carried out from its early conceptualization to the point where it is turned over to others for implementation. As the major systems and perspectives are identified and the action system (discussed in a later section) is formed, the coordinating functions are shifted to the action system.

The work of the change agent system begins with carrying out the problem identification and analysis described in Chapter 8. This planning effort continues as each of the systems and participants is defined and a strategy is developed for getting the change accepted.

Task 3: Identify the Client System.   The client system is made up of those individuals who are asking for and will become the direct beneficiaries of the change if it is implemented. In Chapter 8, we pointed out that macro change efforts begin with identification of a target population and a problem. The client system would be a subset of the target population for whom the specific change effort is being undertaken. In some cases it is possible that the target population and the client system could even be synonymous. For example, if the target population is all homeless people in the town of Liberty, and the purpose of the community change effort is to provide housing and services for all homeless people in Liberty, then the target population and client system are the same.

Different terms are used for conceptual purposes. A target population brings focus to the problem analysis and usually represents a broader spectrum of people. A client system refers to the people who are intended to benefit from the change effort. In the town of Liberty, for example, for a specialized project, the client system could be homeless women and children.

In defining the client system, the change agent should resist the temptation to jump to the easy and obvious definition of the primary beneficiaries, and should patiently and carefully analyze details. For example, if the identified problem is drugs in the schools, several potential beneficiaries could be considered as the client system. A partial list of people who would benefit from eliminating drugs from the schools would include students, teachers, administrators, parents, local police, campus security, neighbors, the school board, and the community as a whole. The question, then, becomes one of establishing priorities for direct benefits, and distinguishing between primary and secondary beneficiaries. The decision will have an important impact on the change effort. If "students who want a good education in a drug free environment" are identified as primary beneficiaries, then the intervention may well be directed toward tighter security and stricter discipline. If, on the other hand, primary beneficiaries are described as "students who use drugs and are unable to maximize their educational opportunities due to impairment," then the intervention may be directed toward treatment.

However the primary beneficiaries are defined, the remaining groups should be identified and listed as secondary beneficiaries. Secondary beneficiaries may be important and may need to be called upon when the change effort needs public support. We will refer to this group as the support system.

Task 4: Identify the Support System. The support system refers to that segment of the community or organization who have an interest in the success of the proposed change and who may receive secondary benefits. This group is expected to be involved in supporting and advocating for the change if they are needed. The boundaries for macro-level changes tend to be defined in a way that the primary focus is on a segment of a community or organization. Total communities as defined by political boundaries (entire towns, cities, counties) or total organizations are rarely the focus of a change effort.

The support system is defined largely by the target population (or client system) and the problem. People have an interest in certain populations and problems for a variety of reasons: a loved one is afflicted with the problem, their employment brings them into close contact, their church or service organization has selected this population for assistance. They are sometimes described by the related concern or issue, such as the "mental health community," or the "foster care community." These are the people the change agent will count on to become involved if decision makers need to be persuaded that the change is necessary. Figure 9.1 illustrates the relationship between initiator, change agent, client and support systems.

Initiator, change agent, and client systems can be seen as incorporated within the boundaries of the support system in that they all have an interest in addressing the need for change. Initiator, client, and change agent systems may overlap, or may represent separate and distinct constituencies.

Task 5: Identify the Controlling System. The controlling system is defined as that group of individuals with the formally delegated authority and the power to approve and order the implementation of the proposed change. Macro-level

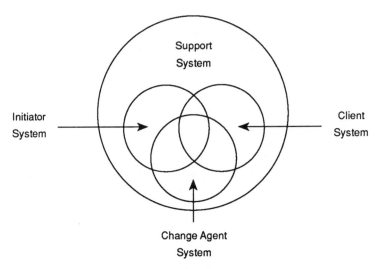

FIGURE 9.1 Relationship of Systems

change invariably involves approval by some formally designated authority. If the change involves a public agency or publicly funded or regulated services, control may rest with a body of elected officials. If the change involves a private agency, control may rest with a board of directors. These bodies are significant to acceptance and implementation of the change effort, and their positions on the proposed change must be known and considered.

Task 6: Identify the Host and Implementing Systems. The host system is the organization or group responsible for implementation of the change. Within the host system is a smaller group who will have day-to-day responsibility for carrying out the change. We refer to this as the implementing system. Implementers are employed by or volunteer for the host system. In most instances of macro-level change the host system will be an organization that will be expected to implement a policy change, a new program, or a project. The listing of systems in Table 9.2 identifies controlling, host, and implementing systems in a school system and in a law enforcement system.

The change agent should be careful not to assume that the positions of the controlling system, host system, and implementing system are identical. It is not unusual for those involved in the execution of policy to disagree with the policymakers

TABLE 9.2 Examples of Controlling, Host, and Implementing Systems

	Controlling	Host	Implementing
School System	School Board	A particular school and its principal	Teachers in the school involved in the change
Law Enforcement System	City Council	Police Chief and department	Police officers involved in the change

and vice versa. Each system should be assessed separately. Figure 9.2 depicts the typical relationships of the controlling, host, and implementing systems.

Task 7: Identify the Target System.   The target system is the individual, group, structure, policy, or practice that needs to be changed for the primary beneficiaries to achieve the desired benefits. The target system is a complex concept that cannot always be defined in clear and simple terms. Often what needs to be changed may include philosophy, values, attitudes, practices, and policies as well as the provision of services. Another complicating factor is that many change efforts must address multiple targets. For example, in addressing the high school's drug problem it may be necessary to educate the faculty and staff about what is happening before they are willing to allow the change to occur. They are targeted for change first. Next, it may be necessary to target the school board to gain their approval to intervene. Finally, having gained the approval and support of teachers and school board members, the intervention, focusing on the "real" target group—high school students using drugs—can be implemented.

Two questions need to be answered in defining the target system: (1) what change (or series of changes) needs to take place in order for the primary beneficiaries to achieve the desired benefits? and (2) what individuals or groups need to agree to the change (or series of changes)? We have defined these individuals or groups as controlling, host, and implementing systems. The target system may lie within the boundaries of any or all of these systems, or it may lie entirely outside of any of them. Target could include, for example, selected school board members, a principal and assistant principals, or a subgroup of teachers, or the target system could be a selected group of students.

Task 8: Identify the Action System.   As all other systems are being defined and participants selected, an action system is being formed. The action system is made up of those individuals from other systems who have an active role in

FIGURE 9.2   Relationships between Controlling, Host, and Implementing Systems

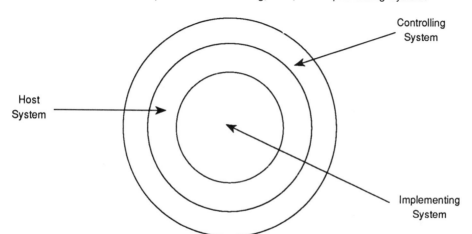

planning the change and moving it toward implementation. Clearly there is a good deal of overlap here with the change agent system, earlier defined as the professional change agent, sanctioning organization, and sometimes a core planning group. While the change agent system forms the core of the action system, other actors also have important roles in providing input into decision making. The action system should include, whenever possible, representatives from all other systems, including those systems in need of change, if the relationship is not excessively adversarial.

For example, if the social problem under consideration is the unmet needs of the homeless, the concern might first be raised by a person who passes by a few old men sleeping in doorways every day on her way from the bus to her place of work (initiator). She finds that several other employees at her place of work have the same concern and raises the issue to the city council (controlling system), where it is assigned to the City Department of Human Services (change agent system and host system). The social worker (change agent and possibly implementer) forms a task force which includes those who brought the issue to the council. As the condition is researched and analyzed, more people are added to the task force. Professionals who work with the homeless (support system) would be asked to join, as would some current or former homeless people (client system) and someone from the city's political or administrative structure who understands the potentialities and limitations of the city's participation (controlling system). When all the significant participants have been identified, this group would become the central decision-making body in the change effort and would be defined as the action system.

Systems in Interaction. In examining these systems in interaction, it is important to remember that we distinguish among them and define them separately for conceptual purposes only. In actual practice, all systems could be within one organization, and it is highly probable that many systems will overlap. The interrelationships of all systems is depicted in Figure 9.3.

FIGURE 9.3 Systems in Interaction

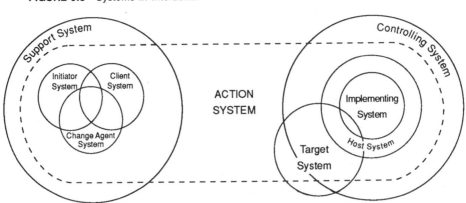

One side of the diagram includes those systems proposing and favoring change. The larger system is the support system, and includes all systems favoring change. Contained within the support system we find the initiator, client, and change agent systems, all with possible varying degrees of overlap. On the other side of the diagram we find those systems identified as in need of change. The controlling, host, and implementing systems are represented by concentric circles in that each subsystem is typically contained within the span of control of the next larger system. The target system may lie within any of these systems or even outside all three. The action system may overlap any or all of these systems.

An example illustrating all systems within one organization would be a situation in which an organizational change is proposed. For example, a human service agency may have a special program for "crack babies" and their mothers (the client system) which includes detoxification, rehabilitation, counseling, and parent training. After six months, a supervisor (initiator system and change agent system) notices that the case managers (implementing system) have been practicing "creaming," providing the bulk of services to the most highly motivated clients and ignoring the needs of the least motivated. In this example, this practice of "creaming" would be the target—that which is to be changed. The supervisor calls the problem to the attention of the executive director (representing the host system) and the executive director raises it with the board (the controlling system), and recommends that incentives (the proposed change) be developed for case managers to work with less motivated clients. A task force (action system) made up of the supervisor, a case manager, a board member, administrator, and an ex-client now volunteering for the agency examine the problems and possibilities of directing more service to unmotivated clients.

All this has taken place within the boundaries of a single organization with essentially no input from extraorganizational sources. This illustrates the nature of the shifting boundaries of systems, while demonstrating the value of retaining conceptual clarity in defining the systems. Even though the terms *controlling, host,* and *implementing* may never be used, it is important that the change agent understand the domain, authority, and power of each, and keep roles, responsibilities, and expectations for each clear and distinct.

Focus B: Examining System Readiness for Change

As the change process unfolds, each of the systems defined above should be assessed for its readiness to support the proposed change. An assessment of readiness should include consideration of an openness to change in general, commitment to the proposed change, availability of resources to implement the proposed change, and the degree of outside resistance to the proposed change. These considerations will most likely be assessed differently for different systems. However, it is likely that there will be some similarities among those systems promoting change (initiator, change agent, client, support, and action systems) and among those with whom they are hoping to bring about change (controlling, host, implementing, and target).

Task 9: Assess General Openness to Change.   General openness to change involves an informal assessment, based on experience, of how people in decision-making positions have dealt with earlier proposals. This is not likely to be a consideration for those systems promoting change, since few are likely to have a history, with the possible exception of the support system and the change agent's employing organization. Furthermore, the significant issue is that these systems are clearly in support of change in this instance. However, when examining the systems to be changed, it can be a very different story. Much has been written about the difficulties of getting organizations (especially bureaucracies) to change (see, for example, Brager & Holloway 1978). Analyzing past experiences may be helpful in finding those subsystems or individuals that are most likely to be responsive to the proposed change.

Task 10: Identify Anticipated or Actual Response.   Commitment to the proposed change should be examined in terms of each system's enthusiasm in endorsing the change in its existing form. It is characteristic of community and organizational change that there will be differences in perspective on what form changes should take, even when there is enthusiastic agreement that change is needed. Low levels of commitment to the change as proposed can have a negative effect on its acceptance and eventual implementation. Assessment of commitment should involve examination of degree of enthusiasm as well as degree of internal consensus about the design of the proposed change.

Task 11: Determine Availability of Resources.   Availability of resources, for many change efforts, will be the key question. While openness to change and commitment to the proposed change are helpful, availability of resources is a sine qua non. Resources for the systems to be changed usually refers to budgeted dollars, but should also be understood to include reassigning staff, use of volunteers, in-kind resources such as computer time, supplies, space, and others. Resources for the systems promoting change usually refers to numbers of people, time available, and the willingness to persist if opposed.

Task 12: Examine Outside Opposition to Change.   The final factor to be explored with each system is the degree of external resistance or opposition experienced. There may be instances where a controlling system—elected local officials, for example—supports a proposed change but the constituency it represents—grassroot groups, for example—is opposed. Almost any proposed change that requires public funds will find external resistance from those groups that are competing for the funds. If pressure tactics are to be used, the change agent should ascertain whether the pressures that can be brought about through this change effort will be able to offset pressures brought by those resisting the change. For the systems promoting change it is important to identify possible vulnerable targets within its ranks. People who can be pressured to back down may represent a liability, and those promoting change should be aware of it. A summary of considerations is illustrated in Table 9.3.

TABLE 9.3 Assessing System Readiness for Change

	Systems Promoting Change	Systems to Be Changed
	Initiator, Client, Change Agent, Support, Action	*Controlling, Host, Implementing, Target*
General Openness to Change	Probably not an issue, since these groups are promoting change.	If these systems have shown tendencies in the past to resist changes of this type, this should serve as an early warning.
Anticipated or Actual Response to Proposed Change	How committed are those promoting change to the type of change being proposed? What are the differences, if any? Are some committed only to a highly specific solution?	Is there consensus or disagreement about the type of change being proposed? How strong are feelings for and/or against it?
Availability of Resources for Proposed Change	Do the systems promoting change have the skills and human resources to see the change effort through to completion, even if there is resistance?	Do the systems to be changed have the funding, staff, facilities, equipment, or other resources needed to implement the proposed change?
Opposition to Proposed Change	What forces outside these systems are opposing change? How strong is the opposition?	What is the source of outside opposition? How strong are the pressures to reject the proposed change? What significant actors are most vulnerable to pressures?

Focus C: Selecting a Change Approach

One of the first agenda items for the action system is selecting a change approach. As the change agent moves toward completion of all of the problem identification and analysis tasks covered in Chapter 8, the nature of the problem and significant supporting information should be coming into focus. This makes clear what needs to be changed. An important question yet to be answered is how the change should come about. For example, if one of the client service programs within an agency is providing a poor quality of services, improving the services may require a policy change (e.g., redefining eligibility). This same situation could also require a program change (e.g., changing the type of counseling provided), or a project change (e.g., testing out a new service with a limited number of clients). Changes in personnel and practices are also options, but we recommend that their use be limited to situations in which policy, program, or project approaches are determined not to be feasible. These five change approaches will be discussed below.

Task 13: Select a Policy, Program, Project, Personnel, or Practice Approach.   The professionally assisted change efforts discussed in these chapters are intended to fall into two very general categories: (1) those that lead to an improved quality of life for the clients served, or (2) those that lead to an improved quality of work life for employees so that their energies can be devoted toward providing the best possible services to clients. In order to address these two categories, we propose five approaches to change.

Policy.   Policy is represented by a formally adopted statement that reflects goals and strategies or agreements on a settled course of action. Policies may be established by elected representatives, boards, administrators, or by a vote of the people affected.

In some instances, a policy may be needed in order to change a situation. For example, a new policy that outlines a grievance process for clients may be empowering to those persons who feel they have no recourse when they disagree with agency practices. In other situations, existing policy may be unnecessarily restrictive and need to be amended. For example, administrators of congregate housing for the elderly may find that policies created to facilitate transfers and relocations actually tie their hands rather than enable them to make individualized and caring decisions.

Program.   Programs are prearranged sets of activities designed to achieve a set of goals and objectives. In macro practice, programs are usually intended to provide services directly to clients. Sometimes they are of a supportive nature, such as fund-raising or public relations programs.

Program change will vary. Some change efforts will result in the establishment of new programs to serve a special population group. Other change efforts may focus on altering existing programs so that they are designed to be more sensitive to client needs.

Project.   Projects are much like programs but have a time limited existence and are more flexible so that they can be adapted to the needs of a changing environment. Projects, if deemed successful and worthwhile, are often permanently installed as programs.

Often change agents will find that creating a project that demonstrates a new or different intervention is more palatable to decision makers than making a long-term program commitment. Therefore, it is likely that change will result first in a demonstration or pilot project before a program change is possible.

Personnel.   Many types of activities take place in communities and organizations. Sometimes people experience seemingly insurmountable differences and engage in ongoing conflict. Employees occasionally get involved in an attempt to depose an unpopular administrator. The professional change agent should proceed very carefully before getting involved in personnel-related issues. Several factors should be considered. First, is the proposed personnel-related change effort being considered because of the reasons stated above: improvement of the quality of life of clients or improvement of work life so that clients can be better served? Second, will the proposed change be dealt with above board through regularly established channels? When the target of a change effort is an individual, there is often a temptation to proceed "underground."

Brager and Holloway (1978) suggest that, under certain circumstances covert tactics may be appropriate. First, one must determine if agency officials are ignoring client needs in favor of their own interests. Second, the change agent must decide if the use of formal, overt sources may jeopardize self, clients, or colleagues. Third, if overt means have failed or are clearly not feasible, one may consider covert tactics. In any case, the professional change agent should recognize the potential risks, including loss of job, should be convinced that the change is worth the consequences, and should be prepared to accept them if necessary. Ethical practice is basic to social work, and ethical dilemmas often emerge in which either side in two opposing perspectives could be the "right" one. Ethical dilemmas will be discussed more thoroughly in the final chapter.

Practice.   The fifth focus of change, practice, refers to the way organizations or individuals within them go about doing business. Practices tend to be less formal than policies. They may even be specific to individuals or groups, and, therefore, are more elusive than policies. Well-designed policy, together with monitoring and evaluation capability, is usually a stronger and more permanent remedy for inappropriate or offensive practices. For example, if a receptionist treats clients rudely and proves to be insensitive to their concerns, several options are available. He or she could be reprimanded, sent for training, or even fired. These actions may or may not change behavior, but even if they do, they are unlikely to solve the problem because they focus only on the practice of one person. A more permanent solution would be to incorporate into the personnel processing system for receptionists an expectation of courtesy to clients. This would include job description, recruitment literature, and criteria for hiring, performance evaluation, merit increases, and promotion. Dealt with in this way, not only is one employee encouraged to change practices or behaviors but all future employees as well.

Approaches in Interaction.   A decision about the change approach is obviously intimately connected to a decision about the nature of the problem and the target system. The important issues to be resolved in defining the change approach are: (1) what is needed to remedy the problem, and (2) how ready are the people in decision-making positions to recognize, accept, and implement the remedy. For example, many changes can be handled in a very simple and straightforward manner. More day-care slots are needed for single mothers in employment training programs; the change agent calls this to the attention of the appropriate people in the human service department and more slots are added. Parents want drug and alcohol education in the high schools; the school board agrees to provide it.

Other changes, however, may require, first, policy, then program change. The state department of human services may recognize a need to provide preventative educational and counseling services to teens who are at high risk of becoming pregnant. Conservative legislators may be opposed to allocating funds seen as violating parental prerogatives. The change may require that enabling legislation be passed first and that a project or program then be implemented. The change agent and action system should carefully analyze the proposed change and system readiness for change, and should prepare a plan that allows for the appropriate sequencing of policy, program, and/or project changes.

Focus D: Assessing Political and Interpersonal Considerations

Several times throughout the book we have discussed the importance of politics in bringing about change. We address these considerations more directly in this section. *Politics* is used here in a broad sense of having to do with the different ways individuals important to a change effort may respond when asked to support the change. This includes consideration of partisan politics, but is not limited to that arena.

Task 14: Address Public Image and Successful Change.   An early question to ask is: Who is involved in promoting the proposed change, and how are they perceived by decision makers? Preparing a list of participants in each system and assessing the political and interpersonal strengths and liabilities of each participant can assist the change agent and action system in making the best use of each participant. Some people with valuable technical expertise may be seen as highly controversial and a liability when viewed from the interpersonal/political perspective. This applies to both community and organizational change efforts, but may be more important in organizational change because of the closeness of working relationships and the greater likelihood of people knowing more about each other than they would in the community arena. An additional question to be asked all the way through is: Has anyone critical to the success of this change been left out? Failure to involve people who can help can be as damaging as involving people who may harm the effort.

Task 15: Identify Alternative Perspectives.   A second consideration is perspective. People involved in change in the field of human services are often amazed to learn that there is almost no concern raised that does not have an opposing view. For every advocate of a woman's right to have control over her own body, there is one who will support a fetus's right to survive. For every person concerned about child abuse, there is one who is equally concerned about perceived abuses of parental prerogatives by child welfare workers.

It is tempting to dismiss opponents' views as uninformed and unenlightened, but in undertaking macro-level change it is unwise to do so. Alternative perspectives should be carefully analyzed for their merit and their potential or actual political appeal. Even plotting a spectrum of opinions, together with some educated estimates of levels of public support of each, can be an informative exercise for action system participants. Each perspective should also be weighed for the intensity of its support. The likelihood is that the closer to the extremes, the more intense the feelings. Figure 9.4 illustrates a continuum of possible perspectives on services to AIDS patients.

Task 16: Assess Duration and Urgency.   A third area of consideration that affects perception of a problem is the length of time a problem has existed and the extent to which it is considered threatening to individual or organizational survival. We refer to these as duration and urgency, and deal with them together because in many ways they are interrelated.

I————————I————————I————————I————————I

| AIDS patients should be cared for entirely in publically run facilities that also provide support services. | The public should supplement AIDS medical programs with support services. | AIDS patients who can afford it or are insured should pay for their own care. Others should be cared for in public hospitals. | Selected AIDS patients who cannot afford medical treatment should be cared for in a private facility but not paid for with public funds. | AIDS patients should be responsible for their own care. |

FIGURE 9.4 A Continuum of Perspectives

Longstanding problems are hard to change. People become desensitized and community and organizational leaders are not easily persuaded that there is really a problem that needs attention. For example, it took a class action suit on behalf of the chronically mentally ill citizens of Arizona to force the state legislature to address their needs. Recently emerging problems like homelessness among young families tend to have more popular support for change. Occasionally, longstanding problems can be presented in a new way, as has been done with alcohol abuse in the campaign against drunk driving over the last decade.

For newly emerging or newly defined problems, the change agent should examine the issue of urgency. The closer the problem is to threatening survival needs such as food, clothing, shelter, safety, and medical care, the more likely those in a position to make changes will attend to it. Within organizations, problems that directly or indirectly affect the budget, and therefore the capacity of the organization to survive, tend to receive a relatively higher priority than non-budget-related problems. The proposed change should be weighed in terms of their duration and urgency, and these factors used appropriately in preparing a strategy for promoting the proposed change.

Focus E: Assessing Resource Considerations

The major concern of decision makers about proposed change in most cases comes down to how much it will cost. Whether or not social workers agree with this value perspective, we operate within a money-oriented system. Decision makers often look at the cost before they even consider the rationale for implementing the change. Improved quality of life is not, in itself, enough of a rationale for persons responsible for managing limited resources to agree to support a particular change effort.

Task 17: Determine the Cost of Change.   The change agent must, therefore, make some estimates of what the proposed change will cost. This can be difficult, because in many cases the details of the intervention design are not even worked out until there are some assurances that the change will be accepted. Take, for example, a situation where the parents in a community want the school board to sponsor more organized and supervised after-school activities. Some may want arts and crafts, some athletic activities, some drama and music options. These details have probably not been addressed at the point where the school board is approached. The change agent must be prepared for a response that "the proposed change will cost too much and resources are not available." To counter this, some preliminary calculations must be prepared at least to the point of estimating the number of staff persons and approximate salaries required. Technical expertise may have to be consulted to arrive at realistic cost estimates. While most decision makers will want to conduct their own analysis of costs, estimates by the proposers of change can at least serve as standards for comparison.

Task 18: Determine the Cost of Doing Nothing.   A very valuable statistic for comparative purposes, if it can be calculated, is the cost of nonresolution of this problem or nonimplementation of the proposed change. It is important to impress upon decision makers that there are also long-term costs associated with doing nothing. For example, costs for in-patient or residential services can run as high as $4,000 to $5,000 a month. At first blush, an intensive vocational training program for high-risk adolescents costing $10,000 per client per year may appear outrageously expensive. However, if presented side by side with data demonstrating that 90 percent of the clients who complete this program become self-sufficient, decision makers may be persuaded that it really represents a long-term cost savings.

Focus F: Weighing the Likelihood of Success

When the major participants, the proposed change, and the political and economic issues have been identified, the time has come to weigh the relative strength of supporting and opposing forces and to decide if the change effort is to be a "go" or a "no-go." This can be done in an orderly fashion by adapting Kurt Lewin's techniques of force-field analysis (1951). The issue for consideration here is whether or not to invest additional time, energy, and resources. The experienced change agent recognizes that there is little value in moral victories. If a change effort is to be undertaken, there should be some chance of succeeding. Force-field analysis can enable the change agent to make an informed decision about the likelihood of success.

We propose a modification of Lewin's framework which examines two areas: (1) support from individuals, groups, and organizations, and (2) support from facts and perspectives.

Task 19: Assess Support from Individuals, Groups, and Organizations.
Applying the force-field analysis model, support from individuals, groups, and organizations should be laid out in three columns. Column one represents the driving or supporting forces. Column two represents neutral forces, and column three represents the restraining or opposing forces. Identifying each of the systems involved, together with their key individuals or groups will provide a graphic depiction of supporting and opposing forces, and will help in determining the possibility of success if the change effort goes forward. Figure 9.5 illustrates a force-field analysis.

SUPPORT FROM INDIVIDUALS, GROUPS, AND ORGANIZATIONS			
System	**Driving/ Supporting Forces**	**→ Neutral Entities ←**	**Restraining/ Opposing Forces**
Initiator System	Homeless advocates, T. Johnson, L. Stearns		
Change Agent System	St. Catherine's parish and youth worker, J. Foster		
Client System	Homeless teens in Douglas County		
Support System	Homeless advocates, Parents of Runaways, Inc., existing homeless programs		
Controlling System	City council members supporting change	City council members not yet taking position	City council members opposed to teen shelter
Host System		City Department of Human Services	
Implementing System	Potential contract agencies		
Target System		City council member votes in favor of funding proposed teen shelter	
Action System	Youth worker, J. Foster, advocates, two homeless teens, two social workers from existing shelters		
Other Systems		A large percentage of the general public	Taxpayers Against Increased Public Social Services (TAPS) City newspapers Task force on CMI Homeless (who are competing for funding)

FIGURE 9.5 Force-Field Analysis of Individuals, Groups, and Organizations Supporting and Opposing a Proposed Project to Serve Homeless Teens

Task 20: Assess Support from Facts and Perspectives.   Following the identification of individuals, groups, and organizations supporting and opposing the change effort, we propose that facts and perspectives be identified in the same way. It is unlikely that any new research or analysis is necessary at this point. Identifying supporting and opposing facts and perspectives involves drawing on everything now known and available in terms of statistics, history, theory, research, etiology, interpersonal and political factors, or resource considerations. Each should be examined for its potential driving or restraining effects on the change effort. Figure 9.6 illustrates examples of support from facts and perspectives.

Using this format, action system participants next initiate a discussion session focused on making the "go/no-go" decision. An option, of course, is to gather more facts or to postpone the decision to a more opportune time. Additional fact gathering, if absolutely necessary, is considered advisable only if it is highly focused and time-limited. If, however, fact gathering is proposed as a delaying tactic or intended simply to avoid making a difficult decision, it should be recognized for what it is and rejected. It should also be recognized that this may be the point where some participants will believe the proposed change to be unattainable and will decide to drop out, while others may choose to pursue the effort. Here again, it should be emphasized that the professional person acting as change agent must make as rational, non-emotional a decision as possible. Necessary changes that have a good chance of success should be supported. Causes that are likely to be defeated as currently conceptualized should be tabled until they are more fully developed or the timing is better.

Focus G: Setting Goals and Objectives

Goals are brief, one sentence or phrase, general statements of expected outcomes (e.g., To reduce the number of dropouts in the Jefferson district). Objectives spell out the details for each goal in measurable terms, including expected outcomes and the processes to achieve them. Activities are lists of tasks that must be undertaken and completed in order to achieve each objective.

If the decision is made to proceed, the final step before selecting tactics is to establish a set of goals, objectives, and activities for the change. Goals and objectives are intended to act as a beacon to aid in keeping the change effort on track. Activities specify precisely what is to be done, by whom, and within what time frame.

Setting goals and objectives is probably as much art as it is science. The purpose is to take what can be a very large and complex undertaking and to break it up into manageable subsets. Each subset has its own set of goals, objectives, and activities.

FIGURE 9.6 Support from Facts and Perspectives on the Problems of Homeless Teens

Driving/Supporting Forces →|←	Restraining/Opposing Forces
1. Teen homelessness is increasing by 20 percent per year	1. Resources are already inadequate to meet existing needs of homeless families
2. Homeless teens have been drawn into drug trafficking, prostitution and many property crimes	2. No federal or state funding is available; homelessness is considered a local problem
3. Media have increased coverage of the problem; the public increasingly favors some action	3. Suburban cities are not willing to contribute needed support; major urban city council feels it should be considered a regional problem

The process begins with re-examining the change effort and organizing it into categories or sections. This takes some practice and requires knowledge of the subject area, which is why problem analysis is so important in macro-level change. The problem, as analyzed and conceptualized in the problem analysis phase, becomes a theme that is repeated throughout the change episode. The following examples illustrate how one might go about this first step of breaking a large and complex change effort into subsections or categories. They are built on the assumption that the preceding community or organizational analysis and the problem analysis work have been completed.

Example 1

The proposed change is a three-year project to reduce teen pregnancy and enable at-risk teens to graduate from high school.

Project Subcategories

1. Building self-esteem
2. Providing health, hygiene, and sex education
3. Providing academic support
4. Providing financial support

In the example, we have depicted a four-part program designed to achieve the purpose as stated above. In both examples, each of the four areas listed above would have its own set of goals, objectives, and activities.

Example 2

The proposed change is a policy change that provides for financial incentives for programs demonstrating measurable improvement with alcohol-abusing clients.

Project Subcategories

1. Developing valid and reliable indicators
2. Developing the fiscal incentive package
3. Developing quality assurance measure

By dividing the change effort into subcategories, each part of the effort can proceed toward achieving its own set of goals and objectives in a way that is more concentrated and focused than if all objectives and activities were organized under a single goal. The exception to this principle of subdividing is when the change effort is so clear and simple that it does not require subcategories. For example, a project to conduct a client satisfaction survey might be a project that requires only a single set of goals, objectives, and activities. It is often true, however, that simple, unopposed change efforts come about without complications, and do not require the type of change process described in this book. If one follows the steps recommended in this book, it is likely that one is dealing with relatively complex change.

Once the subcategories are selected, a set of goals, objectives, and activities should be developed for each. They should always be thought of as a set or package, not as items that stand alone, even though they are occasionally used alone.

Task 21: Identify Goals.   A goal is a general statement of expected outcomes or a desired future state (Kettner et al. 1985). It need not be observable or measurable. It is simply a statement of hopes or expectations, stated in a positive and general enough way to get agreement and support. Continuing with the above examples, the following goal statements would be appropriate.

Teen Pregnancy Project

    Goal 1: To improve client self-esteem.

    Goal 2: To increase client knowledge of health, hygiene, and contraception.

    Goal 3: To strengthen client academic abilities.

    Goal 4: To increase client financial resources.

Measuring Client Outcomes

    Goal 1: To develop indicators of client change.

    Goal 2: To develop fiscal incentives to promote client improvement.

    Goal 3: To develop methods for assuring service quality.

Task 22: Formulate Outcome and Process Objectives.   Once a goal statement is written, the next step is to specify objectives. Objectives are intended to move the change effort toward the goal. They are highly specific and measurable. There are two types: (1) outcome objectives, and (2) process objectives. One outcome objective is written for each goal, and specifies the results or outcomes to be achieved. One or more process objectives then specify the process to be followed in order to achieve the result. When the outcome objective and all its related process objectives are completed and written out, it should be evident that the process objectives, when completed, will lead to achievement of the outcome objective, and that the outcome objective, when accomplished, will move the effort toward the goal. A complete objective, whether outcome or process, has four parts: (1) a time frame, (2) a target, (3) a result, and (4) a criterion for measuring or documenting the result (Kettner et al. 1985). In the following pages, examples will be given of both outcome and process objectives.

The time frame is stated in terms of the month, day, and year by which the result will be achieved. In situations where a project's start date is unknown, the time frame may be specified in terms of time elapsed from the beginning of the project (e.g., ''within three months of the beginning of the project,'' or "by the end of the first year"). Once a start date is known, it is wise to go back and fill in actual dates, since objectives are often also used as monitoring tools.

The second part of an objective, the target, specifies the individuals or focal point for which the objective is written. Outcome objectives are focused on a quality of life change and will identify the individuals for whom the change is intended. Process objectives may have an object (such as a program or a department) as a target, instead of a population.

Statements should be as precise as current knowledge will allow. A drug treatment program, for example, might specify "twenty-four cocaine addicts at least eighteen years of age and currently employed" as its target. A process objective might specify "the counseling program" or the "performance evaluation system" as its target or focal point. For reasons stated in earlier chapters in this text, the more precise the target, the greater the likelihood of a successful intervention. As an example, the teen pregnancy program mentioned above will be used to illustrate how outcome and process objectives fit together to form a plan of action. The following diagram illustrates partial objectives, including a time frame and a target.

Outcome objective:

[time frame   ]
By June 30, 19XX,

[target   ]
at least fifty teens considered to be at risk of pregnancy . . .

Process objective:

[time frame   ]
By February 1, 19XX,

    . . . will be developed for

[target   ]
a group of teens considered to be at risk of pregnancy . . .

In this illustration, the target is the same. The reason will become evident as the objectives are developed further.

The third part of an objective is a phrase that specifies the expected outcome or result to be achieved when all activities are completed. This phrase differs depending on whether the objective is an outcome or a process objective. An outcome objective focuses on a quality of life change for the target population. Outcome objectives refer to such factors as improved knowledge and skill, improved relationships with spouse, reduction of alcohol abuse and other such changes. Process objectives focus on the result expected at the completion of the process. Results might include such objects as a report, a plan, or a new data collection form. Continuing with the example of the outcome and process objectives used above, we add the following outcome and result.

Outcome objective:

    [time frame   ]
    By June 30, 19XX,

    [target   ]
    at least fifty teens considered to be at risk of pregnancy . . .

    [outcome   ]
    will increase their knowledge of health, hygiene, and contraception . . .

Process objective:

    [time frame   ]
    By February 1, 19XX,

    [result   ]
    a training curriculum on health, hygiene, and contraception will be developed

    [target   ]
    for teens considered to be at risk of pregnancy . . .

The final part of an objective is the criterion which will be used to determine whether or not the objective has been achieved. Objectives must be precise and measurable, yet sometimes the result to be achieved seems vague and elusive. Some programs, for example, are designed to improve self-esteem. The question is, how does one know whether or not self-esteem has been improved? The criterion specified in the objective insures that only one standard will be used. If improving self-esteem is the result, then it must be measured by a standardized test designed to measure self-esteem. The criterion for an outcome objective usually begins with the phrase, ". . . as measured by . . ." Increased self-esteem might be measured by the Index of Self-Esteem (Hudson, 1982). Process objectives generally produce products or achieve milestones in a process, and use a different type of criterion to measure the result. In most cases, process objectives will use the phrase, ". . . as documented by . . ." indicating some formal product or result that will be accepted as documentation that the process objective has been completed. Continuing examples of outcome and process objectives on the teen pregnancy project follow.

Outcome objective:

    [time frame   ]
    By June 30, 19XX,

    [target   ]
    at least fifty teens considered to be at risk of pregnancy . . .

    [outcome   ]
    will increase their knowledge of health, hygiene and contraception . . .

    [criterion   ]
    as measured by a pretest/posttest developed for the course.

Process objective:

[time frame   ]
By February 1, 19XX,

[result   ]
a training curriculum on health, hygiene, and contraception will be developed

[target   ]
for teens considered to be at risk of pregnancy . . .

[criterion   ]
as documented by receipt of a completed training package.

When all four parts—time frame, target, result, and criterion—have been written, the objective is complete. The foregoing examples are reproduced in Table 9.4 to reinforce the understanding of the differences between outcome and process objectives.

Typically a set of goals and objectives will include one goal, one outcome objective, and several process objectives. For example, in the program outlined in Table 9.4, the following might be the focus of goals and objectives.

Goal

To increase knowledge about health and pregnancy for teens at risk.

Outcome Objective

By June 30, 19XX, to increase knowledge of health, hygiene, and contraception for fifty teens considered to be at risk of pregnancy as measured by a pretest/posttest developed for the course.

Some possible process objectives:

1. Develop training curriculum
2. Develop and reproduce training materials
3. Recruit fifty teens at risk of pregnancy
4. Secure a suitable training location
5. Hire trainers
6. Implement the program
7. Evaluate the program

Task 23: Plan Activities.   The final step in Focus G is to itemize activities. Activities represent the highest level of detail incorporated into the plan. Each activity represents a step which, when accomplished, moves the project closer to achievement of a process objective. Activities should specify the work to be done, the person responsible, and a time frame. The Gantt chart, originated early in the century by management pioneer Henry L. Gantt, has proved to be a useful format for setting up activities. A Gantt chart is made up of columns and rows.

TABLE 9.4 Sample Outcome and Process Objectives

	Outcome	Process
Time Frame	By June 30, 19XX	By February 1, 19XX
Target	50 teens considered to be at risk of pregnancy	for teens considered to be at risk of pregnancy
Outcome/Result	will increase their knowledge of health, hygiene, and contraception	a training curriculum on health, hygiene, and contraception will be developed
Criterion	as measured by a pretest/posttest developed for the course.	as documented by receipt of a completed training package.

Each row represents an activity, and columns are used to identify activity number, person responsible, and the beginning and ending month. Illustrated below is an example of a Gantt chart applied to one of the process objectives for the pregnancy prevention program.

The Gantt chart in Figure 9.7 depicts a training project beginning July 1, phasing in each activity sequentially over the next seven months, and delivering the completed training package as promised on February 1. The horizontal lines across the columns indicate the approximate anticipated beginning and ending times for those activities. The *1* in the February column next to activity number 7 indicates that the completed training package is due on that specific date.

In preparing an action plan for a macro-level change, each subsection of the intervention should include a set of goals, objectives, and activities. When these are developed at an acceptable level of precision, with responsibilities and time

FIGURE 9.7 A Gantt Chart

Process Objective: By February 1, 19XX, to develop a training curriculum on health, hygiene, and contraception for teens at risk of pregnancy, as documented by receipt of a completed training package.

Activity Number	Activity	Person Responsible	Time Frame J F M A M J J A S O N D
1.	Develop course objectives.	J. Smith	
2.	Prepare content outline modules on health, hygiene, and contraception.	J. Smith/ L. Black	
3.	Select teaching methods for each module.	L. Black	
4.	Prepare workbooks and handouts for each module.	C. Rich	
5.	Print up workbooks and handouts.	B. Wood	
6.	Develop pretest/posttest.	J. Smith	
7.	Deliver complete training package.	J. Smith	1

frames clearly specified, the action plan is complete. The last steps in macro-level change involve the selection of tactics and the development of a written plan. These final steps are discussed in the next chapter.

REFERENCES

Brager, G., and S. Holloway. (1978) *Changing human service organizations: Politics and practice.* New York: Free Press.

Brager, G., H. Specht, and J. L. Torczyner. (1987) *Community organizing.* New York: Columbia University Press.

Hudson. W. W. (1982) *The clinical measurement package.* Homewood, IL: Dorsey Press.

Katz, D., and R. L. Kahn. (1966) *The social psychology of organizations.* New York: John Wiley & Sons.

Kettner, P. M., J. M. Daley, and A. W. Nichols. (1985) *Initiating change in organizations and communities.* Monterey, CA: Brooks/Cole.

Lewin, K. (1951) *Field theory in social science.* New York: Harper & Row.

Tropman, J. E., and J. L. Erlich. (1987) Introduction to strategies. In F. M. Cox, J. L. Erlich, J. Rothman, and J. E. Tropman, eds., *Strategies of community organization* (2nd ed., pp. 257–69). Itasca, IL: F. E. Peacock.

von Bertalanffy, L. (1950) An outline of general system theory. *The British Journal for the Philosophy of Science, 1*(2): 493–512.

CHAPTER **10**

Selecting Appropriate Tactics

INTRODUCTION

Chapter 9 addressed strategy, which refers to the development of a written plan directed at bringing about the proposed change. Deciding on a strategy can be a time-consuming and detailed process. Although many may agree that a problem exists, getting agreement on just how the situation should be changed is seldom easy. Special efforts must be concentrated on tactics designed to get the change accepted.

Tactic selection tests the professional judgment of the change agent, particularly in how to approach the target system. Certain tactics can raise ethical dilemmas. Selecting tactics calls for mature, professional judgment in community and organizational change. Social workers should be open to the possibility that practices in many of the arenas in which they operate are well entrenched and there will be a natural tendency to resist. The fact that agency missions are stated in inspiring words does not mean that all agencies carry out those missions. Practitioners must be aware that they are a part of legitimized systems that often contribute to the oppression experienced by the client group they are trying to serve. Selecting appropriate tactics requires one to think critically and to carefully analyze the target system.

FOCUS A: SELECTING APPROPRIATE TACTICS

The choice of tactics is a critical decision point in planned change. Tactics have been defined as "any skillful method used to gain an end" (Brager et al. 1987, 288). Whereas strategy is the long-range linking of activities to achieve the desired goal, tactics are reflected in day-to-day behaviors (Brager & Holloway 1978). As the change agent engages in tactical behavior, it is important not to lose sight of the goal toward which these behaviors are directed.

Brager, et al. (1987), identify four essential properties of tactics used by professional change agents: "(1) they are planned . . . (2) they are used to evoke specific responses . . . (3) they involve interaction with others . . . and (4) they are goal-oriented" (p. 288). In addition, it is our contention that a fifth property must be in place in professional social work change efforts: (5) the tactic will do no harm to members of the client system and, whenever possible, members of that system will be involved in tactical decision making.

Change almost always involves influencing the allocation of scarce resources—authority, status, power, goods, services, or money. Decisions about tactics, therefore, must take into consideration whether the resources are being allocated willingly or whether someone must be persuaded to make the allocation. If there is agreement on the part of the action and target systems that the proposed change is acceptable and that resources will be allocated, a collaborative approach can be adopted. If there is agreement that the proposed change is acceptable but a reluctance or refusal to allocate resources, or if there is disagreement about the need for the proposed change, then a more coercive approach may be necessary if the change effort is to proceed.

For example, a change effort may focus on the inability of physically disabled people to get around the city and travel to needed service providers. A thorough study documents the problem, and a dial-a-ride transportation service is proposed. The planning commission and city council graciously accept the report, agree on the need, and thank the Transportation for the Disabled Task Force. Three city council members favor funding, three are opposed, and one is undecided. If the undecided council member can be persuaded to favor funding, then collaborative tactics can be adopted. If, however, he or she decides to oppose funding or if a compromise would undermine the change effort, then tactics designed to coerce support must be adopted. For collaborative approaches to be adopted, there must be agreement on both the proposed change and the allocation of needed resources.

In the social work literature, tactics have been divided into three broad categories: collaboration, campaign, and contest (Brager & Holloway 1978; Brager et al. 1987). In this chapter, we use these terms to describe the relationship between the action and target systems. *Collaboration* implies a working relationship where the two systems agree that change must occur, whereas contest tactics indicate disagreement between the two systems. *Campaign* tactics are used when the target must be convinced of the importance of the change, but when communication is still possible between the two systems. The effectiveness of the "campaign" may determine whether collaboration or contest follows. *Contest* tactics are used when neither of the other two are possible any longer. Change efforts that begin with one set of tactics may progress to other sets, depending on the evolving relationship between the action and target systems. The continuum along which these tactical categories fall is as follows:

Collaboration ↔ Campaign ↔ Contest

Although we categorize these relationships, success may hinge on the change agent's ability to keep the action and target systems in a state of continual interaction. It is possible that what begins as a collaborative relationship will move to conflict when new issues arise during the change process. It is equally likely that the relationship will vascillate between various gradations of communication, with both systems uncertain about the other, even when compromise can be reached. In short, these relationships ebb and flow, sometimes unpredictably, given the political situation, and sometimes all too predictably, given the change agent's prior experience with the target system.

Our concern is that the social worker never take the relationship between the action and target system for granted. To assume that the target is immovable before communication has been attempted demonstrates poor use of professional judgment. To assume that the target will embrace the cause once the facts are known is naive. Assumptions have little place in assessing the relationship between the action and the target system. We believe that regardless of what types of tactics are used, communication should be maintained with the target system if at all possible. If communication ceases, it should be because the target system refuses to continue interaction.

Within each of the three categories are tactics that are typically used. The framework in Table 10.1 guides our discussion. Some of the following conceptualization is drawn from previous literature (Brager & Holloway 1978; Brager et al. 1987). In some areas, we offer slightly different perspectives and add new tactics. Throughout the following discussion, we attempt to provide an analytical framework to guide an action system in selecting the most appropriate mix of tactics.

Collaboration

Implementation. Collaborative approaches include instances when the target and action systems agree that change is needed. Under collaboration, we place (1) implementation and (2) capacity building tactics.

Implementation tactics are used when the action and target systems work together cooperatively. When these systems agree that change is needed and allocation of resources is supported by critical decision makers, the change simply needs to be implemented. Implementation will most likely involve some problem solving, but it is not expected that adversarial relationships will be a concern in these type of collaborative efforts.

Capacity Building. Capacity building includes the tactics of participation and empowerment. Participation refers to those activities that involve members of the client system in the change effort. Empowerment is the process of "helping

TABLE 10.1 Tactical Behaviors

Relationship of Action and Target Systems	Tactics
Collaboration	

Target system agrees (or is easily convinced to agree) with action system that change is needed and supports allocation of resources	1. Implementation
	2. Capacity building
	   a. Participation
	   b. Empowerment

Campaign	

Target system is willing to communicate with action system, but there is little consensus that change is needed; or target system supports change but not allocation of resources	3. Education
	4. Persuasion
	   a. Cooptation
	   b. Lobbying
	5. Mass media appeal

Contest	

Target system opposes change and/or allocation of resources and is not open to further communication about opposition	6. Bargaining and negotiation
	7. Large-group or community action
	   a. Legal (e.g., demonstrations)
	   b. Illegal (e.g., civil disobedience)
	8. Class action lawsuit

a group or community to achieve political influence or relevant legal authority" (Barker 1987, 49).

For example, a problem may be defined as exclusion of a neighborhood from decisions that affect them. The focus of the intervention is on building a capacity for greater self-direction and self-control—that is, actually teaching people how to get involved in the decision-making processes in their communities and taking greater control over the decisions that affect their lives. This approach often emerges in situations where disenfranchised communities become targets for development, freeways, airport expansion, and other such encroachments.

Through professionally assisted change efforts, perhaps led by a neighborhood social service organization (change agent system), neighborhood resident (client system), and city council (controlling system and perhaps target system) agree that community citizens should have a greater voice in developments that affect their community. The focus of the change or intervention, however, is not on the target system (city council/planning commission) but on educating, training, and preparing community citizens for a fuller participation in decisions that affect their communities. Tactics would include education, training, and actual participation in civic organizations and activities.

Empowerment involves enabling people to become aware of their rights, and teaching them how to exercise those rights so that they become better able to take control over factors that affect their lives. Mobilizing the efforts of self-help groups and voluntary associations identified in Chapter 5 as well as the client system's informal support structure may be used to assist in guiding the target system toward consensus with the change effort.

Campaign

Campaign implies a group effort to convince target system members that a cause is just or a change is needed, and that resources should be allocated. Campaign tactics require a good deal of skill on the part of the change agent and action system. Lack of consensus rules out collaboration, yet a firm disagreement has not been established. Under this heading we include the use of education, persuasion, and mass media appeals designed to influence public opinion.

Education. Educational tactics can be an integral part of campaigns. Therefore, we use educational tactics to describe those interactions in which the action system presents perceptions, attitudes, opinions, data, and information about the proposed change with the intent of convincing the target system to think or to act differently. The objective is to inform. The assumption is that more and better information will lead to a change in behavior. It is a difficult tactic to use because opponents of the change can also be expected to inform decision makers armed with different sets of data and information, and there is seldom an absolute "truth" in dealing with complex organizational and community problems. In many cases where education fails to produce the desired result or falls short of having the desired impact, the change agent turns to persuasion.

Persuasion.   Persuasion refers to the art of convincing others to accept and support one's point of view or perspective on an issue. Social workers must frequently use persuasive tactics in addition to collaboration because their causes are not always embraced by decision makers, who often must be convinced through persuasion that the change is worth pursuing. This means that the change agent must understand the motives and reasoning of the target system in order to identify what incentives can be used to negotiate an agreement.

Skillful communication requires that the action system must carefully select its leadership from those persons who have the ability to persuade. Persons who are seen as nonthreatening to the target system and who can articulate the reasoning behind the planned change are particularly useful. For example, in a change effort, particular actors may be perceived as unreasonable, as trouble-makers, or as chronic complainers by members of the controlling system. It is not in the best interest of the client system for those persons to be the only spokespeople for the change. Clients themselves can also be powerful spokes-persons, providing information and a viewpoint that persuades people of the need for change.

Framing the problem statement to make it more palatable to target system members is a persuasive technique. This requires the ability to think as the target thinks. For example, a social worker hired as a long-term care ombudsperson was working closely with a coalition of advocates for nursing-home reform to end abuse in long-term care facilities. Nursing-home administrators were very upset over the nursing-home reform coalition and perceived them as not understanding the difficulties with which they coped on a daily basis. They sincerely wanted to provide quality care, but were frustrated by staff who were not properly trained to work with geriatric populations. By framing the problem as a training problem designed to better prepare employees and reduce turnover, the ombudsperson was able to persuade administrators to cooperate with the action system. When the ombudsperson met with the local nursing home association, she acknowledged that she was aware that the administrators wanted to operate high-quality facilities. She also noted that recent studies revealed that high staff turnover rates often contributed to lack of continuity and lower patient care, sometimes leading to abuse. She explained that she and her colleagues would be willing to develop training for nurses aides because they interacted most intimately with patients, yet were most vulnerable to high turnover. Essentially, one of the contributing factors leading to abuse was being addressed, but it was framed as reducing an administrative nightmare—high staff turnover.

Cooptation is defined as minimizing anticipated opposition by absorbing or including members of the target system in the action system. Once target system members are part of the planned change effort, it is likely that they will assume some ownership of the change process. Persuasion is used to coopt new persons into the action system. This is valuable to the success of the change effort because it is important to include persons who are viewed as powerful by the target system. These persons may be relatively neutral and may have little interest in obstructing the change effort. However, if they can be convinced to support the change effort (or even to allow their names to be used in publicity), their participation may sway others who respect their opinions. Cooptation is most effective as a tactic when opponents or neutral parties can be helped to recognize a self-interest in the proposed change.

Cooptation can be formal or informal. Coopting individuals is called informal cooptation, whereas coopting organized groups is referred to as formal cooptation. Formal cooptation means that an entire group agrees to support a cause. Because their governing structure agrees that the change effort is worthwhile, the group may issue a statement to that effect. This formalizes the commitment, even though there are always members of any group who may, as individuals, disagree with the proposed change.

Formal cooptation of a number of groups leads to coalition building. A coalition is a loosely woven, ad hoc association of constituent groups, each of whose primary identification is outside the coalition (Haynes & Mickelson 1986). For example, the purpose of the National Health Care Campaign is to provide health care coverage to all American citizens. This change effort brings together hundreds of organizations such as the National Association of Social Workers and the American Public Health Association. On a state by state basis, health care campaign chapters are forming. Interested change agents have encouraged local groups to join in the efforts—forming a coalition dedicated to the stated goal. The diversity of the coalition contributes to a powerful alliance of individuals and groups that vascillate between collaboration and campaign tactics as they attempt to address health care needs.

Lobbying is a form of persuasion that addresses policy change under the domain of the controlling system. The action system will have to determine if it is necessary to change agency policy, to amend current legislation or to develop new legislation in order to achieve their goal. Haynes and Mickelson (1986) delineate three essential concepts for social work/lobbyists to consider. First, one should always be factual and honest. Trying to second guess or stretching the facts to support one's position is devastating to one's professional reputation as well as to the change effort's credibility. Second, any presentation should be straightforward and supported by the available data. The problem identification and analysis process discussed in Chapter 8 will assist the change agent in organizing the rationale for change. Third, any discussion should include the two critical concerns of decision makers—cost and social impact of what is proposed. If the cost is high, the social worker is advised to calculate the costs of allowing the identified problem to remain unresolved.

Mass Media Appeal. Mass media appeal refers to the development and release of newsworthy stories to the print and electronic media for the purpose of influencing public opinion. This tactic is used to pressure decision makers into a favorable resolution to the identified problem. The expectation is that if the proposed change can be presented to the public in a positive way and decision makers' refusal to support the proposed change can be presented as obstructionist or somehow negative, then decision makers will feel pressured to change their position. Where decision makers are high-profile people like elected representatives who depend on a positive public perception, this can be an effective tactic. Use of mass media depends on news reporters' agreement that the proposed change is a newsworthy story, and assurance that one's cause will be presented accurately. Use of any media must always include consideration of clients' rights to privacy.

Contest

Under the heading of contest we include the use of bargaining and negotiating, the use of large group or community action, or class action lawsuits. Large groups in community action can be further divided into legal and illegal tactics. Contest tactics are used in situations where: (1) the target system cannot be persuaded by the action system, (2) the target system refuses to communicate with the action system, or (3) it is perceived that only lipservice is being given to the proposed change. Contest tactics mean that the change effort becomes an open, public conflict as attempts are made to draw broad support and/or to pressure or even force the target system into supporting or at least accepting the change. Once this occurs, the action system must be prepared to face open confrontation and to escalate its coercive techniques.

Conflict is inevitable in social work practice. There will be times in the experience of every macro practitioner when incredible resistance is encountered in addressing the needs of oppressed population groups. Social work as a profession developed in response to a basic societal conflict—the persistent anatagonism over individualism and the common good. Conflicts over the rights of various population groups have spawned violent confrontations rooted in basic value systems and beliefs. We believe that physical violence and terriorism can not be condoned in any change efforts in a civilized society. Nonviolent confrontation, however, including civil disobedience, is an option when there is a communication stalemate between the target and action systems.

Contest tactics will require widespread commitment and possible participation from members of the support system. It is critical to the success of these tactics that the support system and its subsystems—initiator, client, and change agent—are comfortable with contest tactics because there are risks that are not present when using collaboration and campaign tactics. It is likely that the time and energy necessary for effective change will increase and relationships can become disrupted. When collaborative and campaign tactics are employed, tactics can move toward contest. However, once contest tactics are employed it is not likely that one can return to collaborative or campaign tactics. Without a clear understanding of what contest tactics involve and without full commitment from the support system, contest tactics are not advised.

Bargaining and Negotiation. Bargaining and negotiation refer to those situations in which the action and target system confront one another with the reasons for their opposition. Bargaining and negotiation occur when there is a recognized power differential between parties and a compromise needs to be made. These tactics are more formalized than persuasion, often involving a third-party mediator. Members of the target system will typically agree to negotiate when the following factors are in place: (1) there is some understanding of the intentions and preferred outcomes of the action system, (2) there is a degree of urgency, (3) the relative importance and scope of the proposed change is known, (4) there are resources that facilitate the exercise of power, and (5) they perceive the action system as having some legitimacy. In order to negotiate, both the action and the target systems must perceive that each has something the other wants, otherwise there is no reason to come together (Brager et al. 1987).

Bargaining and negotiation can result in a win-win situation, where both target and action systems are pleased with and fully support the outcome. The result can be a win-lose where one system is clearly the victor, or a lose-lose where both systems give something up and are disappointed in the results.

Large Group or Community Action.   Large group or community action refers to the preparing, training, and organizing of large numbers of people who are willing to form a pressure group and advocate for change through various forms of such collective action as picketing, disruption of meetings, sit-ins, boycotting, and other pressure tactics. Peaceful demonstrations are legal activities, often used by both groups at either extreme of an issue, to express their views. Civil disobedience activities intentionally break the law. When action system members deliberately engage in illegal activities, they must be ready to accept the consequences of their actions. The change agent is responsible for making potential participants fully aware of these risks before the decision is made to proceed.

Class Action Lawsuits.   Class action lawsuits refer to those instances where an entity is sued for a perceived violation of the law and it is expected that the finding of the court will apply to an entire class of people. These tactics are often used with highly vulnerable populations such as the chronically mentally ill, the homeless, or children, where it is unlikely that they have the capacity or the resources to protect their own rights. Public interest law organizations may be resources for the action system in developing class action tactics.

Considerations in Selecting Tactics

A few salient considerations need to be weighed in selecting the best tactic or mix of tactics. These considerations include:

1. What are the current *objectives* of the change effort?
2. What is the perception (by those promoting change) of the *controlling and host systems?*
3. What is the perception (by those promoting change) of the role of the *client system?*
4. What *resources* are needed and available for each tactic?
5. What are the *ethical* dilemmas inherent in the range of tactical choices?

Objectives.   Objectives often tend to evolve as the change process moves along, and a re-examination prior to selection of tactics is in order. For example, with the problem of domestic violence, the condition may have been brought to public awareness by the perceived need for additional emergency shelter space for battered women. However, as the problem is analyzed and better understood, the objectives may shift toward consciousness raising for all women in the community who are perceived to be at risk of violence. Thus strategy and tactics would move from advocating for service provision to educating for empowerment. Since tactics can change as objectives change, it is worthwhile to make one last check to insure that all are clear and in agreement on current objectives. The following questions can be used to guide the action system's re-examination of the change objectives.

---

1. What are the stated objectives of this change effort?
2. Given what has been learned in the change process thus far, do the stated objectives need to be revised?
3. Which best describes the intent of the current objectives?
   a. to solve a substantive problem or provide a needed service
   b. to increase self-direction or self-control of the client system
   c. to influence decision makers
   d. to change public opinion
   e. to shift power
   f. to mandate action
4. Do members of the action system have any concerns about the intent of the current objectives that require further discussion?

The range of objectives and likely accompanying tactics are indicated in Table 10.2.

TABLE 10.2 Relationship of Current Objectives to Tactics

Current Objective	Relationship of Target and Action System	Possible Tactics
1. Solving a substantive problem; providing a needed service	Collaborative	Implementation through joint action
2. Self-direction; self-control	Collaborative	Capacity building through participation and empowerment
3. Influencing decision makers	In disagreement but with open communication	Education, and persuasion through cooptation, lobbying, etc.
4. Changing public opinion	In disagreement but with open communication	Education, persuasion, mass media appeal,
	Adversarial	Large group or community action
5. Shifting power	Adversarial	Large group or community action
6. Mandating action	Adversarial	Class action lawsuit

Controlling and Host Systems.   The controlling and host systems can be perceived in a variety of ways. If they are seen as employers or sponsors of the change, then collaboration is likely. If they are seen as supporters of, but not participants in the change, capacity building (through participation and empowerment) may be the tactic of choice. If they are seen as neutral or indifferent, a campaign strategy may be in order. If, however, they are seen as oppressive or unresponsive to their primary clientele, then some type of contest approach will likely be selected. Discussion of the following questions may assist the action system in assessing their relationship with the controlling and host system.

---

1. Who are the critical actors in the host and controlling system(s)?
2. What term(s) best describe(s) the action system members' perceptions of the host and controlling system actors?
   a. sponsors, supporters, co-participants, or colleagues
   b. neutral or indifferent actors
   c. uninformed barriers who are not sure about change
   d. informed barriers or opponents
   e. oppressors
   f. violators of rights
3. Are action system members' perceptions similar or dissimilar?
4. If they are dissimilar, what are the different perceptions and what are the implications of this divergence of opinion for the change effort?

Table 10.3 illustrates the various perceptions of roles that might be assigned to the controlling and host systems, and the logical tactic for each.

Primary Client.   *The role of the primary client* can vary, and the way in which this role is perceived can affect selection of change tactics. Sometimes it may be difficult to determine who the primary client really is. For example, in addressing

TABLE 10.3   Relationship of Controlling and Host System Roles to Tactics

Perception of Role of Controlling and Host Systems	Relationship of Controlling, Host, and Action Systems	Possible Tactics
1. Sponsors; supporters; co-participants; colleagues	Collaborative	Implementation through joint action
2. Neutrality or indifference	Collaborative	Capacity building through participation and empowerment
3. Uninformed barriers; not sure about change	In disagreement but with open communication	Education and persuasion
4. Informed barriers; opponents to successful change	Adversarial	Bargaining; large-group or community action
5. Oppressors	Adversarial	Large-group or community action
6. Violators of rights	Adversarial	Class action lawsuit

the needs of the elderly, the change agent may discover that caregivers are suffering from stress and fatigue. In this situation, one must ask if the primary beneficiaries of a change effort will be the older persons themselves or their caregivers?

If the primary client is seen as a consumer or recipient of service, then a collaborative change approach is the most likely tactic. If the primary role is as a resident of a community or potential participant in an effort to achieve self-direction and control, then a capacity building approach is, perhaps, more appropriate. If the primary client is seen as a person who needs a service (but this need is not acknowledged by the controlling system), as a victim, or as a voter or constituent with potential power to influence decision makers, then some type of contest approach is likely to be employed. The following questions guide the action system in assessing the role of the primary client.

---

1. Who is defined as the primary client?
2. How do members of the action system describe the primary client?
   a. consumer or recipient of service
   b. resident of the community in need of self-direction or self-control
   c. citizen/taxpayer not permitted full participation
   d. victim, underserved needy person
   e. victim, exploited person
   f. person denied civil rights
3. Do action system members agree or disagree in their descriptions of the primary client? Do clients agree or disagree?
4. What role does the primary client play within the action system?
5. How much overlap is there between the client and the action systems?
6. What mechanisms does the action system use to obtain input from the client system?

Table 10.4 displays client roles, approaches, and tactics.

TABLE 10.4 Relationship of Client-System Role to Tactics

Perception of Role of Client System	Relationship Client and Target Systems	Possible Tactics
1. Consumer; recipient of service	Collaborative	Implementation through joint action
2. Resident of the community in need of greater self-direction and self-control	Collaborative	Capacity building through participation and empowerment
3. Citizen/taxpayer not permitted full participation	In disagreement but with open communication	Education and persuasion
4. Victim; underserved needy person	Adversarial	Mass media appeal
5. Victim; exploited person	Adversarial	Large group or community action
6. Person denied civil rights	Adversarial	Class action lawsuit

Resources. Finally, *resources available to the action system* should be examined in relation to each of the tactics being considered. If collaboration is the tactic of choice, then several resources are needed. These include technical expertise capable of understanding whether or not the change is being properly implemented, monitored, and evaluated. In order for a capacity building tactic to be used, grass roots organizing ability, together with some teaching and training expertise, must be available to the action system. If there is conflict, either skilled persuaders, media support, large numbers of people willing to do what is necessary to bring about change, or legal expertise must be available. The following questions may assist the action system in assessing resources.

---

1. What tactics are being considered at this point?
2. What resources will be needed to adequately use these tactics? (e.g., expertise, training, time, funding, equipment, etc.)
3. What members of the action system have access to the needed resources?
4. If additional resources are needed, should the boundaries of the action system be expanded to include persons/groups who have access to additional resources?

Resource considerations are illustrated in Table 10.5.

Professional Ethics. In Chapter 3, we discussed the importance of values in social work practice. Ethics are the behaviors that bring values into action. An ethical dilemma is defined as a situation in which a choice has to be made between equally important values. Tactical choices are no exception. Decisions regarding what tactics to use are based on the values held by action system members. It is often the clash of action and target system values that leads to the selection of contest tactics.

TABLE 10.5 Resources Needed by Action System for Each Tactic

Tactic	Resources Needed
1. Collaboration—joint action or problem solving	Technical expertise; monitoring and evaluation capability
2. Capacity building	Grass roots organizing ability; teaching/training expertise; opportunities for participation; some indigenous leadership; willing participants
3. Persuasion	Informed people; data/information; skilled persuaders/lobbyists
4. Mass media appeal	Data/information; newsworthy issue or slant; access to news reporters; technical expertise to write news releases
5. Large group or community action	Large numbers of committed people (support system); training and organizing expertise; informed leadership; bargaining and negotiating skills
6. Class action lawsuits	Legal expertise; victims willing to bring action and provide information; at least enough money for court costs

Three ethical principles were discussed in Chapter 3: autonomy, beneficence, and justice. These principles are deeply emeshed in macro-practice change. A clash between autonomy and beneficence occurs when the client system is not willing to risk the little they have, yet, when the action system wants to push for a quality of life change. The client system may have limited control over their lives, but their right to decide (self-determination) that they do not want to risk the little control they have must be respected by action system members if it is clear that client system opinion is being fairly represented. Alternately, the action system may be heavily composed of professionals who are acting on the principle of beneficence. They may sincerely believe that they know what is best for the client system. Rights of clients take precedence over the wishes of the action system when such a conflict emerges.

This clash was illustrated in a social work intern's first field experience. Working for a small community center in the southwest, she discovered that many of her Hispanic clients lived in a crowded apartment complex with faulty wiring and inadequate plumbing. With the backing of her agency, she began talking with clients to see if they would be willing to engage in a change process directed toward their living conditions. As she analyzed the situation, she realized that any change process would involve housing and public health personnel in the action system. Her clients begged her not to bring these concerns to the attention of local authorities. Many members of the client system were illegal aliens and they feared that their exposure to public authorities would assure their deportation. The client system was willing to accept poor housing conditions rather than risk the consequences of exposure. The client system's autonomy was in conflict with the change agent system's beneficence.

The clash between justice and autonomy is exemplified when the action system demands redistribution of resources and the target system believes that in giving up their control over valued resources they have less freedom. Macro change frequently appeals to the principle of justice, for it is usually through the redistribution of valued resources (e.g., power, money, status, etc.) that change occurs. Because justice is a basic ethical principle that raises emotions when it is violated, change agents can become so obsessed with injustice that any means is viewed as an appropriate tactic if it leads to a successful end. It is our contention that this type of thinking can lead to professional anarchy whereby tactics are perceived as weapons to punish the target system rather than as actions to enrich the client system. In these situations it may be too easy for the change to take on a life of its own and for the professional to assume a beneficent role. Righteous indignation may overtake sound judgment.

In the previous chapter, we discussed the use of covert tactics in certain situations where legitimate channels of communication have been tried and where clients agree that covert means may be their only chance for success. These considerations must be carefully weighed because the use of covert tactics usually raise ethical concerns.

To guide the action system in discussing professional ethics, we pose the following questions:

1. What are the value conflicts between the target and action systems?
2. What ethical principle(s) appear to be guiding the activities of the action system?
3. Is there the potential for a clash of ethical principles between the client and action systems?
4. If covert tactics are being considered, what conditions have led to this decision?
   a. The mission of the target agency or the community mandate is being ignored.
   b. The mission of the target agency or the community mandate is being denied for personal gain.
   c. Change efforts have been tried through legitimate channels but the target system will not listen.
   d. Client system members are fully aware of the risks involved, but are willing to take the risks.
   e. Other _____

There are very few situations where there is clearly a right or wrong tactic. Berlin (1990) explains, ''we are all vulnerable to oversimplified bipolarizations. We search for order, find meaning in contrasts, and learn by maintaining an 'essential tension' between divergent experiences, events, and possibilities. It is this allowance of contrasts that differentiates either-or, narrowing and excluding bipolarizations from those that are encompassing or transforming'' (p. 54).

It is common to think dichotomously (e.g,. win-lose, right-wrong, good-bad, consensus-conflict). In conflict situations, dichotomous thinking may assist the radical change agent in believing that the target system represents evil, whereas the action system represents good. This fuels the fire of confrontation and is appropriate in some situations. However, we believe that the professional social worker has a responsibility to carefully analyze what is happening before making assumptions that lead directly to the use of contest tactics. This means that the majority of change efforts will utilize collaboration and campaign tactics as the action and target systems attempt to communicate with one another. Although consensus-conflict is a dichotomy, we believe that the majority of interactions happen in the various gradations in-between—where varying degrees of communication occur.

If the action system attempts to collaborate or is willing to compromise but the target system remains unmoved, then contest tactics may have to be employed. What professionals must guard against, however, is action system members making assumptions about target system members without attempting to communicate with them. In short, decisions about what tactics to use depends on the situation, the proposed change, and the relationships among actors in the action, client, and target systems.

FOCUS B: PREPARING A WRITTEN PLAN

When all the foregoing tasks have been completed, the proposed change should be written up in the form of a short, concise plan. This will include a few pages on the purpose, the problem, and the proposed change. A page on costs, and a few pages on expected benefits should make clear what resources will be requested, how they will be spent, and what benefits will be derived from implementation of the proposed change.

A few pages should be used to lay out the strategy and tactics, outlining roles, responsibilities and time lines in Gantt chart form. This will be helpful in insuring that the proposed strategy and tactics are well coordinated as they are implemented. Any documents from the data collection and problem analysis phases that are felt to be helpful and are clear and concise can be attached to the plan.

This brings the change effort up to the point where it is ready for action. A community or organizational problem affecting a target population has been identified and thoroughly thought out. A general approach to an intervention has been proposed, and a hypothesis developed proposing a relationship between problem, intervention, and outcomes. Alternative strategies have been carefully thought through, participants selected, issues weighed, and tactics selected.

Clearly there is more to be done prior to the full implementation of change. It is not the intent of this book, however, to get into the details of project or program planning. The macro practitioner, as conceptualized here, could reasonably be expected to withdraw at the point of acceptance of the proposed change and turn responsibilities over to those who will provide leadership in implementation of the policy, program, or project experts.

CONCLUSION

We began this book with a chapter on the history and values of the social work profession. We discussed the struggles of gaining a professional identity and the ethical dilemmas those struggles impose on macro practice. Parts II and III focused on approaches to understanding community, social service systems, and health and human service organizations.

Part IV has proposed a systematic approach designed to produce the strategy and tactics that offer the best chance of successful change. The approach includes a carefully thought out series of tasks intended to maximize participation, to think through all possible types of change, and to select the options that will most likely achieve the desired results.

Next, the planners of change consider a number of political, interpersonal and economic factors in order to be able to assess strengths and weaknesses of the proposed change. Itemizing the supporting and opposing people and factors allows the planners of change visually and cognitively to assess the likelihood of success. If it appears that the chances for success are good, the change effort moves to the stage of selecting appropriate tactics. Finally, a proposed plan of action is sketched out, including specification of key participants, activities, and time lines.

As with all professional practice, the approach is modified by the practitioner to fit the situation. If conditions dictate immediate action, some procedures will be shortened or streamlined. If time allows and the significance of the proposed change dictates, each task will be carried out with careful attention to detail.

In any case, it is our position that some changes will always be needed in the field of human services, both in organizations and in communities. These changes, we believe, require the professional assistance and consultation of social workers knowledgeable about macro-level change. They require informed, and sometimes scholarly participation and guidance in order to insure that what is achieved is what is most needed to address the social problem in the best interest of the target population.

We believe that social workers are well qualified to lead or coordinate the planning stages of such change efforts and to bring them to the point of action, and this book is intended to assist in that process. As the change effort moves into its next stages, we would expect that the necessary expertise—legal, media, organizing, planning, designing, managing, or whatever is needed—would be sought from additional available sources and from elsewhere in the social work literature.

REFERENCES

Barker, R. L. (1987) *The social work dictionary.* Silver Spring, MD: National Association of Social Workers.

Berlin, S. B. (1990) Dichotomous and complex thinking. *Social Service Review, 64*(1): 46–59.

Brager, G., and S. Holloway. (1978) *Changing human service organizations: Politics and practice.* New York: Free Press.

Brager, G., H. Specht, and J. L. Torczyner. (1987) *Community organizing.* New York: Columbia University Press.

Haynes, K. S., and J. S. Mickelson. (1986) *Affecting change: Social workers in the political arena.* New York: Longman.

Action System Discussion in Consideration Tactics

Objectives

1. What are the stated objectives of this change effort?
2. Given what has been learned in the change process thus far, do the stated objectives need to be revised?
3. Which best describes the intent of the current objectives?
   a. to solve a substantive problem or provide a needed service
   b. to increase self-direction or self-control of the client system
   c. to influence decision makers
   d. to change public opinion
   e. to shift power
   f. to mandate action
4. Do members of the action system have any concerns about the intent of the current objectives that require further discussion?

Controlling and Host Systems

5. Who are the critical actors in the host and controlling system(s)?
6. What term(s) best describes the action system members' perceptions of the host and controlling system actors?
   a. sponsors, supporters, co-participants, or colleagues
   b. neutral or indifferent actors
   c. uninformed barriers who are not sure about change
   d. informed barriers or opponents
   e. oppressors
   f. violators of rights
7. Are action system members' perceptions similiar or dissimiliar?
8. If they are dissimiliar, what are the different perceptions and what are the implications of this divergence of opinion for the change effort?

Primary Client

9. Who is defined as the primary client?
10. How do members of the action system describe the primary client?
    a. consumer or recipient of service
    b. resident of the community in need of self-direction or self-control
    c. citizen/taxpayer not permitted full participation
    d. victim, underserved needy person
    e. victim, exploited person
    f. person denied civil rights
11. Do action system members agree or disagree in their descriptions of the primary client?
12. What role does the primary client play within the action system?
13. How much overlap is there between the client and the action systems?
14. What mechanisms does the action system use to obtain input from the client system?

Resources
15. What tactics are being considered at this point?
16. What resources will be needed to adequately use these tactics? (e.g., expertise, training, time, funding, equipment, etc.)
17. What members of the action system have access to the needed resources?
18. If additional resources are needed, should the boundaries of the action system be expanded to include persons/groups who have access to additional resources?

Professional Ethics
19. What are the value conflicts between the target and action systems?
20. What ethical principle(s) appear to be guiding the activities of the action system?
21. Is there the potential for a clash of ethical principles between the client and action systems?
22. If covert tactics are being considered, what conditions have led to this decision?
    a. the mission of the target agency or the community
    b. mandate is being ignored
    c. the mission of the target agency or the community mandate is being denied for personal gain
    d. change efforts have been tried through legitimate channels but the target system will not listen
    e. client system members are fully aware of the risks involved, but are willing to take the risks and accept the consequences
    f. other _____

Case Example: Jackson County Foster Care

The following example illustrates the major components of a written plan for a macro-change effort.

BACKGROUND

In the child welfare division of a major urban county, an analysis of five years of foster-care data was recently undertaken. Findings revealed that the likelihood of a child's returning to his or her natural parents after being placed in foster care was significantly less for ethnic minority children than for white children.

In response to a newspaper article which reported these results, over thirty representatives of minority communities attended an open hearing held by the county board of supervisors. They expressed serious concerns about the findings. The county director of child welfare services was instructed to appoint a task force to study the situation and to make recommendations. The fourteen-member task force included:

three minority parents who had children in foster care,

four minority community leaders,

two foster parents,

two foster-care social workers,

a foster-home recruitment coordinator,

a child welfare researcher from the local university, and

the top administrator from the foster-care program.

The task force examined five-year statistics, looked at other research on minority children and families, studied the available literature on several major ethnic minority groups, and familiarized themselves with the issues associated with foster care and return to natural families. As they concluded their study, the following alternative explanations emerged:

1. Minority children with adjustment problems tend to remain in their natural homes longer than white children and therefore exhibit more serious problems by the time they are placed in foster care. This reduces the chances that foster care can help them adjust and return to their homes.
2. Minority families whose children go into foster care tend to have fewer economic, social, emotional, or family support resources than white families, and this reduces the likelihood that they will be able to make the changes needed to take the child back into their homes.
3. Many child welfare workers and foster parents demonstrate a lack of any real in-depth understanding of the meaning of culture and tradition to ethnic minority families. A child's behavior tends to be interpreted from a white perspective, and expectations are inconsistent with those established within ethnic minority cultures.
4. Support services offered to help families deal with problems when a child has been removed seem to lack the cultural sensitivity necessary to help strengthen ethnic minority families.

The task force concluded that the focus of any change effort should be on the child welfare system and the minority families whose children go into foster care. It was felt that natural families needed more resources and supportive services. Foster families and child welfare workers needed a better understanding of the family context and the variables critical to a healthy family environment for minority children. The following intervention hypothesis was proposed:

If minority families who place children in foster care can be recruited into a program of supportive services, and

if the number of ethnic minority foster families and child welfare workers can be increased, and

if child welfare workers and foster parents can increase their knowledge of and sensitivity to the needs of minority children and their families,

then the number of successful post-foster care returns to natural families will be increased.

After proceeding through each of the tasks outlined in Chapters 8, 9, and 10, they produced the following written plan.

PART I: THE PROBLEM AND THE PROPOSED CHANGE

In the Jackson County Division of Child Welfare Services it was recently discovered that the rate of return of minority children from foster care to their natural families was significantly less than the rates for white children. A task force was appointed and a study was undertaken. A number of causal factors have emerged from the study.

There is some evidence that minority families whose children go into foster care have more serious economic, social, and emotional problems and are in need of a network of supportive services that will enable them to strengthen the family and better parent the child. On the whole, such services, with a special emphasis on serving ethnic minority families, have generally not been available to these families.

Second, there is evidence that child welfare workers and foster parents lack knowledge about minority families that could be important in the decision-making process about the needs of minority children and what should be considered realistic behavioral and performance expectations for return to natural families.

The task force proposes a series of interventions aimed at improving the cultural sensitivity of child care workers and foster parents and strengthening families who place children in foster care.

The first set of interventions will be directed toward child welfare workers and foster-care parents. Cultural sensitivity training for these persons will include:

assessing one's values and perceptions as they relate to work with minority children and their families,

understanding African American families and children,

understanding Hispanic families and children,

understanding Native American families and children,

understanding Asian American families and children.

For those foster parents who complete cultural sensitivity training courses, they will:

receive a higher level of payment, and

be certified to receive minority foster children.

The second set of interventions will include support services, under contract with agencies that have demonstrated an understanding of and sensitivity to ethnic minority cultures. These services will be directed toward minority families. They are:

case management,

economic incentives,

individual and family assessment and counseling,

remedial education and GED opportunities,

job preparation, training, and placement,

self-esteem building workshops, and

self-help groups.

PART II: KEY ACTORS AND SYSTEMS

1. *Initiator System:* Black Families United, a community organization that organized the effort to meet with the county board of supervisors.
2. *Change Agent System:* the task force, staffed by an experienced child welfare supervisor.
3. *Client System:* ethnic minority children who are placed in foster care and their families.
4. *Support System:* at least eight ethnic community organizations, two child welfare advocacy groups, several minority clergy and their congregations, many child welfare professionals and the foster parents' association.
5. *Controlling System:* the county board of supervisors.
6. *Host System:* the Jackson County Division of Child Welfare.
7. *Implementing System:* three units within the Jackson County Division of Child Welfare—(1) the foster care unit, (2) the staff development and training unit, and (3) the purchase of services contracting unit.
8. *Target System:* Since this will be a multiphase process, there will be phase specific targets. The initial target will be those funding sources needed to underwrite the proposed interventions. This includes the board of supervisors and several local foundations. Subsequent targets include (1) child welfare workers and foster parents who need to become more ethnic sensitive, and (2) minority families with children in foster care.
9. *Action System:* the task force, together with key representatives from the division of child welfare and potential service providers.

PART III: GOALS, OBJECTIVES, AND ACTIVITIES

This change effort is proposed as a three-year pilot project during which time the division of child welfare will experiment and correct any problems discovered in implementing the original design. Following the three-year trial period, it is to be implemented as a permanent part of Jackson County Child Welfare Services.

Goal 1

To improve and strengthen the cultural sensitivity of the Jackson County Child Welfare system.

Outcome Objective 1.1

By December 31, 19XX, to increase the knowledge of four ethnic minority cultures of at least fifty trainees (including child welfare workers and foster parents), as measured by a 50 percent increase between pre- and posttest scores on tests developed for the training course.

Process Objectives

1.1 By July 19XX, to present a proposal to the county board of supervisors for funds to develop culturally sensitive curriculum for child welfare workers and foster parents in Jackson County.

1.2 By September 19XX, to develop four training courses on understanding African American, Hispanic, Native American, and Asian American families designed for child welfare workers and foster parents who serve minority children.

1.3 By October 19XX, to produce fifty copies of all handouts associated with the training courses and distribute them to the child welfare staff development and training unit.

1.4 By November 19XX, to recruit at least fifty child welfare workers and foster parents to take the training courses.

1.5 By January 19XX, to administer pretests and to train at least fifty child welfare workers and foster parents in cultural sensitivity.

1.6 By March 19XX, to administer posttests to trainees and to analyze the pre- and post-test results.

Goal 2

To strengthen ethnic minority families who have children who are placed in foster care.

Outcome Objective 2.1

By September 30, 19XX, at least 100 ethnic minority families with children in foster care will demonstrate greater economic, social, emotional and/or family strength as measured by at least 30 percent higher scores on the Multidimensional Family Assessment Scales.

Process Objectives

2.1 By November 19XX, to inventory economic, social, emotional, and family support resources needed to serve African American, Hispanic, Native American, and Asian American families in Jackson County.

2.2 By April 19XX, at least 100 ethnic minority families with children in foster care will have been initially assessed to determine what resources are currently used and what resources are needed but not available or accessible.

2.3 By June 19XX, gaps between available and needed resources for minority families will be documented in writing.

2.4 By September 19XX, contracts to provide needed services designed for minority families will be implemented.

2.5 By September 30, 19XX (one year later), at least 100 ethnic minority families with children in foster care will have been served through these special contracts.

Activity Chart for Process Objective 2.1																
Process Objective 2.1: By November 19XX, to inventory economic, social, emotional, and family support resources needed to serve African American, Hispanic, Native American, and Asian American families in Jackson County.																
Activity Number	**Activity**	**Person Responsible**					**Time Frame**									
			J	F	M	A	M	J	J	A	S	O	N	D		
1.	Form task force to identify resources	Change agent	—													
2.	Hold meeting of task force	Change agent		—												
3.	Develop subcommittee	Members of task force			—											
4.	Conduct inventory of resources: a) economic b) social c) emotional d) support	Members of task force					————————									
5.	Prepare final report	Task force chair										————				
6.	Report results along with identified gaps in available resources	Task force chair												—		

PART IV: TACTICS

It is anticipated that this change effort will proceed through a series of phases, as follows:

Phase 1

The objective of Phase 1 is to get the change accepted by potential funding sources. The focus of this phase is on the county board of supervisors, several private foundations interested in minority concerns, and people capable of influencing their decisions. Campaign tactics will include education, persuasion, and lobbying. In the event that campaign tactics are not successful and that funding sources are not open to change, contest tactics may be used. These tactics would include mass media appeals to mobilize the support system as well as bargaining and negotiation and large group social action.

Phase 2

The objective of Phase 2, if the project is funded, is to increase cultural sensitivity awareness and knowledge. The focus of this phase is on child welfare staff and foster parents who serve minority children and their families. Collaborative tactics will include joint action, capacity building, and education.

Phase 3

The objective of Phase 3 is to insure that improved services are provided to minority families who have placed children in foster care. Services should be adapted to the unique needs, concerns, interests, and traditions of each ethnic group, and will involve application of knowledge and skill gained in Phase 2. The focus of this effort will be on child welfare workers, foster parents, and contracted service providers. Collaborative tactics will include capacity building and joint action. Services will be measured by improvement in economic, social, emotional, and overall family strength of minority families who have placed children in foster care.

Index